SATELLITE TELEVISION
An Impact on Social Participation

DR. TARJEET SABHARWAL

KANISHKA PUBLISHERS, DISTRIBUTORS
NEW DELHI-110 002

KANISHKA PUBLISHERS, DISTRIBUTORS
4697/5-21 A, Ansari Road, Daryaganj
New Delhi-110 002
Phones : 2327 0497, 2328 8285
Fax : 011-2328 8285
E-mail: kanishka_publishing@yahoo.co.in

First Published 2008

ISBN 978-81-8457-064-9

PRINTED IN INDIA

Published by Madan Sachdeva for Kanishka Publishers, Distributors, 4697/5-21A, Ansari Road, Daryaganj, New Delhi-110 002, Typeset by Sunshine Graphics, Delhi, and Printed at Nice Printing Press, Delhi.

To

my father

Shri Mohinder Pal Singh

Preface

This book presents readers with an overview of the impact of satellite television on social participation. It attempts to draw together in a single volume a wide range of factors that contribute to changes in the daily life of viewers with the presence of round-the-clock TV.

The prime focus of the book is to compare viewers and non-viewers of satellite TV in three different socio-economic groups on many dimensions of social participation. The fact that there is a decline in some forms of social participation within and across families has been reflected upon in this book. It also traces the nature and form of social participation of members in the family, ties at the informal level with kinship and neighbours and formal social relationships among urban dwellers.

The book provides a detailed account of the ways families construct their media world. It also highlights the structuring of the daily and weekly scheme of activities of both viewers and non-viewers. Besides this, it explains the patterns of lesiure activities adopted by families in relation to the presence of 24-hour television at home. The restriction of physical mobility and an over-all decline in the expenditure of leisure time from 'out of home' to 'in home' activities have been highlighted.

Television viewing can enrich the possibilities of verbal and non-verbal communication is addressed in terms of family, kinship and neighbourhood ties. It also elaborates on the family interaction patterns, inter-personal relationships across families, power relations and intra-familial conflicts in the context of family television viewing.

The intra-city variations in terms the selection and preferences of TV programmes and viewing patterns have been detailed. It also elaborates the ways families respond to western based content. That satellite TV has transformed the socio-cultural landscape of most countries cannot be denied. It brings into homes the popular cultural and western value system. The book seeks to explore the impact of the western media as perceived by the audience in the Indian situation. The profound effect on children reflected through academic and non-academic dimensions is explained in detail. The role of parents in this context was examined and provides readers with deep insight into the changing dynamics in parent-child relationships. The book reveals some interesting facts of the substantial impact of satellite TV affecting every unit within and across families and how it makes a differential impact upon different categories of urban dwellers and various forms of social participation.

AUTHOR

Contents

1
Introduction

Technological advances in the industrial and modern periods of history have not only changed the physical "equipment" of societies but also their social and cultural melieu. Industrialization and modernization have stimulated social and cultural changes leading to several common trends: the adoption of urban values, the increased employment of women in the non-family economy, greater freedom in sexual behaviour and marital choice, higher expectations in marital relationship, more permissive parent-child relationships, greater emotional involvement of fathers with their children and rising survival rates of the very old (Yorburg, 1983).

Other social and cultural changes resulting from modernization that have been widely noted include the creation of the job of housewife, an increased standard of living, a paring down of the size of the nuclear family, greater dependence on the home and reduction of contact with neighbours, an increase in the role of the family for emotional interdependence, a decrease in the authority of individual members, a struggle for more space in which to live, an increase in family mobility and consequent lessening of ties with extended kin, and an increase in the disparity in life style between city and rural dwellers. While these changes have been felt in the more developed countries of the world, the fallout of industrialization and modernization has been experienced everywhere. While all nations may not be equally industrialized or entirely modern, there is industry and modernity in every culture and a fundamental awareness of desire for a better life exists among people everywhere (Allan, 1985).

It has been established that there is an ineluctable link between technology and economic factors on the one hand and social change on the other (Veblen, 1904). In every historical epoch, the technological innovations and scientific achievements have left significant repercussions on the social organisation. However, whether the relationship is one-way i.e., flowing from technological to the social change or mutual, depends upon the way one looks at it. Thus, it is possible to delineate a number of theoretical perspectives emphasizing on different dimensions of the interplay between technology and social change.

William F. Ogburn (1938), giving primacy to technological developments, talks of the cultural lag theory. It involves the identification of atleast two variables that can be shown to have been in adjustment at one time. One of the variables is then shown to have changed to a greater extent than the other because of a discovery or invention. In other words, whenever the rates of change of the interdependent parts of culture are unequal, we have a condition of cultural lag, and the consequent adjustment is "less satisfactory" than that which existed initially.

To support the notion of cultural lag, the two variables of family size and religious doctrine may be considered. The religious doctrine may make the large family 'sacred'. Then, with modernization, and the use of new techniques of birth control, family may shrink in size. The religious doctrine, however may oppose this trend and the use of birth control methods, causing maladjustment between religion and family.

Ogburn's thought revolved basically around technology and culture. He points out that non-material aspects of the culture must adjust to the material developments, and the gap between the two will be areas of social problems. Technology is the driving mechanism of change; according to Ogburn people seem to be gasping to keep up and adapt to the world that technology is ever creating anew (Lauer, 1992).

A similar emphasis on the technological factors as an independent variable may be found in the conceptualization of 'pre-industrial cities' made by Gideon Sjoberg (1951). He too ascribes the differences in the social, religious, political and ecological structures between societies in terms of their level of industrialization (Hatt and Reiss, 1951).

However, the empirical variations between the western and non-western societies on the one hand and developed and developing on the other, indicate the difficulty of treating technology as an independent variable in the process of social change. An important consequence of such a comparative analysis of societies is provided in the views of Max Weber who found religious ideology to be acting as an important independent variable for the emergence of capitalism in some western societies (Olsen, 1968). Weber (1958) argued that in addition to economic, social and political requirements, industrialization may itself be dependent upon a set of cultural values and norms which must be internalized by individuals so as to motivate their activities. Such values and norms which he found in the "Protestant Ethic", stress the importance of hard work, self-denial, self-discipline, thrift, frugality, self-reliance and individual initiative. Industrialization requires the investment of large sums of money or capital into machinery, buildings, raw materials and trained man power. Weber argued that without the values and norms of the Protestant Ethic, individuals lack the motivation and drive, necessary to carry out the process of industrialization. Weber supported his thesis by showing that Protestant England, Germany and Scandinavia industrialized long before Europe. Numerous critics (Sammuelsson, 1961) have since attacked Weber's thesis and have conclusively demonstrated logical and factual errors in his linkage between Protestantism and this set of cultural values and norms.

Thus, scholars like Weber and Hoselitz (1960) maintain that traditional societies like India have failed to industrialize at a similar pace owing basically to their social, structural and cultural pecularities which have hindered economic growth. Despite the varying emphases, it can hardly be denied that the strides made in technological and industrial areas have affected societies in more than one way. There are some aspects of this technological advancement which directly and constantly have influenced social life.

Of all technological changes which have been sweeping through the traditional societies of the underdeveloped world in the last decade, the most fundamental and pervasive in their effects on human society, have been the changes in communication (Millikan, 1961). All these changes began with the industrial revolution during the latter half of the 18th century. Along the path of development, a society finds that it can use communication to implant and extend the idea of change to raise aspirations of the society in which it operates. Raising aspirations of the people would make them want a larger economy and modernized society (Schramm, 1967). Communication, while spreading knowledge among the people can also help to create specific attitudes and a type of personality which is necessary in order for traditional societies to become modern (Lerner, 1958).

The mass media are largely responsible in bringing about change in the economic and social spheres, especially in the context of modern welfare state. Progressive changes in the communication networks and mass media have not only brought the distant culture within a society together, but more importantly, they have literally contributed to a conception of a 'global society'. The initial attempts of the mass media for generating desired kinds of attitudes among members of a society may be thwarted by the exposure of audience to an even greater variety, thus leading to a number of implications.

While examining the relationship between technological factors and social change, one must be clear that the different segments of a society may not be uniformly affected due to definite reasons. Therefore, it is evident that the urban societies due to a greater exposure to almost all technological innovations, may experience these changes more drastically and strongly than their rural counterparts. Especially in the case of mass media, the urban population in a developing society like India would definitely have different experiences than the rural. Thus, mass media may serve as one of the many factors influencing the social and cultural life of urban dwellers. Since urban social networks and participation constitute a fertile area for empirical research in the transitional societies like India, the nexus between mass media and changing behaviour in an urban context becomes an important area for investigation.

Urbanization for a long time has been treated as an independent variable in bringing about social change. It has been emphasized on the basis of empirical evidence that urban societies tend to have different social and cultural characteristics (Redfield, 1947 and Wirth 1938). Contacts in the city are impersonal, superficial, transitory and segmental so that the urbanite loses the spontaneous self-expression, the morale and the sense of participation that comes from living in an integrated society. Wirth's notion was that an increase in the size and density of the population leads to increased anonymity; which together with the more widespread division of labour would in turn produce social heterogeneity. Under these conditions, relationships would inevitably become more impersonal and formally prescribed, and prestige would be allocated according to criteria other than personal acquaintance. Wirth listed out secondary contacts, weakening of bonds of kinship, declining social significance of family which resulted into the city dweller to become anonymous, isolated, secular, relativistic, rational and sophisticated. The various dichotomies and continual that were set forth later by the sociologists were derived primarily from the works of Durkheim (1933) and Tonnies (1940).

That urban societies tend to have peculiar social and cultural features is an observation made much earlier by Tonnies in terms of Gemeinschaft and Gesellschaft, by Maine of status and contract and by Durkheim of mechanical and organic solidarity.

That social bonds, relationships and ties are qualitatively different in urban societies is impressively elaborated upon by Tonnies. Such an emphasis is evident from his argument that an essential condition of the social relationship in the Gesellschaft is the 'contract' (De Fleur, 1970). The contract is a formal relationship into which a deliberate entry is sought. In the new society of complex credit, world markets, large formal associations and a vast division of labour, the contractual relationship is widely found between members. In other words, throughout all the major social institutions, the economic, the political structure, the educational system, religion and even in some instances the family, Gemeinschaft is being replaced by the relationships of the contractual type. While no society has been or probably ever will be exclusively Gesellschaft, it is clear that this type of social bond has become ubiquitous and pervasive.

For a long period of time urbanisation was equated with the emergence of cities as a result of which the entire emphasis of the analysts remained on the big cities. It is important to note that urbanism as a way of life is not restricted to the areas which are defined as urban. The continuous interaction between city and the hinterland results in diffusion of urban life style. Urbanism, besides being centripetal is at the same time centrifugal, radiating its influence outward (Anderson, 1960). Wirth was probably the first to make a systematic and detailed analysis of 'urbanism' in the social context. He differentiated between 'urbanism' and urbanisation by considering the former as that complex of traits which makes up the characteristic mode of life in cities; and urbanisation as a process of development and extension of these factors. For him, the three demographic conditions i.e., a large size, greater density and heterogeneity of population led to the emergence of secondary, segmental and artificial social relationships. Commenting on Wirth, Lewis (1965) observed:

> "Because Wirth thinks of the city as a whole, as a community, he assumes that all people who live in cities are affected by this experience in profound and similar ways."

As Wirth had borrowed Redfield's concept of folk-urban continuum, a study by Glass (1964) showed the futility of such a demarcation between urban and rural settlements and of the conception of a undirectional change from rural to an urban end. While Lewis found the way of life of the city dwellers to vary with their socio-economic status, Gans (1968) emphasized that the lack of uniformity found within the urban population with respect to the way of life depended on the socio-economic status.

Therefore, there is a need for conducting studies of the areas with varying degrees of urbanisation within the framework of their social, economic and demographic background. However, before going into these it would be appropriate to examine the relationship between mass media and urbanisation.

On lines similar to the folk-urban continuum, Lerner (1958) contrasts the oral or the traditional society to the medial system or the modern society. Lerner assumes that communication systems are agents of social change in his book, "The Passing of Traditional Society" (1958). He contrasts the traditional system to the modern system. He lists out the characteristics of the channel of communication of the traditional society as personal (face to face) communication. He also describes the audience of the traditional society as belonging to primary groups, basically rural, non-representative and illiterate. In contrast, the modern society has a heterogeneous (mass) audience and the channel of communication is the broadcast media. Also, their other characteristics include being urban and literate.

Lerner regards modernization as primarily a communication process. He takes into consideration in his explanation of what he regards as a modernization trend taking place on a global scale and irreversible, four variables, (1) Urbanisation, (2) Literacy, (3) Participation (divided into economic and political participation) and (4) Media consumption.

Lerner then makes two important conclusions:

1. Urbanisation everywhere leads to a reduction of illiteracy. This brings about a higher consumption of media. This in turn is inter-related with more intensive economic and political participation.
2. There is an inter-relationship between media consumption and education as well as the dependence of participation on these two variables.

Schramm and Ruggels (1967) examine Lerner's thesis keeping in view the fact that mass media growth is highly related to general economic and social development and concluded that the basic variables of urbanisation, literacy, GNP seem to be related in different ways in the several regions to the developing media. This suggests that there are different patterns of change in different countries.

Srivastava (1986) pointed out that media would continue to be urban in location and orientation. However, with a declining significance of the folk-urban continuum in understanding the contemporary urban situation in India, socio-economic status and class differences have emerged as important indices to be preferred in such an analysis (Lewis, 1965; Gans 1968; Chandra, 1977; Gill and Dhawan, 1991). Therefore, it becomes more meaningful to examine the changes in urban social organisation in terms of the variety of socio-economic groups within a settlement. A greater involvement informal organisations on the one hand, and a weakening of kinship and neighbourhood ties on the other, have already been identified among the upper socio-economic groups in the urban milieu.

In this background then, the invasion into the life of urban dwellers by the cable media is bound to produce innumerable transformations within the small unit of family as also beyond it at varying levels of social participation.

Existing Theoretical Perspectives on Effects of Mass Media

The potentiality of mass media for bringing about planned and desired change in society has been assessed in different theoretical perspectives. The relationship between the communicator/sender of the message on the one hand, and the receiver on the other, has been projected differently in these formulations. Before going into these, however we must give a brief account of the initial environment in which the most important mode of mass media i.e., television and later on Cable TV emerged as a major technological change inducing social change.

In the aftermath of the World War I, there emerged quite a general belief in the great power of mass communication. The media were thought to be able to shape public opinion to sway the masses toward almost any point of view desired by the communicator. This first set of beliefs about the nature and power of mass communication was never actually formulated at that time into a systematic statement by any communication scholar. But in retrospect it has come to be called the 'magic bullet theory' or the hypodermic needle theory which assumes that media messages are received in a uniform way by every member and that immediate and direct responses are triggered by such stimuli. The audience are assumed to be passive according to this theory. This theory was criticized by researchers of mass media as it depicted a one-way relationship between media and its audience (Katz and Lazarsfeld, 1954).

During the 1920's and early 1930's scholars developed an interest in the media as objects of research. They were beginning to turn from mere speculation about their effects to systematic studies of impact of particular communication upon particular kinds of people. Such an interest led to the emergence of various theories relating to the effects of the media on different aspects of society.

Contrary to the initial perspectives discussed above, mass media was believed to exercise varying impact on the audience, thus recognizing the significance of selectivity in acceptance or rejection of the media messages. Further, the variables along which variations among the receivers occurred were delineated. The empirical investigations in this direction proved to be highly relevant since these exposed the complexity involved in the interplay between mass media and the consequent change at individual and group levels.

An important contribution in this direction came from Lazarsfeld (1949) who contends that the *social categories perspective* is a central focus in media studies. It assumes that there are broad collectivities, or social categories, particularly in urban industrial societies, whose behaviour in the face of a given set of stimuli is more or less uniform. Such characteristics as age, sex, income level, educational attainment, rural-urban residence or religious affiliation provide a reasonably accurate guide to the type of communication content, a given individual will or will not select from available media.

The most obvious contemporary expression of the role of individual differences in the process of media exposure and effects is the *uses and gratification approach* (Blumler and Katz, 1974). Uses and gratification is an unsystematised set of specific theoretical viewpoints tied together by a shared emphasis on an active media audience (Katz, 1979; Swanson, 1979). These researchers have portrayed the individuals that constitute any mass audience as active selectors and interpreters of media messages who utilize media messages to gratify their individual needs. Individuals not only selectively expose themselves to media messages but also selectively avoid media messages (Becker, 1979).

Another theory which has been used by media researchers is the *cultural norms theory*. De Fleur states that the cultural norms theory postulates that the mass media through selective presentations and the emphasis of certain themes creates impressions among their audiences and that cultural norms concerning the emphasized topics are structured or defined in some specific way (De Fleur, 1970). In essence, this theory assumes that people identify themselves with particular demographic and social groups.

Close to this theory, Riley and Riley (1959), point to the role played in the communication process by *primary groups* and *reference groups*. The communicator influences his receivers through transmitting specially designed messages. The researchers distinguish primary groups by intimate relations among their members, a family being a typical example. A reference group is a group with the help of which an individual may define his attitudes, values and behaviour. He does not need to be member of the group but its norms nevertheless guide him. Primary groups close to the individual often serve as reference groups for him as well. As a communicator or a receiver in the communication process, an individual is influenced by the primary group. As a receiver, he may be guided by these groups in how to select, perceive and react to messages.

In the light of the above discussion, the medium of communication, Cable TV in this case, may create new reference groups for the viewers. The selection and adoption as well as rejection of these media messages may be greatly influenced by group norms, so that different messages may be received differently by various groups with different group norms. Also, different individual personalities would accept and reject media messages differently. Thus, in the same ecological situation, a city in this case with a similar media i.e., Cable TV – members of different socio-economic groups may select, adopt and reject different messages. But before getting on directly to the effects of Cable television on social life in a city, it would be appropriate to familiarize ourselves with its historical emergence.

Emergence of Cable Television

Cable television had a humble start, conceived of as a way to sell TV sets. An appliance store owner in Mahanoy City, Pennsylvania, John Walson, Sr., was frustrated because when TV sets were first marketed in 1947, he couldn't even demonstrate the new technology to his customers. The town was surrounded by the Appalachian Mountains, which entirely blocked TV reception. Later that year, Walson erected a large antenna on a nearby mountain and strung wire down the mountain, using amplifiers to boost the signal, to a television set in a warehouse in town. He was successful in selling several TV sets to towns people who also paid Walson $100 for a cable connection plus $2 monthly fees. In a short time, other cities that couldn't receive TV signals adopted Walson's methods. Thus Cable television was born in 1948. It was named Community Antenna Television (CATV) because it provided households with limited or non- existent TV reception with a connection via cable to a 'master' antenna that could pick up TV signals. Early Cable TV merely extended the reach of commercial TV by enabling small communities access to broadcasts from major cities and by improving the quality of TV reception.

Satellite communication systems have also expanded the horizons of cable operators. Apart from being able to relay TV signals over oceans, domestic satellite operators provide instant transmission of programmes over vast distances. By relaying signals to a satellite transponder (device which receives and then retransmits TV signals) a programme can be received anywhere in the country by anyone with a receive-only earth station.

Development of Cable television is a relatively inexpensive and simple technological matter where in large dish antennas receive satellite transmissions. These transmissions are then sent via coaxial cable to the subscribers. The initial cost of connecting households with CATV antenna is made relatively modest by piggybacking coaxial-cable lines on existing telephone-pole routes and by using the conventional TV set as the receiver.

CATV appealed to urban residents because it increased both picture fidelity and the number of channels they could receive. Channel capacity and picture fidelity are increased because cable transmissions are relatively unaffected by the airspace limitations and interference problems of conventional over the air television.

As the terms Satellite television, CATV (Community Antenna Television) and Cable TV have the same meaning, these terms have been used interchangeably in the study.

In India, the cosy world of home-green television is no longer what it was. In more and more homes, viewers are able to change channels and get a variety of programmes not only off the satellites, though these are the main source of the new stream of programmes, but from cable networks which are beginning to sprout all over the big cities and in some cases in not so big cities as well.

What started with CNN during the Gulf War in January 1991 was carried forward by STAR TV (Satellite Television Asian Region). CNN, MTV, STAR PLUS, BBC, PRIME SPORTS, ATN and ZEE TV are commanding prime viewership and in the process are edging out not just Doordarshan and films but are also affecting the social life within as well as across families (The Tribune, December 21, 1992).

Satellite television hence treated as a carrier of social change has had several consequences. Although, in its growing stages, it has opened up numerous tangible benefits in the economic and entertainment arenas. Dua (1992) observed that CATV will generate employment for the rapidly expanding self-employed entrepreneurial youth in cities and towns. Retail and small advertisers will get an opportunity to advertise their products and services on cable networks. This will thus contribute to increasing the market size. Also, cabling will prove to be an important source of revenue for the government as there will be an opportunity to collect licence fees.

On the other hand, CATV is also sometimes perceived as having deleterious effects on Indian culture (Sharma, 1992). The pervasive influence of such alien norm based television viewing can have several consequences. The process of non-Indian acculturisation of the urban middle class, which had set in even earlier, is perhaps getting consolidated now. More and more Indians are expected to identify with and adopt values and norms of men and women being projected on the screen. Since the presentation is so life-like the process of identification is greatly facilitated. This may lead to initiate the screen models in language, dress, life-styles etc. This process is so subtle and at an unconscious level, that most people would not even be aware of it. If such a situation continues over a period of time, a whole group of Indians may change and such a change would be in a non-Indian direction (Patri, 1992).

Vasantha, R. Patri (1992) further observes that the invasion of satellite television has had considerable and varying impact on the viewers in India. Clearer role models are being provided for the westernization of the urban youth. Further, among adults, satellite television with its many serials that cater to the fantasy of the starved urban upper-middle class lives, may have an impact on socialising, family outings and gatherings.

The undeniable feature of satellite television is that it caters to the needs of different people. The young and old, males and females of different classes and soon even the non-urban group may be drawn into it.

Regarding the viewership of the various channels by STAR TV, i.e. STAR PLUS, PRIME SPORTS, MTV, BBC (the entertainment channel, the sports channel, the music channel, and BBC world service channel respectively), Dyal (1992) found an increased relevance of factors such as age and socio-economic status.

India has earned the distinction of being the first developing country to have her National language satellite channel, i.e., the Asia Television Network. ATN is credited to have first realised the potential of Hindi language software in the Asia region. Also with a wide variety of programmes on ZEE TV, it is meaningful and appropriate for the researcher to study and examine the popularity of the various channels among viewers in different socio-economic groups in the urban context.

Television and Family

Cable television as a strong invader especially in the life of the urbanities is expected to influence a number of aspects of human life. Even with an analysis of the changing urban and social fabric, specific areas directly under its influence may be delineated. Perhaps first among these would relate to the influence Cable TV may have on the smallest unit of society, i.e., family, which also constitutes the most crucial primary group.

There is no doubt that the Indian families are changing under the influence of urbanization and modernization. Exposure to mass media, education, greater physical mobility and wider job opportunities in non-traditional sectors are the major contemporary developments in urban India. Keeping these factors in mind, it is therefore important for us to define 'family'.

Generally, families are composed of persons who are related by blood or marriage or sharing the same roof, food, dining table, money, material goods or emotions could define any group of family (Lull, 1988). Families in ethnically diverse countries are especially heterogeneous. Still differences often persist in the form of values and these values are present in the ways that families think and act. Socio-economic classes within individual cultures are another critical determinant of difference, as is the number of persons in the living space, whether or not there are children present and when there are children, whether or not both parents live at home.

A careful review of studies on family change in India at once makes one conscious regarding the usage of the term 'family' and its definition. Whether it is defined as a "dwelling unit" or a "network of relationships" would make a tremendous difference on such an analysis. With this in view a distinction is preferred between 'family' and 'household' for the subsequent discussion to avoid ambiguity. The term household is preferred both for its conceptual as well as the methodological appropriateness. However, while analysing the ties among members i.e., between spouses, parents and their children and their ties with other such units at both formal and informal levels, the concept of nuclear family would be more useful with a focus on relationships rather than a common residence.

Family is the first and most important social unit to experience the influence of media especially in the form of television, and thus it constitutes a fertile area of research.

Formulation of the Problem

An impact of Cable television on urban society could be observed in several ways through various dimensions. However, for the present purpose, the difference that cable viewing makes to the degree and nature of social participation within the primary as well as the secondary groups, is emphasized.

The review of literature clearly indicates that Cable TV may not work as an independent variable in transforming the values and behaviour patterns of the viewers. On the contrary, the process has been found to be both sided and mutual. Audience must not be considered as totally passive and the heterogeneity within the viewers in terms of age, sex, socio-economic status, rural-urban background, culture etc., may be quite prominent in the whole process.

Also, it must be pointed out, that due to limited availability of literature on Cable television, studies relating to television can be appraised for the present purpose. There are divergent opinions of social scientists regarding the interaction patterns among viewers of television.

Dorr (1986) came out with an interesting finding that even when television viewing is not on, it can be a stimulus to social interaction. Television facilitates discussion as it provides a subject for interaction. This leads to greater interaction among household members. This view has been highlighted by Lull (1980), Brodie *et. al* (1983) and Goodman (1983). However, contradictory to this view, Robinson (1972), Szalai (1972) and Noelle-Neumann (1981), observed that television in the household reduced conversation among married couples. Comstock (1978) also held a similar view that television had reduced interaction among family members.

Various social scientists have examined the influence of the intervening variables like age, sex, cultural values etc. on television viewing. Lull (1988) indicates a two-way relationship between television and family. He, on the one hand discusses the effects of television on the dynamics of the family and on the other, he brings out the fact that familial social and cultural ethos and norms influence television viewing patterns as well as interpretations of the programmes. Also, Cantor and Cantor (1986) reported that it is the audience in each country with its own system of cultural values and beliefs that ultimately decides the popularity of programmes. They further add that audience world-wide have the power to watch or not watch programmes that others select for them. But, given a choice audience almost invariably prefer their own local programmes to those produced in the US or elsewhere. Further, research by Greenberg and Dominick (1969) shows that low status minorities consume more hours of television than does any other social group. Such studies reveal the significant intervening role of cultural background of viewers.

It has been observed that sex and age of the viewers may influence their motivation for watching different programmes and channels on Cable TV. Differences in programme preferences held by men and women all over the world follow a predictable pattern. Men everywhere prefer sports, action-oriented programmes, and information programming (especially news), while women prefer dramas (including serials, soap operas and films) and music/dance/comedy-based programmes (Morley, 1988). These findings by Morley (1988) were held to be true not only in the West but also in China, Venezuela, India and West Germany. He further adds that males assert cultural power within the realm of domestic relations, including the construction of routine acts of television viewing. Men plan their viewing carefully and also control the technical aspects of television, including the remote control device, which they may use for unnegotiated channel switching, thereby asserting their preferences and weilding "cultural power" even more. Women, on the other hand, do not have as much say as men in the selection of shows or in possession and use of the technical aspects. They watch television far less attentively (more "distractedly") because they are constantly trying to manage their domestic responsibilities in addition to whatever viewing they can do at night.

Television and Children

Studies have been conducted on a limited scale on the viewing habits of children. There has been a great deal of public speculation that television cuts into the time for school work and serious study and ultimately affects academic performance. Once addicted to this medium, children become listless; this leads to passivity and poor concentration in other spheres. Some programmes, such as imported serials, which glorify violence, can lead to aggression or create hallucinations in childrens' minds (Kunhikrishnan, 1990).

Kunhikrishnan (1990) further states that television is bound to create displacements in children's schedule of daily activities, to make time for viewing programmes. It has a dominating influence on general family life, and this can cause conflict; often parents feel they are losing control and have no authority over their children; sometimes such conflicts may result in a total collapse of the family and bring in material change in the value system. This change is further contributed by the western channels of Satellite television.

Dyal (1992) adds that MTV, the musical programme of STAR TV was the most popular channel amongst the younger age group. Therefore, the role of age and sex plays an important role and it may be inferred that different types of programmes elicit different styles of viewing for different people at different times of the day. Thus, longer hours of cable viewing are bound to influence the activities of viewers in terms of their social interaction at different levels. The role of socio-economic status cannot be overlooked in the relationship between television and social participation. In practice, family forms in the industrial urban centres differ according to social class. On the basis of an extensive survey of literature, Goode (1963) contends that the contacts of upper strata families with their kin form a smaller proportion of their total social participation, since the higher strata belong to more voluntary organisations, clubs and formal groups than the lower strata. On the other hand, they have more resources with which to maintain their ties with kin and because of these means mutual exchanges are also more frequent than in the lower strata. The positive association between socio-economic status and formal participation is further substantiated by various other studies in India (Chandra, 1977 and Gill and Dhawan, 1992). Also, research by Buley (1977) reveals that if subscribers of Cable TV spend more and more time interacting with cable, then there will be less chance for social contacts and it would isolate individuals and families. Such a process then is expected to enhance anonymity, reduce social participation at the informal level and social interaction in general, thus, resulting into changes in the direction of urbanism.

The very definition of urbanism as a way of life involves a change from a folk to an urban society basically flowing from the perspective of folk-urban continuum. The conceptualization by Wirth and Redfield predicts a change from social participation based on predominantly primary ties which are face to face, informal, conventional, traditional, personal and emotional, towards predominantly secondary ties which are formal, superficial, segmental, impersonal and transitory.

Although the characteristics of urban-dwellers as listed out by Wirth have not been found to be relevant in many of the western as well as non-western cities (Lewis, 1965 and Gans, 1968), still the nature of social participation from an informal to formal participation has been empirically confirmed in different types of cities including the Indian (Chandra, 1977 and Gill and Dhawan, 1992). Therefore, formal participation has usually been taken as an indicator of urbanism although it has been found to be positively associated with education, occupation and economic status of urban-dwellers.

An important inference that can be drawn from such studies is that although the nature and degree of social participation would normally undergo change with urbanism, such a change may not be uniform among the urban dwellers in view of the internal variations within them.

In yet another study in an Indian city, different patterns of change were found between formal and informal participation within the urban dwellers among various socio-economic groups. Further, while informal participation among all these groups was found to have declined, an increase informal participation was basically a characteristic of the upper socio-economic groups, thereby creating a kind of vacuum for the lower and middle socio-economic groups (Gill and Dhawan, 1992).

Hence, the relationship between urban residence and specific types of social participation is evident. However, one factor within the urban milieu which is bound to play a significant role in transforming both the degree as well as the nature of social participation, relates to the strong influence exercised by viewership of Satellite television.

In view of the empirical studies mentioned above, it is evident that television has made a considerable impact on social interaction within the families. But, *we lack any studies to examine its impact on social participation beyond the unit of family*. Whether Cable television exercises a uniform effect on formal and informal social participation or not, also remains to be explored. Secondly, whether such an impact on the two types of social participation takes place uniformly among the urban dwellers constitutes an important question. These are some of the *important gaps in existing theoretical understanding* regarding the impact of *Cable television on social* participation and the present study addresses itself to these.

Major Objectives of the Study

In view of the existing literature it may be inferred that as a society undergoes the process of urbanisation, the degree as well as the nature of informal ties among families as well as within them tend to weaken. A similar kind of effect has been found empirically to follow the inception of Satellite television due to its capacity to glue the viewers to the TV sets for long periods. Hence, it may be assumed that Satellite TV would be expected to further reduce the degree of informal ties among families as well as within them, thus making urbanism as a way of life even more pronounced. However, whether it has a similar impact on formal participation too, needs to be explored. We intend in this study to test these assumptions. However, the specific objectives are listed below :

1. To study the socio-economic and demographic profile of Cable TV viewers and DD viewers.
2. To examine the association of the time devoted to TV and selectivity of programmes with income, education and occupation.
3. To analyse the association of duration of viewing TV with selectivity of programmes on the one hand and

degree of social participation (both formal and informal) on the other.

4. To examine the association between socio-economic status and social participation of the respondents.
5. To analyse if viewing of Satellite TV has led to a change in the degree and nature of social participation (both formal and informal) from the point of view of viewers themselves.
6. To assess the impact of Satellite TV on social participation within and outside the family by comparing the Cable TV viewers and DD viewers in terms of the degree and nature of social participation.
7. To examine the reactions of the respondents towards the western media dominating on the Satellite television among various socio-economic groups, especially in terms of its impact on the children.

Hypotheses

The following hypotheses were drawn for the study:

1. Formal participation has a positive association with income education and occupation.
2. Viewing Cable television (with longer duration and variety of channels) would reduce intra-family communication.
3. Viewing Cable television (within a household) would have the most profound effect on children reflected through both academic and non-academic dimensions.
4. The various socio-economic groups would differ significantly in terms of the perceived effects of Cable TV on social participation.

Rationale of the Study

Initially, this study intended to undertake a comparative study of Cable TV viewers and non-viewers. The assumption was that TV viewing presupposes a certain level of physical immobility of the viewers, so that they would spend most of their time glued to the TV sets. This tendency is expected to curtail social participation of the viewers in a significant manner. Viewers would naturally curtail their outdoor activities, interaction with relatives, friends and neighbours when they are busy watching their favourite programmes. Further, the presence of TV that offers entertainment for 24 hours through the cable network, may further affect interactional patterns within the members of a family. Hence, TV is expected to isolate the individuals from *(a)* the outside world, as well as *(b)* from their family members. Instead of performing a socializing function, it is expected to 'individuate' or 'isolate' the viewers both physically and socially. The present study makes an endeavour to analyse this main hypothesis. The importance of the study increases in view of the paucity of studies on the above issues. Whatever literature we have has mainly focussed upon the intra-familial communciation only, that too in the western context.

For conducting this study, it was intended to compare the patterns of social participation among subscribers of Cable TV and others who do not have it. But, then it was found that while it was possible to identify the Cable subscribers, it was not possible to locate any 'non-viewers' since television had become an essential part of almost every household. Therefore, a comparative study was designed between Cable viewers on the one hand and the Doordarshan viewers on the other. Such a comparison was justified because at the time when the survey was conducted i.e., 1994, Doordarshan had only two channels i.e., DD I and DD II. Also with the advent of Cable TV, Doordarshan in an effort to compete with it, started increasing the timings of its telecast to woo the viewers. Initially, Doordarshan had limited telecast timings during morning, afternoon, evening and night with ample space in between each of these sessions of telecast. Also, with the lack of good programmes, manpower and expertise available in the country that many 'quick and easy to make' type of programmes were produced although efforts are now being made to improve quality (Sinha, 1996). On the other hand, Satellite TV was offering round the clock programmes. Secondly, in addition to the quantity, the two kinds of viewerships differed in quality too, with a greater content of western culture in the Satellite TV. The nature of programmes, themes of serials, predominant life styles depicted were considerably different. With round-the-clock programmes, viewers are engrossed in selecting programmes to suit their choice and hence are glued to the TV, thus rescheduling their daily activities. On the other hand, DD provides limited channels thus limiting the choice of programmes as well as giving ample time for its audiences' to continue their daily routine.

The time available for DD viewers may lead to a greater involvement in social participation both within and outside the family, whereas in the case Cable viewers, social participation may be curtailed at both these levels. Hence, it was meaningful to study the impact of Satellite TV on social participation among people as well as comparing Cable viewers with DD viewers.

For the present study, social participation has been treated as the key dependent variable. Social participation is one area on which Satellite television is expected to have exercised its influence to a great extent. Therefore, it is assumed that the impact of such a media will create different patterns in the nature and degree of social participation within and across families.

Definition of Social Participation

Social participation has been defined as all those actions or dispositions that reflect an individual's interest, concern or identification for an organisation, programme, group etc. (Chandra, 1977, p. 31).

Social participation may be located in various social situations – in family and kinship groups, in groups of friends, neighbours and informal and informal associations.

Operationalization of Social Participation

For the present study, social participation in an operational context would cover all activities related to the urbanite's joining formal social-cultural organizations and all varieties of informal interactions within the family, with neighbours, relatives and friends.

Social participation has been operationalized on two main dimensions, namely formal and informal participation.

Definition of Formal Participation

For this study, formal participation is defined as the voluntary membership of any social-cultural or religious organisation by an individual. This does not include an organisation where a person is employed. Formal participation as defined by Wirth is also the symbolic manifestation of the urban ethos characterized by segmental and transitory relationships, secondary contact, sophistication, cosmopolitanism etc.

Definition of Informal Participation

For the present purpose, informal participation would include the interactions within the family, and across families with neighbours, relatives and friends. Participation of this type refers to all varieties of interactions within the family, membership of friendship circles, neighbourhood participation and participation in informal interest groups. This informal participation is generally considered to be at its minimum in an urban milieu.

Formal and informal participation can be measured from two dimensions – nature and degree.

Operationalization of Nature and Degree of Formal Participation

Regarding the nature of formal participation, a typology of formal organizations to which respondents belong were developed on the basis of a pilot study. Thus, the nature of formal participation was measured in terms of:

1. nature of the organisation to which the respondent belongs, i.e., religious, political, entertainment based, sports etc.
2. nature of the membership of the respondent in terms of the following:
   (a) Only consumers of services.
   (b) Contribute money only.
   (c) Contribute money and participate actively.
   (d) Office-holding.

The *degree of formal participation* was measured in terms of the frequency of attendance in the organizations mentioned above.

Operationalization of Nature and Degree of Informal Participation

The *nature of informal participation* with neighbours, friends and relatives was measured in terms of the levels of intimacy and casualness. An index was developed to measure the nature of informal participation in terms of the intensity of the ties. Due to the difficulty in quantifying the interaction among the members of a household, respondents was asked to give their perceived effects of Cable TV on the interaction within the household unit.

The *degree of informal participation*, on the other hand was measured in terms of the frequency of contacts of the respondents with the neighbours, friends and relatives. A separate index for this purpose was constructed. The time spent together by members of a household, viewing patterns etc., were analysed to measure the degree of social participation within the household.

Reactions to the Western Media

Since the Satellite television contains a heavy dose of the western media, thus exposing the viewers to the western culture through its various channels, people may respond differently to it depending on their selectivity of programmes. Thus, it is intended here to elicit their reactions to the western media in terms of sexuality, nudity or obscenity. It is expected that these reactions will vary among various socio-economic groups.

Viewership

In the present study, by viewership we mean watching the Satellite television which of course includes watching of the local Doordarshan programmes. Therefore, by CATV viewers we mean

(i) all those who have subscribed to the Cable TV and
(ii) all those having the connections through private dish antennas.

On the other hand, by DD viewers we mean all those without a provision of Satellite television through either of the above two means. Hence, the DD Viewers would not be regular viewers of Satellite television, although they may be viewing television as such. Since viewing of TV as such (Doordarshan) may be a common factor between CATV viewers and DD viewers, the differences between the two groups can be safely ascribed to Satellite TV.

Method of Study

Most of the descriptive studies in Sociology lay a substantial focus on "describing" a certain aspect of the social phenomena. As and when an attempt is made to explain the transforming social phenomena in terms of certain independent variables, the first problem encountered by the researcher is, how to ensure that the phenomenon under study is an effect of the independent variable/s in question. Indeed, it is admitted at the very outset that it is neither feasible nor a desirable goal for a social scientist to aspire for a causal analysis in view of the tremendous degree of heterogeneity as well as changeability of the phenomenon under study. Since the present study is intended to examine the extent to which the patterns of social participation and interaction within and across families are being influenced by Cable TV as an important technological factor, I as a researcher am faced with a similar problem. However, the difficulty in arriving at causal explanations in no way can minimize the importance of examining the association between a particular social dimension and a factor directly influencing it. I have tried to achieve this by the following steps.

Universe and Sampling Frame

Since the CATV viewers and DD viewers may not form neat and homogeneous categories within themselves, there is a need to specify the universe precisely. Thus, roughly we may find the following categories:

- *(a)* subscribers to Cable TV and those who own private dish antennas.
- *(b)* those who own television.
- *(c)* those who do not own a television, but watch it at any other place (neighbours, friends etc.).
- *(d)* Non-viewers – those who neither own a television nor watch it elsewhere. On the basis of a preliminary survey conducted by me, in the localities under study, the third and fourth categories are almost non-existent except negligible exceptions in the case of low socio-economic group.

Therefore, it is feasible and quite practical to delineate the viewers of Satellite TV from DD viewers.

The study was conducted in the city of Chandigarh. This city represents a typical case where uniformity of houses in each sector indicates socio-economic distinctions within its population, making it easy to distinguish one socio-economic segment from the other.

The city on the whole comprises of 54 sectors and each sector is further sub-divided into four sub-sectors i.e., A, B, C and D. Due to its planned nature, residential plots of an equal size are cut in different sectors, thus providing homogeneously structured neighbourhoods on the basis of socio-economic status, although all the sectors are not absolutely homogeneous in terms of the housing units.

Since the present study undertakes a comparative analysis among upper, middle and low socio-economic groups of urban-dwellers and since it is not possible to stratify the total population of Chandigarh on the basis of socio-economic status, three sectors were purposely selected as they are homogeneous within themselves in terms of the housing units. During the pilot study, it was noticed that there was no cable operator in Sector 9 and the residents of Sector 9 subscribed to Cable TV from the neighbouring sectors or had installed their own dish antennae. Due to heavy installation charges most residents were without cable connections. Hence, the researcher included the two kanal or bigger houses of Sector 8 and Sector 18 too, where there were local operators. Hence, the universe for this study comprises of the population residing in two kanal or bigger houses in Sectors 8, 9 and 18, which is representative of the upper socio-economic group and Sector 22 and Industrial Area 'B' which are representative of the middle and low socio-economic groups respectively. The rationale behind selecting Industrial Area 'B' i.e., Ram Darbar are *(a)* Cable television exists in this low socio-economic locality, *(b)* It consists of pucca houses occupied by relatively settled households with well-developed informal and formal networks. In no other low socio-economic locality with comparable size of population, such a permanent settlement was found. Hence, Ram Darbar represents the low socio-economic segment for the present study.

The sampling frame for this study consisted of all 2 kanal and bigger than 2 kanal houses in Sectors 8, 9 and 18; all households in Sector 22 and in Ram Darbar. The information regarding number of households in these sectors was obtained from the Town planner, UT Secretariat Office, Sector 9, Chandigarh.

It was observed that there were a total of 282 (2 kanal plus) houses in Sector 9, 313 houses in Sector 8; 318 houses in Sector 18; 1472 houses in Sector 22 and 344 houses in Ram Darbar. Thus, there were 913 households in the upper socio-economic group; 1472 households in the middle and 344 households in lower socio-economic group which constituted our sampling frame. At the next stage, these households were stratified on the basis of CATV viewers and DD viewers in each of these sectors. This was done on the basis of information obtained from the cable operators within these sectors as also the identification of privately owned dish antennas. The cable operators were contacted during December 1994 at the time when the survey began and from each of these sectors all the cable operators (in sectors where there were more than one cable operator, all were contacted) were asked to give a list of the households which had cable connections. It was observed that there were a total of 363 households in the upper socio-economic group, 637 households in the middle economic group and 72 households in Ram Darbar who had either cable connections or private dish antennae. In the final stage 100 households from each of these three socio-economic groups were selected by using the method of systematic random sampling with an equal proportion of CATV viewers and DD viewers in each case. In households where there was more than one married couples residing together, the youngest married male was chosen in the sample.

Limitations of the Study

Due to the non-availability of a sampling frame for the total population of Chandigarh on the basis of socio-economic status, the sampling frame consists of only the selected sectors. Hence, the inferences drawn in the study will be generalizable only to these sectors.

Collection of Data

An interview schedule was constructed to elicit relevant information from the heads of the households. However, an effort was made to conduct the interviews in the presence of other members to get a glimpse and sensitization to their reactions too. Both, open ended as well as fixed alternative questions were framed to obtain relevant information. During the pilot survey it was observed that the lady of the household (wife of the respondent) was intervening to give answers to some questions pertaining to her husband's TV viewing habits. As the study was focussing on intra-familial relationships some questions were posed to the lady of household in the context of TV viewing by her husband and children. Also, at times, as the male head of the household was being interviewed, the wife too started responding, which was quite advantageous. Such responses helped me in getting more information especially regarding children which was used while drawing inferences.

Theoretical Framework

The present study aims to examine the impact of Satellite viewing on social participation among urban dwellers. Various theoretical frameworks have been developed in the area of communication studies to understand the role of mass media in transforming the different aspects of society. On the other hand, the changing pattern of social participation in an urban milieu has also been examined from a number of perspectives. It is therefore necessary here to specify the theoretical framework to which the present study belongs.

Perspectives on Impact of Mass Media

The impact of mass media on various aspects of society has been understood differently by scholars. The initial theoretical perspective thus projected this relationship as one-sided, with a determining role to the mass media and is known as 'magic-bullet' or the 'hypodermic needle theory'. Contrary to this perspective, the later theories ascribed a more active role to the audience, thus making sufficient scope for the variations within the effects of media on society (Lazarsfeld, 1949). Thus, according to the 'social categories perspective', there are broad collectivities, particularly in urban industrial societies, whose behaviour in the face of a given set of stimuli is more or less uniform. Thus individuals constituting a social category may experience a similar effect as a consequence of exposure to a media. 'Uses and gratification approach' is another unsystematized set of specific theoretical viewpoints tied together by a shared emphasis on an active media audience (Katz, 1979; Swanson, 1979).

The theory that comes close to a sociological way of looking at the phenomenon is the 'cultural norms theory' (De Fleur, 1970). In this perspective, Riley and Riley (1959) underline the role played in the communication process by primary groups and reference groups. As a communicator or a receiver in the process, he may be guided by these groups in how to select, perceive and react to messages.

Perspectives on Changing Patterns of Social Participation in Cities

The most prominent theoretical perspective developed to understand the changing nature of social participation in urban societies is the 'folk-urban continuum' perspective (Redfield, 1947 and Wirth, 1938).

According to this perspective, urban dwellers have been found to be substituting the traditional, informal, personal and primary group ties by the transitory, formal, impersonal and secondary ties. Such a viewpoint owed a lot to the dichotomous conception of societies developed by Emile Durkheim, Tonnies, Max Weber and others. However, later empirical research has put some of the major assumptions of the continuum theory into question. Change in social organization following urbanization has not been found to be uniform and is greatly intervened by factors such as socio-economic status, suburbanism, life-cycle, age and ethnic background (Gans, 1968 and Gill and Dhawan, 1992).

In the backdrop of these theoretical perspectives then, the present study focussing on the impact of Satellite television on social participation is based on the assumption that this impact would be influenced by the socio-economic status of viewers. Thus, the 'social categories' perspective seems to be most useful in delineating specific social categories among the audience and studying the impact of a specific kind of media exposure on them. Since the present study undertakes the task to examine the changing patterns of social participation among urban dwellers as a consequence of cable viewing, the analysis will be made following this framework, using socio-economic groups as the social categories under study.

Significance of the Study

Ever since the concept of Cable TV emerged in India after the Gulf War in 1991, there has been very limited research conducted in this field by social scientists in the country. Although studies regarding viewership of Cable TV have been conducted by a few research organisations in India, there is little literature available on the effects of Cable TV especially in the social context. Research into mass communication and the study of media effects, which is almost 50 years old or more can be discussed in terms of three main stages. In the first phase, the media were attributed considerable power to shape opinion and belief, change habits of life, actively mould behaviour and impose political systems. Such views were not based on scientific investigation but were based on empirical observation of the sudden extension of the audience to large majorities and on the great attraction of popular press, cinema and radio. The second phase extending from 1940 to early 1960's was concerned with the application of empirical method to specific questions about the effects and effectiveness of mass communication. The third phase which still persists is, one where new thinking and new evidence is accumulating on the influence of mass communication, especially television. The availability of variety of effects research makes comparisons across studies difficult. Yet, the numerous dimensions on which the effects studies differ, can also serve to point out the parameters of the field. These include empirical design (experimental, correlational, field study, etc.), and type of effect studied (short-term or long-term effects, media-induced change, effects on beliefs or behaviour etc.), target population studied (children, adolescents, youth etc.), and type of media content studied (news reports, cartoons, violence, advertisements etc.). Differences between studies must also be understood in their historical context: the media have themselves changed over the past 50 years of research, in terms of technology, content, availability and in relation to the changing practices of everyday life.

Hence, this researcher, in the light of the prevailing scenario, feels the need to examine the emerging patterns of social organisation among urban-dwellers as a consequence of a exposure to Cable television.

Although researchers in the US have studied the effects of Cable TV, the same may not be applicable to Third World countries especially India. It is therefore felt that the study is of significant importance for understanding the contemporary urban society in India. Moreover, a number of studies in our country have clearly brought out the varying patterns of formal and informal participation among upper, middle and low socio-economic groups. But, we lack any attempts to identify the factors contributing to such a tendency. Therefore, the present study gains relevance in its effort to find out the association between viewing of Cable television on the one hand, and the nature and level of social participation within and across families on the other.

2

Viewers of Satellite Television and Doordarshan: A Demographic Profile

Before analysing the data, relating the variables and drawing inferences, it is imperative to first present the demographic profile, socio-economic characteristics and family background of the respondents. The aim of this chapter thus, is to describe the socio-economic and demographic profile of the respondents under study. Besides this, an attempt has been made to compare the respondents in the three different socio-economic groups with regard to the demographic variables.

The data presented in this chapter will reflect the nature and extent of heterogeneity characterizing the city dwellers. While the selection of the three neighbourhoods was made on the basis of varying size of plots, houses and general observation, it is yet to be seen in what other respects these neighbourhoods differ from one another. Since, the study takes socio-economic background as an important intervening variable, the educational, economic and occupational attributes of the respondents will be examined in this chapter. The association of these variables with social participation will be analysed subsequently in the following chapters.

In view of the major objectives of the study i.e., to draw inferences regarding the impact of Satellite television on social participation among urban dwellers, demographic variables which are supposed to have an association with TV viewership as well as social participation, have to be first examined.

In the following discussion, therefore, a familiarity with the age structure, social and economic status of respondents, the structure of their families, patterns of subscription to Cable TV and viewership etc. will be gained. Having accomplished this, it will be easier then to proceed to further analysis of data. In this and the subsequent tables, the three samples collected from the upper, middle and low income groups/neighbourhoods will be designated as Locality I, Locality II and Locality III respectively.

Age

For the purpose of analysis, the age of the heads of the households was divided into six categories. While conducting the survey, it was found that the age of the heads of the households in our sample ranged from a minimum of 20 years to a maximum of 78 years. Therefore, six categories i.e., 20-29 years, 30-39 years, 40-49 years, 50-59 years, 60-69 years and 70 years and above were made.

The data indicates that on the whole, around 38 per cent of the total respondents belonged to the 40-49 years age group category and 25.3 per cent and 26 per cent of the respondents belonged to the 30-39 years and 50-59 years categories respectively. Also, only 6.3 per cent of the respondents belonged to the 20-29 years age group category. In Locality I, 36 per cent belonged to the 50-59 years category while 24 per cent and 28 per cent belonged to the 30-39 years and 40-49 years categories respectively. In Locality II, 43 per cent of the respondents were in the 40-49 years category while 25 per cent each belonged to the 30-39 years and 50-59 years categories respectively. Also, 3 per cent and 4 per cent of the respondents belonged to 20-29 years and 60-69 years age group categories respectively.

In Locality III, 42 per cent of the respondents were in the 40-49 years category while 27 per cent and 17 per cent belonged to 30-39 and 50-59 years categories respectively. Also, 12 per cent and 2 per cent of the respondents belonged to 20-29 years and 60-69 years age groups respectively.

The data reveals that a majority of the respondents (89%) belonged to the three middle aged categories, i.e., 30-39 years, 40-49 years and 50-59 years. On the whole, most respondents belonged to the 40-49 years age group category. In Locality I, majority of the respondents (36%) belonged to 50-59 years age group category while in Locality II and Locality III majority of the respondents belonged to the 40-49 years age group category.

Table-2.1
Distribution of Respondents According to Age in the Three Localities

Age (in Years)	*Locality* I	II	III	*Total*	*%*
20-29	4	3	12	19	6.3
30-39	24	25	27	76	25.3
40-49	28	43	42	113	37.7
50-59	36	25	17	78	26.0
60-69	5	4	2	11	3.7
70 +	3	–	–	3	1.0
Total	100	100	100	300	100

Mean age :

Locality I : 46.8 years

Locality II : 44.7 years

Locality III : 41.5 years

The mean age of the respondents was calculated for all the three localities and it was observed that the mean age was the lowest in Locality III (41.5 years) while it was the highest in Locality I (46.8 years). It is inferred that the respondents of Locality III were younger than the respondents of other two localities.

As the study also aims to compare CATV viewers and DD viewers, the data shall be presented separately for these two categories of respondents.

In the present study, by CATV viewers we mean respondents watching the Satellite television which of course includes watching the local Doordarshan programmes. Therefore, by CATV viewers we mean all those having the connections through private dish antennas or through cable operators. On the other hand, by DD viewers we mean all those without a provision of Satellite television through a private dish antenna or connections through cable operators. Hence, the DD viewers would not be regular viewers of CATV although, they may be viewing TV as such.

On the whole, 8 per cent of the CATV viewers and 4.7 per cent of the DD viewers belonged to the 20-29 years age group category while 28.6 per cent of the CATV viewers and 22 per cent of the DD viewers belonged to the 30-39 years age group category. Further, 29.3 per cent of the CATV viewers and 46 per cent DD viewers belonged to the 40-49 years age group category while 30 per cent CATV viewers and 22 per cent DD viewers belonged to the 50-59 years age group category. Only 2 per cent CATV viewers and 5.4 per cent DD viewers were above 60 years of age.

In Locality I, 42 per cent of the CATV viewers and 30 per cent of the DD viewers belonged to the 50-59 years age group category while 22 per cent of the CATV viewers and 34 per cent of the DD viewers belonged to the 40-49 years age group category. Also, 22 per cent of the CATV viewers and 26 per cent of the DD viewers belonged to the 30-39 years age group category while 4 per cent each among CATV and DD viewers belonged to the 20-29 years age group category. About 10 per cent CATV viewers and 6 per cent DD viewers were above 60 years of age.

In Locality II, 32 per cent among CATV viewers belonged to each of the age group categories 30-39 years, 40-49 years and 50-59 years. Also, 18 per cent each among DD viewers belonged to the 30-39 years and 50-59 years age group categories while 54 per cent belonged to the 40-49 years age group category. Further, 4 per cent CATV viewers and 2 per cent DD viewers belonged to the 20-29 years age group category while 8 per cent DD viewers belonged to the 60-69 years age group category.

In Locality III, 34 per cent CATV viewers and 50 per cent DD viewers belonged to the 40-49 years age group category while 32 per cent CATV viewers and 22 per cent DD viewers belonged to the 30-39 years age-group category. About 16 per cent CATV viewers and 8 per cent DD viewers belonged to the 20-29 years age group category while 16 per cent CATV viewers and 18 per cent DD viewers belonged to the 50-59 years age group category. There were no respondents in Localities II and III both among CATV and DD viewers who were above 70 years of age.

The data reveals that the respondents were fairly spread in the three middle age categories i.e., 30-39 years, 40-49 years, and 50-59 years among CATV viewers and DD viewers. The data also indicated

Table–2.2
Distribution of CATV Viewers and DD Viewers According to Age in the Three Localities

Age (in Years)	*Locality* I	II	III	*Total*	*%*
20-29	2 (2)	2 (1)	8 (4)	12 (7)	8.0 (4.7)
30-39	11 (13)	16 (9)	16 (11)	43 (33)	28.6 (22.0)
40-49	11 (17)	16 (27)	17 (25)	44 (69)	29.3 (46.0)
50-59	21 (15)	16 (9)	8 (9)	45 (33)	30.0 (22.0)
60-69	3 (2)	- (4)	1 (1)	1 (7)	0.7 (4.7)
70 +	2 (1)	- (-)	- (-)	2 (1)	1.3 (0.7)
Total	50 (50)	50 (50)	50 (50)	150 (150)	100 (100)

(Figures in parentheses are the frequencies for DD viewers.)

Mean Age	*Cable Viewers*	*Doordarshan Viewers*
Locality I	48.5 years	52.04 years
Locality II	43.7 years	45.7 years
Locality III	40.1 years	42.9 years

that majority of the CATV viewers belonged to the 50-59 years age group category while majority of the DD viewers belonged to the 60-69 years age group category. Hence, it may be inferred that Cable TV viewers were younger in age as compared to the DD viewers.

The mean age of the respondents both CATV and DD viewers was calculated and it was observed that among CATV viewers the highest mean age was in Locality I (48.5 years) and the lowest mean age was in Locality III (40.1 years). Among DD viewers the highest mean age was 52.04 years in Locality I and lowest mean age was 42.9 years in Locality III. It was also observed that the mean age of the DD viewers was higher than the CATV viewers in all the three localities indicating that Cable viewers were younger than the DD viewers.

After the description of the age structure of the respondents it is important to analyse the structure of other variables like family income, educational level and occupational status.

Family Income

Family income is an essential factor in assessing the socio-economic status of a respondent. For the purpose of this study, family income includes income from all sources for a period of one month. In this study, family income has been calculated for one household unit, i.e., members residing together in a house. The income may comprise of income through a working wife and working unmarried children, income through rent and other sources for the household unit.

Table–2.3
Distribution of Respondents According to Family Income in the Three Localities

	Locality				
Family Income (in Rupees)	*I*	*II*	*III*	*Total*	*%*
Upto 2000	–	4	67	71	23.7
2001-5000	–	41	32	73	24.3
5001-10000	70	47	1	118	39.3
10001+	30	8	–	38	12.7
Total	100	100	100	300	100
Mean Income					
Locality I :	Rs. 9750.50				
Locality II :	Rs. 6200.48				
Locality III :	Rs. 1865.17				

The family income was divided into four categories, *(i)* upto Rs. 2000; *(ii)* Rs. 2001-5000; *(iii)* Rs. 5001-10000; and *(iv)* Rs. 10001 and above.

The data indicated that 39.3 per cent of the total respondents had a family income between Rs. 5001-10000. About 24.3 per cent of the respondents belonged to the Rs. 2001-5000 category while 23.7 per cent and 12.7 per cent of the respondents had an income below Rs. 2000 and above Rs. 10001 respectively.

In Locality I, 70 per cent of the respondents belonged to the Rs. 5001-10000 category while 30 per cent had an income above Rs. 10001. There were no respondents who had an income below Rs. 5000 a month. In Locality II, it was observed that 4 per cent, 41 per cent, 47 per cent and 8 per cent of the respondents belonged to below Rs. 2000, Rs. 2001-5000, Rs. 5001-10000 and Rs. 10001 and above categories respectively. In Locality III, 67 per cent and 32 per cent of the respondents had a income of below Rs. 2000 and Rs. 2001-5000 respectively. There was only one respondents with an income between Rs. 5001-10000. Also, there were no respondents who had an income above Rs. 10001.

The data reveals that majority of the respondents had a family income between Rs. 5001 and 10000. Also, in Locality I and Locality II the respondents had an income between Rs. 5001-10000, while in Locality III majority of the respondents had a family income below Rs. 2000 a month. The mean income of the respondents was calculated and it was observed that the mean income was the highest in Locality I i.e., Rs. 9750.50 and lowest in Locality III i.e., Rs. 1865.17.

These data confirm our selection of the three localities as high, middle and low in terms of economic criterion. Whether a similar trend persists in terms of education and occupation too will be examined in the subsequent discussion. Presently, the study explores the variations between CATV viewers and DD viewers in terms of family income.

On the whole, 22 per cent CATV viewers and 25.3 per cent of the DD viewers had a family income below Rs. 2000 a month while 24 per cent CATV viewers and 24.7 per cent of the DD viewers had a family income between Rs. 2001-5000. About 42 per cent of the

Table–2.4
Distribution of CATV Viewers and DD Viewers According to Family Income in the Three Localities

Family Income per Month (in Rupees)	*Locality* I	II	III	*Total*	*%*
upto 2000	-	-	33	33	22.0
	(-)	(4)	(34)	(38)	(25.3)
2001-5000	-	20	16	36	24.0
	(-)	(21)	(16)	(37)	(24.7)
5001-10000	35	27	1	63	42.0
	(35)	(20)	(-)	(55)	(36.7)
10001 +	15	3	-	18	12.0
	(15)	(5)	(-)	(20)	(13.3)
Total	50	50	50	150	100
	(50)	(50)	(50)	(150)	(100)

Mean Income	*CATV Viewers*	*DD Viewers*
Locality I :	Rs. 9750.50	Rs. 9750.50
Locality II :	Rs. 6350.50	Rs. 6050.46
Locality III :	Rs. 1930.17	Rs. 1800.16

CATV viewers and 36.7 per cent of the DD viewers had a family income between Rs. 5001-10000 while 12 per cent of the CATV viewers and 13.3 per cent of the DD viewers had an income above Rs. 10001.

It is observed from the Table 2.4 that no respondent in Locality I had a family income below Rs. 5000 a month among both CATV viewers and DD viewers. There were an equal number of respondents i.e., 70 per cent and 30 per cent each among both CATV viewers and DD viewers who had a family income between Rs. 5001-10000 and above Rs.10001 a month.

In Locality II, there were no CATV viewers who had a family income below Rs. 2000 while there were 8 per cent DD viewers who had a family income below Rs. 2000 a month. About 40 per cent CATV viewers and 42 per cent DD viewers had an income of

Rs. 2001-5000 while 54 per cent CATV viewers and 40 per cent DD viewers had family income between Rs. 5001-10000. Further, 6 per cent CATV viewers and 10 per cent DD viewers had family income above Rs. 10001 a month.

In Locality III, 66 per cent CATV viewers and 68 per cent DD viewers had family income below Rs. 2000 while 32 per cent each among both CATV viewers and DD viewers belonged to the Rs. 2001-5000 category. There was only one respondent among CATV viewers in the Rs. 5001-10000 category. There were no respondents who had an income above Rs. 10001.

There were no considerable differences between CATV viewers and DD viewers in terms of income level except in Locality II in the Rs. 5001-10000 category. Here, about 54 per cent of the CATV viewers and only 40 per cent of the DD viewers had a family income Rs. 5001-10000.

The mean income of CATV viewers and DD viewers was the same Rs. 9750.50 in Locality I while in the other two localities the mean income was higher among CATV viewers (Locality II; Rs. 6350.50; Locality III; Rs. 1930.17) than DD viewers (Locality II: Rs. 6050.46; Locality III: Rs. 1800.16).

It is notable that in the upper income group both the Doordarshan as well as the Cable viewers had exactly similar mean family income. It is yet to be seen therefore as to whether respondents in other two groups do not watch Cable TV due to economic reasons or some other factors.

Education

Another significant variable which may influence TV viewership pattern as well as social participation is educational qualifications. The educational qualifications were classified into five categories for the present analysis, i.e. *(i)* below matric; *(ii)* matric; *(iii)* intermediate; *(iv)* graduation and *(v)* post-graduation.

The data revealed that 38 per cent of the total respondents were graduates, 26 per cent were matriculates and about 19 per cent of the respondents had their education below matric level. Around 4.7 per cent and 12.3 per cent of the respondents were intermediates and post-graduates respectively.

Table-2.5
Distribution of Respondents According to Educational Qualifications in the Three Localities

Educational Qualification	*Locality* I	II	III	*Total*	%
Below matric	-	9	48	57	19.0
Matric	9	24	45	78	26.0
Intermediate	2	8	4	14	4.7
Graduate	67	44	3	114	38.0
Post-graduate	22	15	-	37	12.3
Total	100	100	100	300	100

In Locality I, 67 per cent of the respondents were graduates, 22 per cent were post-graduates and 9 per cent were matriculates. There were no respondents in Locality I who had studied below matric level.

In Locality II, 44 per cent of the respondents were graduates, 24 per cent were matriculates, 15 per cent were post-graduates. Also, 8 per cent and 9 per cent had studied upto intermediate and below matriculation respectively.

In Locality III, 48 per cent of the respondents had studied below matriculation level, about 45 per cent were matriculates, and 4 per cent were intermediate while only about 3 per cent were graduates. There were no post-graduates in Locality III.

The data reveals that majority (38%) of the respondents were graduates closely followed by matriculates (26%). Further, in Localities I and II most respondents were graduates while in Locality III most respondents had their educational qualification below matriculation.

Data in Table 2.5 again substantiate our earlier findings that the three localities vary distinctively in terms of not only family income but educational status too. Consistent differences have been observed among the respondents in localities I, II and III respectively, further confirming their dictinctiveness from one another in terms of educational attributes.

Subsequently, an effort was made to see if there were consistent differences among CATV viewers and DD viewers in the three localities in terms of educational qualifications.

The data in Table 2.6 indicates that on the whole, 18.7 per cent of the CATV viewers and 19.3 per cent of the DD viewers had their education below matriculation level. An equal number of respondents (26%) both among CATV viewers and DD viewers were matriculates. About 4 per cent of the CATV viewers and 5.3 per cent of the DD viewers had their education upto intermediate level. Further, 42 per cent of the CATV viewers and 34 per cent of the DD viewers were graduates while 9.3 per cent of the CATV viewers and 15.3 per cent of the DD viewers were post-graduates.

Table-2.6
Distribution of CATV Viewers and DD Viewers According to Educational Qualifications in the Three Localities

Educational Qualification	*Locality* I	II	III	*Total*	%
Below matric	-	4	24	28	18.7
	(-)	(5)	(24)	(29)	(19.3)
Matric	5	12	22	39	26.0
	(4)	(12)	(23)	(39)	(26.0)
Intermediate	-	4	2	6	4.0
	(2)	(4)	(2)	(8)	(5.3)
Graduate	36	25	2	63	42.0
	(31)	(19)	(1)	(51)	(34.0)
Post-graduate	9	5	-	14	9.3
	(13)	(10)	(-)	(23)	(15.3)
Total	50	50	50	150	100
	(50)	(50)	50 (50)	(150)	(100)

However in Locality I, there were no respondents who had their educational qualification below matriculation level both among

CATV viewers and DD viewers. There were about 10 per cent CATV viewers and 8 per cent DD viewers who had studied upto matriculation level. There were no CATV viewers and only 4 per cent DD viewers had studied upto intermediate level. Also, about 72 per cent CATV viewers and 62 per cent DD viewers were graduates while only 18 per cent CATV viewers and 26 per cent DD viewers were post-graduates in Locality I.

In Locality II, 8 per cent of the CATV viewers and 10 per cent of the DD viewers had studied below matriculation level. An equal proportion i.e., 24 per cent each and 8 per cent each among both the CATV viewers and DD viewers were matriculate and intermediate respectively. About 50 per cent of the CATV viewers and 38 per cent of the DD viewers were graduates while 10 per cent of the CATV viewers and 20 per cent of the DD viewers were post-graduates in Locality II.

In Locality III, an equal proportion i.e. 48 per cent each of the CATV viewers and DD viewers had education below matriculation level. About 44 per cent of the CATV viewers and 46 per cent of the DD viewers were matriculates. An equal proportion i.e., 4 per cent each both among CATV viewers and DD viewers were intermediates. Only 4 per cent of the CATV viewers and 2 per cent of the DD viewers were graduates. There were no post-graduates both among CATV viewers and DD viewers in Locality III.

It was inferred from the above data that in Localities I and II, there were greater number of DD viewers than CATV viewers who were post-graduates. This reveals that majority of the DD viewers were more educated than the CATV viewers in Localities I and II. This establishes and association between viewership and education in Localities I and II, i.e., the respondents with higher level of education were mostly DD viewers.

As education seems to be associated with viewership in Localities I and II, it is important to note if a similar trend is observed in terms of occupational status too.

Occupation

The impact of industrialization, resulting in urbanization has often been manifesting itself through the occupational structure especially in the Indian cities. The economic capacity of the people directly varies with the occupational status. In the previous Table i.e., Table 2.6, it was observed that in higher income group (i.e., Locality I) and the middle income group (i.e., Locality II) the respondents who did not subscribe to CATV were mostly post-graduates. In the present analysis, the association with viewership and occupation shall be examined.

For analysing the occupational status of respondents, the various occupations were divided into seven categories according to their prestige. (For details of occupation prestige, see Appendix B.)

It was observed from the data, that on the whole 32.7 per cent of the respondents belonged to the occupational prestige Category II. About 19 per cent and 16 per cent of the respondents belonged to the occupational prestige Categories III and VI respectively. Further, 11.3 per cent, 9.7 per cent and 8.3 per cent belonged to occupational prestige Categories V, I and IV respectively. Only 3 per cent of the respondents belonged to occupational prestige Category VII.

Table–2.7
Distribution of Respondents According to Occupational Status in the Three Localities

	Locality				
Occupational Prestige	*I*	*II*	*III*	*Total*	*%*
Category I	27	2	-	29	9.7
Category II	70	28	-	98	32.7
Category III	3	52	2	57	19.0
Category IV	-	17	8	25	8.3
Category V	-	-	34	34	11.3
Category VI	-	1	47	48	16.0
Category VII	-	-	9	9	3.0
Total	100	100	100	300	100

However, in Locality I, 70 per cent, 27 per cent and 3 per cent belonged to occupational prestige Categories II, I and III respectively. There were no respondents in any other categories.

In Locality II, 52 per cent, 28 per cent 17 per cent, 2 per cent and 1 per cent of the respondents belonged to occupational prestige Categories III, II, IV, I and VI respectively. There were no respondents in occupational prestige Categories V and VII.

Further, in Locality III, there were no respondents in occupational prestige Categories I and II. About 47 per cent, 34 per cent, 9 per cent, 8 per cent and 2 per cent of the respondents belonged to occupational prestige Categories VI, V, VII, IV and III respectively.

The data indicated that most respondents belonged to the occupational prestige Category II. In Locality I, majority of the respondents belonged to occupational prestige Category II, while in Locality II most respondents belonged to occupational prestige Category III. In Locality III most respondents belonged to occupational prestige Category VI. It is inferred that the respondents of Locality I had a higher occupational status than the respondents of the other two localities – thus indicating an association between occupation and socio-economic status.

It was also observed that the three localities differed distinctively in terms of occupational status. As the data also reveals an association between the occupational and the economic status of the respondents, it is inferred that the three localities vary in terms of income, education and occupational status of the respondents.

It would be interesting to see if the same trend prevails between Cable viewers and DD viewers.

The data from Table 2.8 indicates that on the whole, in occupational prestige Category I there were 12.6 per cent CATV viewers and 6.7 per cent DD viewers. In the occupational prestige Category II, there were 30 per cent CATV viewers and 35.3 per cent DD viewers. Further, there were 20 per cent CATV viewers and 18 per cent DD viewers in the occupational prestige Category III. About 8.7 per cent CATV viewers and 8 per cent DD viewers belonged to the occupational prestige Category IV. In the occupational prestige Category V, there were 10.7 per cent CATV viewers and 12 per cent DD viewers while in the prestige Category VI, there were 13.3 per

Table–2.8
Distribution of CATV Viewers and DD Viewers According to Occupational Status in the Three Localities

Occupational Prestige	*Locality* I	II	III	*Total*	*%*
Category I	17 (10)	2 (-)	- (-)	19 (10)	12.6 (6.7)
Category II	31 (39)	14 (14)	- (-)	45 (53)	30.0 (35.3)
Category III	2 (1)	27 (25)	1 (1)	30 (27)	20.0 (18.0)
Category IV	- (-)	7 (9)	6 (3)	13 (12)	8.7 (8.0)
Category V	- (-)	- (-)	16 (18)	16 (18)	10.7 (12.0)
Category VI	- (-)	- (2)	20 (26)	20 (28)	13.3 (18.7)
Category VII	- (-)	- (-)	7 (2)	7 (2)	4.7 (1.3)
Total	50 (50)	50 (50)	50 (50)	150 (150)	100 (100)

cent CATV viewers and 18.7 per cent DD viewers. In the occupational prestige Category VII there were 4.7 per cent CATV viewers and only 1.3 per cent DD viewers.

However, in Locality I, there were 34 per cent CATV viewers and 20 per cent DD viewers in occupational prestige Category I. In occupational prestige Category II, there were 62 per cent CATV viewers and 78 per cent DD viewers. In occupational prestige Category III there were 4 per cent CATV viewers and 2 per cent DD viewers. There were no respondents in other categories. The data indicated that in Locality I, there were more CATV viewers than DD viewers in occupational prestige Category I. This means that in Locality I, CATV viewers had a higher occupational status than DD viewers. Also, there were more DD viewers than CATV viewers in occupational prestige Category II.

In Locality II, there were 4 per cent CATV viewers and no DD viewers in occupational prestige Category I. There were an equal proportion i.e., 28 per cent each both among CATV viewers and DD viewers in occupational prestige Category II. In the occupational prestige Category III, there were 54 per cent CATV viewers and 50 per cent DD viewers. Also, there were 14 per cent CATV viewers and 18 per cent DD viewers in the occupation prestige Category IV. There were no respondents in occupational prestige Categories V and VII. It was noted that both CATV viewers and DD viewers shared almost the same occupational status in Locality II.

In Locality III, there were no respondents in occupational prestige Categories I and II while there were an equal proportion i.e., 2 per cent each both among CATV viewers and DD viewers in occupational prestige Category III. In occupational prestige category IV, there were 12 per cent CATV viewers and 6 per cent DD viewers while in occupational prestige category V, there were 32 per cent CATV viewers and 36 per cent DD viewers. In the occupational prestige Category VI there were 40 per cent CATV viewers and 52 per cent DD viewers while in occupational prestige Category VII there were 14 per cent CATV viewers and 4 per cent DD viewers. It was observed that CATV viewers and DD viewers differed in occupational status in prestige Categories IV and VII. In both these categories there were more CATV viewers than DD viewers. However, in occupational prestige Category VI there were more DD viewers than CATV viewers in Locality III.

On the whole, there were more CATV viewers than DD viewers in occupational prestige categories I and VII while there were more DD viewers than CATV viewers in the occupational prestige Categories II and VI. It was inferred that CATV viewers had a higher occupational status than the DD viewers indicating a positive association between viewership and occupational status.

The study indicated that the three variables, family income, education and occupation varied among the localities under study. How these variations are associated with the patterns of formal and informal social participation will be examined in the subsequent chapters.

The study, now lays its focus on whether the variables – income, education and occupational status are associated in the three

Table-2.9
Distribution of CATV Viewers and DD Viewers According to Income Level and Educational Qualifications

Educational Qualification / *Income (in rupees)*	*Below Matric*	*Matric*	*Inter-mediate*	*Graduate*	*Post-graduate*	*Total*
Below 2000	19 (22)	13 (14)	- (2)	1 (-)	- (-)	33 (38)
2001-5000	8 (7)	18 (20)	4 (3)	5 (7)	1 (-)	36 (37)
5001-10000	1 (-)	6 (4)	2 (3)	43 (31)	11 (17)	63 (55)
10001+	- (-)	2 (1)	- (-)	14 (13)	2 (6)	18 (20)
Total	28 (29)	39 (39)	6 (8)	63 (51)	14 (23)	150 (150)

CATV viewers $x^2_{cal} = 112.69 > x^2_{tab} = 21.026$ $p < 0.05$, d.f. = 12
DD viewers $x^2_{cal} = 121.203 > x^2_{tab} = 21.026$ $p < 0.05$, d.f. = 12

localities. For the purpose of analysing this, bivarate tables were formed to test the association among these three variables and how they differ in the three localities and between CATV viewers and DD viewers.

As the calculated value of chi-square is greater than the tabulated value in the case of both CATV viewers and DD viewers, it is concluded from Table 2.9 that education and income are associated with each other in the case of both CATV viewers and DD viewers. This means that in this study, income and education are associated for all respondents. It is also essential to see if income is associated with the occupational status of the respondents.

From Table 2.10 it is observed that the variables income and occupation are associated in the case of both CATV viewers and DD viewers as the calculated value of chi-square was found to be greater than the tabulated value. This means that income and occupational status are significantly associated with each other, in this study for all respondents.

Table–2.10
Distribution of CATV Viewers and DD Viewers According to Income Level and Occupational Status

Income (in Rupees) / *Occupational Prestige*	*Below 2000*	*2001-5000*	*5001-10000*	*10001+*	*Total*
Category I	- (-)	- (-)	12 (7)	7 (3)	19 (10)
Category II	- (-)	- (-)	34 (38)	11 (15)	45 (53)
Category III	- (2)	16 (13)	14 (10)	- (2)	30 (27)
Category IV	1 (1)	9 (11)	3 (-)	- (-)	13 (12)
Category V	9 (9)	7 (9)	- (-)	- (-)	16 (18)
Category VI	17 (25)	3 (3)	- (-)	- (-)	20 (28)
Category VII	6 (1)	1 (1)	- (-)	- (-)	7 (2)
Total	33 (38)	36 (37)	63 (55)	18 (20)	150 (150)

CATV viewers $x^2_{cal} = 179.45 > x^2_{tab} = 28.869$ $p < 0.05$, d.f. = 18
DD viewers $x^2_{cal} = 183.87 > x^2_{tab} = 28.869$ $p < 0.05$, d.f. = 18

It is also observed from Table 2.11 that education and occupational status are associated for both CATV viewers and DD viewers as the calculated value of chi-square was found to be greater than the tabulated value.

Hence, it can be concluded from the analysis of the last few tables that the variables income, education and occupational status of the respondents are associated with each other.

It is also inferred from the analysis that income did not have any significant association with the viewership of Satellite TV.

Table–2.11
Distribution of CATV Viewers and DD Viewers According to Educational Qualifications and Occupational Status

Educational Qualification	Occupational Prestige Category I	II	III	IV	V	VI	VII	Total
Below Matric	- (-)	- (-)	3 (4)	2 (1)	6 (9)	13 (14)	4 (1)	28 (29)
Matric	- (-)	5 (5)	9 (7)	7 (5)	9 (8)	6 (13)	3 (1)	39 (39)
Intermediate	- (-)	- (2)	3 (2)	2 (2)	1 (1)	- (1)	- (-)	6 (8)
Graduate	15 (9)	31 (28)	14 (10)	2 (4)	- (-)	1 (-)	- (-)	63 (51)
Post-graduate	4 (1)	9 (18)	1 (4)	- (-)	- (-)	- (-)	- (-)	14 (23)
Total	19 (10)	45 (53)	30 (27)	13 (12)	16 (18)	20 (28)	7 (2)	150 (150)

CATV viewers $x^2_{cal} = 122.04 > x^2_{tab} = 36.415$ $p < 0.05$, d.f. = 24
DD viewers $x^2_{cal} = 109.828 > x^2_{tab} = 36.415$ $p < 0.05$, d.f. = 24

However, there may be other factors which deviate the respondents from the subscription and viewership of Satellite TV.

Table–2.12
Distribution of Respondents According to Religion in the Three Localities

Religion	Locality I	II	III	Total	%
Hindu	62	80	71	213	71.0
Sikh	37	18	27	82	27.3
Christian	1	-	2	3	1.0
Muslim	-	2	-	2	0.7
Total	100	100	100	300	100

It was also observed that in Locality I, CATV viewers and DD viewers did not differ considerably in terms of income level. Therefore, one could relate other factors that intervene in the viewership and subscription of Satellite TV. These factors will be discussed later in the next chapter. Presently the analysis will lay stress on other demographic characteristics like religion, caste, type of ownership of house, duration of stay in Chandigarh and place of origin of the respondents.

It was observed that 71 per cent of the respondents were Hindus, 27.3 per cent were Sikhs and only 1.7 per cent belonged to other minority communities. In Locality I, 62 per cent were Hindus and 37 per cent were Sikhs. On the other hand, 80 per cent were Hindus in Locality II and 18 per cent were Sikhs. In Locality III, 71 per cent were Hindus while 27 per cent were Sikhs and 2 per cent were Christians. It was evident that on the whole, the population was dominated by the Hindu Community. The next table compares the CATV viewers and DD viewers according to religion in the three localities.

Table–2.13

Distribution of CATV Viewers and DD Viewers According to Religion in the Three Localities

	Locality				
Religion	*I*	*II*	*III*	*Total*	*%*
Hindu	27 (35)	40 (40)	45 (26)	112 (101)	74.6 (67.3)
Sikh	23 (14)	9 (9)	3 (24)	35 (47)	23.3 (31.3)
Christian	- (1)	- (-)	2 (-)	2 (1)	1.3 (0.7)
Muslim	- (-)	1 (1)	- (-)	1 (1)	0.7 (0.7)
Total	50 (50)	50 (50)	50 (50)	150 (150)	100 (100)

On the whole, about 74.6 per cent CATV viewers and 67.3 per cent DD viewers were Hindus. About 23.3 per cent of the CATV viewers and 31.3 per cent DD viewers were Sikhs. About 1.3 per cent of the CATV viewers and 0.7 of the DD viewers were Christians while 0.7 per cent each among CATV viewers and DD viewers were Muslims.

The data also indicated that in Locality I, 54 per cent of the CATV viewers and 70 per cent of the DD viewers were Hindus while 46 per cent of the CATV viewers and 28 per cent of the DD viewers were Sikhs. Only 2 per cent of the DD viewers were Christians.

In Locality II, an equal proportion of CATV viewers and DD viewers (80%) were Hindus and also, an equal proportion of CATV viewers and DD viewers (18%) were Sikhs. Further, in Locality II, only 2 per cent each among CATV viewers and DD viewers were Muslims.

In Locality III, 90 per cent of the CATV viewers and 52 per cent of the DD viewers were Hindus while 6 per cent of the CATV viewers and 48 per cent of the DD viewers were Sikhs. Only 4 per cent of the CATV viewers were Christians.

The data reveals that among the Hindus there were more CATV viewers than DD viewers while among the Sikhs there were more DD viewers than CATV viewers. The data also indicates that most of the CATV subscribers were Hindus.

Caste

For the purpose of the study, the various castes of the respondents were divided into three categories namely, upper, middle and low castes. The upper caste category comprised of Brahmins, Jats, Khatris, Banias, Aroras, Rajputs, Thakurs etc. The middle caste category comprised of the artisan class like Sunar, Lohar, Kahar, Tarkhan, Dhobi, Nai etc. The low caste category comprised of the Scheduled Castes and Scheduled Tribes. Those whose castes could not be identified were placed in the miscellaneous category.

Data in Table 2.14 indicates that on the whole, there were 67.4 per cent respondents in the upper caste category while there were 14.3 per cent and 17 per cent in the middle and low caste categories respectively. Only 1.3 per cent of the respondents either did not know their castes or their castes could not be identified to be placed in any of the three categories.

Table–2.14
Distribution of Respondents According to Caste in the Three Localities

Caste	*Locality* I	II	III	*Total*	*%*
Upper	92	84	26	202	67.4
Middle	8	14	21	43	14.3
Low	–	2	49	51	17.0
Miscellaneous	–	–	4	4	1.3
Total	100	100	100	300	100

In Locality I, there were 92 per cent and 8 per cent respondents in the upper and middle caste categories respectively. There were no respondents in the low and miscellaneous categories.

In Locality II, there 84 per cent, 14 per cent and 2 per cent respondents in the upper, middle and low caste categories respectively. There were no respondents in the miscellaneous category.

In Locality III, there were 26 per cent, 21 per cent, 49 per cent and 4 per cent respondents in the upper, middle, low castes and miscellaneous caste categories.

The data reveals that on the whole, majority of the respondents belonged to the upper castes. Also, in Localities I and II majority of the respondents belonged to the upper castes while in Locality III majority of the respondents belonged to the low caste category. This indicates a positive association between caste and economic status.

On the whole, there were 69.4 per cent CATV viewers and 65.4 per cent DD viewers in the upper caste category. There were 11.3 per cent CATV viewers and 17.3 per cent DD viewers in the middle caste category. Also, there were 18 per cent CATV viewers and 16 per cent DD viewers in the low caste category. In the miscellaneous category there were 1.3 per cent each both among CATV viewers and DD viewers.

Table–2.15
Distribution of CATV Viewers and DD Viewers According to Caste in the Three Localities

Caste	*Locality* I	II	III	*Total*	*%*
Upper	50	43	11	104	69.4
	(42)	(41)	(15)	(98)	(65.4)
Middle	-	7	10	17	11.3
	(8)	(7)	(11)	(26)	(17.3)
Low	-	-	27	27	18
	(-)	(2)	(22)	(24)	(16)
Miscellaneous	-	-	2	2	1.3
	(-)	(-)	(2)	(2)	(1.3)
Total	50	50	50	150	100
	(50)	(50)	(50)	(150)	(100)

In Locality I, all the CATV viewers belonged to the upper caste category while 84 per cent and 16 per cent DD viewers belonged to the upper and middle caste categories respectively. There were no respondents in the miscellaneous category.

In Locality II, there were 86 per cent CATV viewers and 82 per cent DD viewers in the upper caste category while 14 per cent each among both CATV viewers and DD viewers belonged to the middle caste category. There were no CATV viewers in the low caste category while there were 4 per cent DD viewers in the low caste category. There were no respondents in the miscellaneous category.

In Locality III, there were 22 per cent CATV viewers and 30 per cent DD viewers in the upper caste category while there were 20 per cent CATV viewers and 22 per cent DD viewers in the middle caste category. In the low caste category there were 54 per cent CATV viewers and 44 per cent DD viewers while there were an equal proportion i.e. 4 per cent each among both CATV viewers and DD viewers in the miscellaneous category.

It was observed that in Locality III, there were more CATV viewers than DD viewers in the low caste category. On the whole, the CATV viewers and DD viewers did not differ in the type of caste in the Localities I and II, as majority of them belonged to the upper caste castegory. This means that the upper and middle income groups were dominated by respondents belonging to upper castes while in the lower income group majority of the respondents belonged to low castes.

Ownership of House

Although the sample size was selected on the basis of socio-economic status, it is important to note the type of ownership of houses in the three localities. Therefore, the researcher questionned the respondents on this dimension.

Table–2.16
Distribution of Respondents According to Ownership of House in the Three Localities

	Locality				
Type of House	*I*	*II*	*III*	*Total*	*%*
Own	88	65	90	243	81.0
Rented	12	29	10	51	17.0
Government	–	6	–	6	2.0
Total	100	100	100	300	100

The data reveals that on the whole, 81 per cent of respondents owned the houses in which they resided, 17 per cent of the respondents lived in rented accommodation while only 2 per cent resided in government accommodation.

The data revealed that 88 per cent in Locality I, 65 per cent in Locality II and 90 per cent in Locality III owned the houses in which they resided. Only 12 per cent in Locality I, 29 per cent in Locality II and 10 per cent in Locality III had rented accommodation. There were no respondents in Locality I and Locality III with government accommodation while only 6 per cent in Locality II had government accommodation.

Thus, the data indicates that in all the three localities majority of the respondents owned houses in which they resided.

On the whole, 84.7 per cent CATV viewers and 77.3 per cent DD viewers owned houses. In the rented accommodation category, there were 13.3 per cent CATV viewers and 20.7 per cent DD viewers. In the government accommodation category there were an equal proportion of CATV viewers and DD viewers (2%).

Table–2.17
Distribution of CATV Viewers and DD Viewers According to Ownership of House in the Three Localities

Type of House	*Locality* I	II	III	*Total*	*%*
Own	46 (42)	38 (27)	43 (47)	127 (116)	84.7 (77.3)
Rented	4 (8)	9 (20)	7 (3)	20 (31)	13.3 (20.7)
Government	- (-)	3 (3)	- (-)	3 (3)	2.0 (2.0)
Total	50 (50)	50 (50)	50 (50)	150 (150)	100 (100)

The CATV viewers and DD viewers break-up in terms of type of accommodation reflected the same trend. About 92 per cent CATV viewers and 84 per cent DD viewers in Locality I; 76 per cent CATV viewers and 54 per cent DD viewers in Locality II and 86 per cent CATV viewers and 94 per cent DD viewers in Locality III owned the houses they resided in. Also, 8 per cent CATV viewers and 16 per cent DD viewers in Locality I, 18 per cent CATV viewers and 40 per cent DD viewers in Locality II and 14 per cent CATV viewers and 6 per cent DD viewers in Locality III had rented accommodation. However, there were no respondents in Locality I and III among both CATV viewers and DD viewers in the government accommodation category. About 6 per cent each among both CATV viewers and DD viewers in Locality II resided in government accommodation.

The data revealed that on the whole majority of the owners of houses were cable subscribers. However, in Locality III more owners of houses were DD viewers.

Place of Origin

Chandigarh is a relatively new city where the residents are migrants from neighbouring states. The study seeks a glimpse into the place of origin of residents in the city of Chandigarh.

(The other states category constituted the states of Kerala, Tamil Nadu, Gujarat, Maharastra and West Bengal.)

Table–2.18
Distribution of Respondents According to Place of Origin

Place of Origin (State)	*Frequency*	%
Punjab	165	55.0
U.P.	33	11.0
Delhi	11	3.7
Haryana	22	7.3
H.P.	29	9.7
Rajasthan	5	1.7
Other States	20	6.6
Other Countries	15	5.0
Total	300	100

Majority of the respondents (55%) had migrated from Punjab to Chandigarh. About 11 per cent were from Uttar Pradesh and around 8 per cent from Himachal Pradesh had migrated to Chandigarh. Migrants from Haryana constituted 7.3 per cent while rest of the states constituted 6.6 per cent of the total respondents. There were 5 per cent of the respondents (all from Locality I)who had migrated to India (Chandigarh) from other countries like Burma, Indonesia, Kuwait, U.K. etc.

The data reveals that most residents of Chandigarh had migrated from Punjab. Also, the city had population which had migrated from the neighbouring states—U.P., Delhi, Haryana, H.P. and Rajasthan. As the residents of Chandigarh are relatively new migrants from Punjab and the neighbouring states it would be important to see the avenues chosen by them for social participation outside the family. This shall be taken up for discussion in Chapter V.

Duration of Stay in Chandigarh

The city of Chandigarh is less than 45 years old and the study also seeks to find out the duration of stay of respondents in the city.

Four categories were made out to assess the duration of stay in Chandigarh i.e.,

(i) less than 10 years
(ii) 11-20 years
(iii) 21-30 years
(iv) more than 31 years.

The data reveals that majority of the residents (32.7%) had been staying in Chandigarh for 11-20 years while about 31.3 per cent of the respondents had been staying in the city for 21-30 years. About 19.3 per cent of the respondents were staying in Chandigarh for less than 10 years while about 16.7 per cent had been residing in Chandigarh for more than 31 years.

In Locality I, 25 per cent, 23 per cent, 27 per cent and 25 per cent had their duration of stay for less than 10 years, for 11-20 years, for 21-30 years and for more than 31 years respectively.

Table–2.19
Distribution of Respondents According to Duration of Stay in Chandigarh in the Three Localities

Duration of Stay (in Years)	*Locality* I	II	III	*Total*	%
- 10	25	17	16	58	19.3
11- 20	23	33	42	98	32.7
21 - 30	27	26	41	94	31.3
31 +	25	24	1	50	16.7
Total	100	100	100	300	100

Mean duration of stay in Chandigarh:

Locality I	:	19.4 years
Locality II	:	21.1 years
Locality III	:	18.1 years

In Locality II, 17 per cent, 33 per cent, 26 per cent and 24 per cent had their duration of stay in the city for less than 10 years, between 11-20 years, for 21-30 years and for more than 31 years respectively.

In Locality III, 16 per cent, 42 per cent, 41 per cent and 1 per cent had their duration of stay in the city in less than 10 years, 11-20 years, 21-30 years and 31 years and above categories respectively.

The data indicates that majority of the respondents had been staying in Chandigarh between 11-20 years. In Locality I, majority of the respondents had been staying in the city for 21-30 years while in Localities II and III majority of the respondents had been staying in Chandigarh between 11-20 years.

The mean duration of stay (in years) in Chandigarh was calculated and it was observed that the highest duration of stay in the city was among respondents of Locality II (21.1 years) followed by Locality I (19.4 years). The mean in Locality III was the lowest (18.1 years). This means that the residents of Locality II were staying in Chandigarh for a longer period than the other two localities.

It was indicated that on the whole, 20 per cent CATV viewers and 18.7 per cent DD had been staying in Chandigarh for less than 10 years while 32 per cent CATV viewers and 33.3 per cent DD viewers belonged to the 11-20 years category. About 29.3 per cent CATV viewers and 33.3 per cent DD viewers belonged to the 21-30 years category while 18.7 per cent CATV viewers and 14.7 per cent DD viewers had been residing in Chandigarh for more than 31 years.

In Locality I, 22 per cent CATV viewers and 28 per cent DD viewers had been staying in the city for less than 10 years while 28 per cent CATV viewers and 18 per cent DD viewers belonged to the 11-20 years category. Further, 22 per cent CATV viewers and 32 per cent DD viewers belonged to the 21-30 years category while 28 per cent CATV viewers and 22 per cent DD viewers were staying in Chandigarh for more than 31 years.

In Locality II, 18 per cent CATV viewers and 16 per cent DD viewers had been staying in Chandigarh for less than 10 years while 26 per cent CATV viewers and 40 per cent DD viewers belonged to the 11-20 years category. Also, 30 per cent CATV viewers and 22 per cent DD viewers belonged to the 21-30 years category while 26 per cent CATV viewers and 22 per cent DD viewers belonged to the 31 years and above category.

Table–2.20
Distribution of CATV Viewers and DD Viewers According to Duration of Stay in Chandigarh in the Three Localities

Duration of Stay (in Years) (in Years)	*Locality* I	II	III	*Total*	*%*
-10	11 (14)	9 (8)	10 (6)	30 (28)	20.0 (18.7)
11-20	14 (9)	13 (20)	21 (21)	48 (50)	32.0 (33.3)
21-30	11 (16)	15 (11)	18 (23)	44 (50)	29.3 (33.3)
31+	14 (11)	13 (11)	1 (-)	28 (22)	18.7 (14.7)
Total	50 (50)	50 (50)	50 (50)	150 (150)	100 (100)

Mean Duration of Stay in Chandigarh

	CATV Viewers	*DD Viewers*
Locality I :	20.9 years	20.1 years
Locality II :	21.8 years	20.4 years
Locality III :	17.4 years	18.8 years

In Locality III, 20 per cent CATV viewers and 12 per cent DD viewers had been staying in the city for less than 10 years while 42 per cent each among CATV viewers and DD viewers had their duration of stay in the city between 11-20 years. Further, 36 per cent CATV viewers and 46 per cent DD viewers belonged to the 21-30 years category while 2 per cent of the CATV viewers had been residing in Chandigarh for more than 31 years.

The data reveals that a majority of the respondents have been residing in Chandigarh for more than 11 years but less than 30 years. There were more DD viewers than CATV viewers who were residing in Chandigarh for more than 11 years but less than 30 years. A similar trend was observed in all the three localities.

There were no respondents in Locality III among the DD viewers who had been staying in the city for more than 31 years. On the whole, there was a general concentration of both CATV viewers and DD viewers in the 11-20 years and 21-30 years category.

The mean duration of stay in Chandigarh of the respondents was calculated and it was observed that the mean in the case of CATV viewers was more than the DD viewers in Localities I and II but the reverse was true in Locality III.

The data reveals some major differences in the demographic profile between the CATV viewers and the DD viewers as well as in between the three localities.

The data indicated that the respondents of Localities II and III were younger than the respondents of Locality I. Further, it was inferred that the CATV viewers were younger than the DD viewers. The mean age of the respondents of Locality I was the highest while it was the lowest in Locality III. Also, the mean age of the CATV viewers was less than the DD viewers in all the three localities. Further, most of the respondents of Localities I and II had an income between Rs. 5001-10000 while majority of the respondents of Locality III had an income below Rs. 2000. It was also observed that the mean income of CATV viewers and DD viewers was the same in Locality I while the CATV viewers of Localities II and III had a higher mean income than the DD viewers. Most of the respondents were graduates in Locality I and Locality II where as majority of the respondents had their education below matric in Locality III. Also, the DD viewers of Localities I and II were more educated than CATV viewers whereas in Locality III there were no considerable differences in the educational qualifications of respondents. It was further inferred that respondents of Locality I had a higher occupational status than those of Localities II and III.

It was concluded that there were consistent differences between respondents in the three localities as well as between CATV viewers and DD viewers in terms of their income, education and occupational attributes. It was further indicated by the study that income, education and occupational status of the respondents were associated with each other among both the CATV viewers and the DD viewers in all the three localities.

The data reflected that majority of the respondents in all the three localities were Hindus. It was also observed that among the Hindus there were more CATV viewers than DD viewers. Further, in Localities I and II majority of the respondents belonged to the upper castes while respondents of Locality III belonged to the low castes. Another inference drawn was that majority of the respondents in all the three localities owned houses in which they resided. Among those who owned their houses, majority of the respondents in Localities I and II were Cable TV viewers. It was also observed that there were more DD viewers than CATV viewers in Locality III among those who owned their houses.

The study shows that majority of the respondents had migrated from Punjab to the city of Chandigarh. Also most of respondents in Localities II and III had been staying in the city of Chandigarh for more than 11 years but less than 20 years. The respondents of Locality I had been staying in the city for 21-30 years. Also, more DD viewers than CATV viewers had been residing in Chandigarh for more than 11 years but less than 30 years. Further, the mean for the duration of stay in Chandigarh was higher among the CATV viewers as compared to the DD viewers in Localities I and II while the reverse was true in Locality III.

It would now be pertinent to see how this demographic background of the respondents would have an effect on the viewership patterns of TV as well as social participation which shall be taken up for discussion in the following chapters.

3

Selection of TV Programmes and Viewing Patterns: The Intra-City Variations

Television provides a window to the world: it brings real life drama, action and happenings into the home of the viewer who can sitting comfortably, even alone, interact with the outside world without having to communicate. The very technology of television determines the nature and impact of its influence on the individual viewer (Thomas, 1990).

Viewing television is not an isolated activity, it is ubiquitious and provides a series of communications, not only entertainment programmes, but also news, commercials and educational programmes, that come to us after others have chosen their message and skillfully used the technology to convey these messages in an interesting and impactful way (Winick and Winick, 1979).

Viewers of television may differ in how they use television. These variations are related to several factors or processes in the viewers' daily life. Families seem to vary according to the degree to which they encourage or inhibit the expression of different ideological viewpoints. Family rules of programme selection and media-related interaction operate in concert with modes of family communication. (Chafee, Mcleod and Atkin 1971; Mcleod *et al.*, 1982).

Satellite television offers a diversity of message choices that facilitates an increase in selectivity in audience exposure behaviour. The key factors are the availability of content choices and the rational analysis of media choice by an individual which may explain the selection behaviour of viewers in the television environment (Williams, Phillips and Lum, 1985). It has been observed that audience members are becoming highly selective in their exposure to channels that provide highly specialized content in contrast to those that offer a more general content (Webster, 1986).

Morley (1988) in his study indicates that women describe television viewing as a fundamentally social activity involving ongoing conversation, and usually the performance of at least one other domestic activity; while men state a clear preference for viewing attentively in silence, without interruption. These distinctive viewing styles are not simply the characteristics of men and women, but characteristics of the domestic roles of masculinity and feminity. Colomina (1968) reported that lower the socio-economic and educational level, more the audience watch television content with their younger children.

Television viewing is also affected by different physical factors. The availability of space for the family, the number of TV sets at home and the set location in such space in a family encourage or discourage viewing (Bryce and Leichter, 1983).

The intention of this research is to illustrate as richly as possible some of the differences in the three localities in terms of how television is used.

The analysis of family space in a household is crucial in examining the social context of television. Depending on this factor, some of the aspects of family environment may be examined. Since we are basically focussing in this study on the impact of Cable television on social interaction, one factor which could be crucial is the number of TV set in a household. This is so because while possession of a single television in the house may bring the members together physically, more than one television on the other hand, may increase physical space between them.

All families with more space and greater economic resources may have more than a single TV set. In such cases, they may distribute the sets around the house in the living room, dining room and bedrooms. Some upper class and middle class families may have as many TV sets as family member units. For example, the parents shall have a separate TV set for themselves and children may have another TV set. In households where another generation, may be vertical or horizontal, stays together, there may be another TV set. This usually depends upon the space and members and also on the economic capacity of the household. A family with little space and only one television set at home normally places the TV set in the central area of the household while the living room happens to be multiuse space Barrios (1988). In such cases, the family members are compelled to watch television together and the experience is affected by several activities at the same time. In cases, where more than one TV set are owned by the family, physical isolation of family members is bound to occur. There may also be cases whereas a matter of decision only a single TV set may be switched on inspite of possessing more than one TV set and other TV sets may be tuned on only when there is a clash in the selection of channels and programmes between family members. In households where there is a single television set, there is extensive selectivity as viewers attempt to search with the remote control device, the most acceptable programme once they are watching. Nevertheless, a very sizeable proportion of the audience at any given time on a typical evening (when all the members are back home after a day's long work) watch a programme because it appears on the channel to which the set is already tuned on or because someone else in the household desires to watch the programme. Comstock (1980) observed that 3 or 4 viewers out of every 10 admit to such daily seduction. Typically TV is consumed as a medium and the decision to view ordinarily takes precedence over the selection of what to view.

As television viewing is affected by different physical factors such as availability of space for a family and the number of TV sets, it would be useful to examine these variations in the three localities before discussing the consumption patterns of the TV content.

Tables 3.1 and 3.2 depict the variations in the ownership of number of TV sets in the three localities as well as the variations among CATV viewers and DD viewers in the same context in the three localities in question.

The analysis indicates that on the whole 79 per cent of the respondents owned one TV set while 19 per cent owned two television sets. Also, 1.7 per cent and 0.3 per cent owned three and four television sets respectively.

The data also indicated that 59 per cent in Locality I, 79 per cent in Locality II and 99 per cent of respondents in Locality III owned only one television set. There were 36 per cent respondents in Locality

Table-3.1
Distribution of Respondents by the Number of TV Sets in a Household in the Three Localities

No. of TV Sets	*Locality* I	II	III	*Total*	*%*
1.	59	79	99	237	79.0
2.	36	20	1	57	19.0
3.	4	1	-	5	1.7
4.	1	-	-	1	0.3
Total	100	100	100	300	100

I with two television sets, 20 per cent in Locality II and only 1 per cent in Locality III with two television sets. On the whole, there were only 4 per cent respondents in Locality I and 1 per cent in Locality II with three television sets. There were no respondents with more than two television sets in Locality III. Only one respondent in Locality I owned four television sets. It was observed that in all the three localities most respondents owned one TV set. However in Locality I, there were about 41 per cent of the respondents who owned more than one TV set. Also, in Locality II, 21 per cent of the respondents owned more than one TV set. It was observed that the number of TV sets varied according to the socio-economic status of the respondents. The higher the socio-economic status and the space available in a household the respondents owned more number of TV sets. It was inferred that the economic capacity as well as the space available in a household were associated with the number of TV sets possessed by respondents. We had already seen in Chapter I that the respondents of Locality I resided in 2 kanal or bigger houses.

The results substantiate the findings of Leoncio Barrios (1988) in a study of television in Venezuela that greater the economic resources and space available in a household, the greater the number of TV sets owned by a family. It would be interesting to see if similar variations persist among CATV viewers and DD viewers in the three localities.

From Table 3.2, it is evident that the majority of DD viewers in all the three localities had one television set. In the two television set category, majority of the respondents were CATV viewers. There were no DD viewers in Locality I with as many as four television sets. In Locality II, there were no DD viewers with three television sets and four television sets. In Locality III there were no CATV viewers and DD viewers with more than two television sets.

Table–3.2
Distribution of CATV Viewers and DD Viewers According to the Number of TV Sets Owned by Them in the Three Localities

	Locality				
No. of TV Sets	*I*	*II*	*III*	*Total*	*%*
1.	25 (34)	35 (44)	49 (50)	109 (128)	72.6 (85.4)
2.	22 (14)	14 (6)	1 (-)	37 (20)	24.6 (13.3)
3.	2 (2)	1 (-)	- (-)	3 (2)	2.0 (1.3)
4.	1 (-)	- (-)	- (-)	1 (-)	0.7 (-)
Total	50 (50)	50 (50)	50 (50)	50 (150)	100 (100)

(Figures in parentheses are the frequencies for DD viewers.)

On the whole, 72.6 per cent of the CATV viewers and 85.4 per cent of the DD viewers owned one television set only. In the two-television set category, 24.6 per cent were CATV viewers and 13.3 per cent were DD viewers. In the three-television set category there were only 2 per cent CATV viewers and 1.3 per cent DD viewers. However, in Locality I, 50 per cent of the CATV viewers and 68 per cent of the DD viewers owned one television set. There were 44 per cent CATV viewers and 28 per cent DD viewers with two television sets. Also, there were an equal proportion of CATV viewers and DD viewers (4%) who owned three television sets. There was a only one respondent who owned four television sets among the CATV viewers.

In Locality II, 70 per cent of the CATV viewers and 88 per cent of the DD viewers possessed one television set. In the two-television set category, 28 per cent were CATV viewers and 12 per cent were DD viewers. There was only one respondent among the CATV viewers who owned three television sets. There were no respondents with four television sets.

In Locality III, 98 per cent of the CATV viewers and all the DD viewers owned one television set. There was only one respondent with two television sets among the CATV viewers. There were no respondents among both CATV viewers and DD viewers with more than two television sets.

The results indicate that in Locality I, the CATV viewers owned more than one TV set while in Locality III both CATV viewers and DD viewers owned one TV set. In Locality II, about 30 per cent of the CATV viewers and only 12 per cent of the DD viewers owned more than one TV set. It is inferred that respondents of Locality I owned more TV sets than respondents of other localities. It was also concluded that viewers of Cable TV owned a greater number of TV sets than DD viewers. This indicates an association between the number of TV sets and the economic status with viewership on the one hand and with the space available in a household on the other hand. As more than 40 per cent respondents of Locality I owned more than one TV set, it is bound to increase physical isolation between family members as well as lead to a reduction in intra-family communication. These issues shall be taken up for discussion in the following chapter.

In the previous chapter, the demographic profile, socio-economic status and family characteristics of respondents were discussed. It was evident from the analysis that socio-economic status and other demographic factors did not have much association with subscription of Satellite TV. Therefore, there may be other extraneous factors which intervene in the viewership of Satellite TV. This chapter deals with a discussion on factors which obstruct respondents from viewership on one hand, and on the other it examines the selection of programmes by respondents and viewing patterns with the socio-economic status.

The present chapter also looks into the various reasons among DD viewers for non-subscription of CATV as well as the reasons pointed out by the DD viewers for withdrawal of the cable connections. The reasons listed out by the DD viewers were divided into six categories as depicted in Table 3.3.

Table–3.3
Distribution of DD Viewers According to Reasons for Not Subscribing to CATV in the Three Localities

	Locality				
Reasons	*I*	*II*	*III*	*Total*	*%*
Children's studies	16	26	19	61	40.7
Waste of time	11	2	1	14	9.3
Enough entertainment on DD	14	5	5	24	16.0
Obscenity on CATV	5	13	10	28	18.7
Sheer nuisance	4	2	-	6	4.0
Economic reasons	-	2	15	17	11.3
Total	50	50	50	150	100

It was observed that most of the DD viewers did not subscribe to CATV due to their children's studies; 16 per cent of them said that there was enough entertainment provided by DD and 18.7 per cent cited obscenity on CATV as a reason for non-subscription to CATV. About 11.3 per cent pointed out economic constraints being responsible for non-subscription to CATV. Only 9.3 per cent considered it a waste of time while 4 per cent DD viewers remarked that it was a sheer nuisance.

Further, 32 per cent of the respondents in Locality I, 52 per cent in Locality II, 38 per cent in Locality III were non-subscribers to CATV due to their children's studies. About 30 per cent of the DD viewers in Locality III said that economic reasons kept them away from subscribing to CATV while 28 per cent in Locality I felt there was enough entertainment provided by DD. In Locality III, 26 per cent said that the obscenity on CATV kept them away from subscribing to it.

The respondents by and large had not subscribed to CATV mainly because they felt it hampered children's studies. They said that children were always glued to the TV even without subscribing to CATV, so there was no question of subscribing to CATV. Most parents complained that the eyesight and health of the children were being badly affected. They also added that CATV was a colossal waste of time while Doordarshan programmes were enough entertainment for the day. Obscenity and vulgarity on CATV was yet another aspect for non-subscription to CATV. Some described CATV as having a nuisance value at home. However, in the middle and lower income groups economic and financial constraints kept them away from subscribing to CATV.

Out of a total of 150 respondents who had not subscribed to Cable TV, many had earlier remained subscribers of CATV. The main reasons for withdrawal of subscription will be discussed later. First let us get a glimpse at the number of respondents who were earlier the viewers of CATV.

Table-3.4
Distribution of DD Viewers Who were Earlier Subscribers to Cable TV

	Locality				
Earlier Subscribers to CATV	*I*	*II*	*III*	*Total*	*%*
Yes	3	25	7	35	23.3
No	47	25	43	115	76.7
Total	50	50	50	150	100

It was observed that in Locality II, 50 per cent of the respondents had been viewing CATV earlier. In Locality I, only 6 per cent of the respondents and in Locality III only 14 per cent of the respondents were viewers of CATV earlier. The main reason cited by respondents in all the localities for withdrawal of CATV, was the bad effect of CATV on childrens' studies. One respondent in Locality II, said that his electricity bills were inflated due to CATV, hence he withdrew its subscription. On the whole, it was observed that parents in middle income locality had decided to withdraw subscription to Cable TV mainly because of children's studies.

Further, on the whole, 23.3 per cent of the DD viewers were earlier viewers of CATV. The withdrawal of CATV subscription was concentrated mainly in Locality II, wherein about 50 per cent of the DD viewers were earlier viewers of CATV.

The respondents were also questioned if they would ultimately install CATV.

The Table 3.5 below depicts distribution of respondents, locality wise, whether they would ultimately install CATV.

On the whole, 25.4 per cent of the DD viewers wanted to install CATV at a later stage while 71.3 per cent of the respondents did not want to subscribe to CATV at all. About 3.3 per cent of the respondents were undecided on this issue.

In Locality I, it was observed that about 14 per cent of the respondents had decided to ultimately install CATV while 84 per cent had a firm 'no' on this aspect. Only 2 per cent of the DD viewers respondents were undecided on this issue.

Table-3.5

Distribution of Respondents According to Whether They would Ultimately Install CATV in the Three Localities

Ultimate Installation of CATV	*Locality* *I*	*II*	*III*	*Total*	*%*
Yes	7	18	13	38	25.4
No	42	29	36	107	71.3
Can't say/undecided	1	3	1	5	3.3
Total	50	50	50	150	100

In Locality II, 36 per cent of the respondents decided to install CATV at a later stage, while 58 per cent of respondents did not want to subscribe to CATV at all. About 6 per cent of the respondents were undecided.

In Locality III, 26 per cent of the respondents wanted to install CATV at a later stage, 72 per cent decided not to do the same and only 2 per cent of the respondents were undecided on this issue.

The study indicates that majority of the DD viewers in all the localities did not want to subscribe to CATV even at a later stage. This means that the non-subscribers of Cable TV did not want to install CATV due to some other factors other than their children's studies. It would be interesting then to look into the factors which kept respondents away from the idea of being viewers of Satellite TV.

Those respondents who were interested in installing CATV at a later stage commented that CATV programmes provided good entertainment and also the transmission was available for the whole day and the viewers could choose any time for entertainment. They also added that CATV was indispensable and one could not remain isolated for long. Others disclosed (from Locality III) that if their financial status improved they would install CATV immediately.

Those who were totally against the installation of CATV said that CATV was having adverse impact on not only the studies of their children but also on their tender minds. "The obscenity, vulgarity and nudity exhibited on CATV is destroying Indian culture", commented most of such respondents.

One respondent said, "With Doordarshan itself the children are not studying; so with CATV it would be impossible to control them." He claimed that DD is enough distraction. Others agreed that DD was providing sufficient entertainment and information. Some respondents said that they did not have much time on hand. They were unable to watch DD programmes fully and so the question of watching CATV programmes did not arise. A few added that CATV was a waste of time and money besides being a nuisance at home. It may be inferred here that most of the DD viewers were concerned about the impact of the western channels on their children. This shall be taken up for disscussion in Chapter VI.

Among DD viewers CATV was considered as a disrupting factor. But, among CATV viewers the TV was tuned on as early as at breakfast time, in some cases even earlier, and it played almost constantly throughout the day and evening-through housework, homework, naptimes, mealtimes, telephone calls and personal conversations. Whether people at home watch it or listen to it or simply coexist with the turned on TV should be taken into account as a major stimulus that is acting upon people continuously (Moody, 1980).

The introduction of television initially made everyone believe that the 'novelty' hypothesis would wear off with the passage of time. But, it has been proved otherwise. In most households TV viewing has become an addiction, a habit. Television viewing measured by hours of set use in the average household has been steadily rising (Comstock, 1980, Yadava and Reddi, 1988). In the United States at the beginning of the 1960's the figure was slightly less than 6 hours a day. By the 1970's it was 7 hours. This upward trend has been accompanied by the convergence of differences in viewing based on social status and education (Comstock, 1980).

The increase in consumption of TV (Steiner, 1963; Bower, 1973; Howe, 1977) respresents the changing norms about the acceptability of TV viewing. Turning on the TV set, whatever the hour, has become more frequently the equivalent of switching on the lights.

Some studies have revealed that viewers tend to exaggerate viewing times, (Betchel, Achelpohl and Akers, 1972; Howe, 1977) over estimating the amount of time during which the set is switched on and hence available for viewing. Once the TV set is turned on, it may remain on over lengthy periods of time, irrespective of whether any member of the family is actually viewing or not. In the US for every 4 hours that families reported in a TV diary, the actual viewing recorded was only 3 hours (Atkin, Murray and Nayman, 1972). As people get more and more accostomed to having a TV in the house, they become more likely to leave it on, even when they are giving little attention to it. Such a tendency has been conceptualized as 'secondary viewing' implying the circumstances in which TV viewing forms an accompaniment to other activities such as housework, reading, eating meals etc. (Robinson, 1969). How the amount of viewing differs in the three localities under study, will be taken up for analysis in the present chapter, while what TV viewing does to daily family life will be discussed subsequently in the next chapter.

As television programmes are telecast constantly throughout the day – during morning, afternoon, evening and night and running into late night on Doordarshan and round-the-clock on CATV, respondents were asked as to how many sessions during the day, they switched on the TV set. The duration of viewing television was measured according to the number of sessions i.e. morning, afternoon, evening and late night, the respondents switched on the TV set in a household.

Table-3.6
Distribution of Respondents According to Duration of Viewing TV in the Three Localities

Duration of Viewing TV	*Locality* I	II	III	*Total*	%
One session	26	32	7	65	21.7
Two sessions	34	35	18	87	29.0
Three sessions	28	25	54	107	35.7
Four sessions	12	8	21	41	13.6
Total	100	100	100	300	100

If respondents switched on the TV set only once during one session of telecast i.e. either morning, afternoon evening or night, the duration of viewing was considered as one session. If the TV set was switched on twice during two separate sessions during the day the duration of viewing considered as two sessions. Similarly, if the TV set was switched on three or four times at three and four different sessions of transmission of programmes, during the day, the duration of viewing was considered as three and four sessions of TV viewing respectively.

The results indicate that on the whole 21.7 per cent of the respondents switched on the TV set for one session in a day while 29 per cent of the respondents switched on the TV set for two sessions in a day. Further, 35.7 per cent of the respondents switched on the TV set for three sessions in a day while 13.6 per cent of the respondents kept the TV set on for almost the whole day till late night.

In Locality I, 26 per cent and 34 per cent of the respondents switched on the TV set for one and two sessions respectively in a day while 40 per cent switched on the TV set for more than two sessions in a day.

In Locality II, 32 per cent of the respondents switched on the TV set for one session in a day while 35 per cent kept the TV set on for two sessions in a day. About 25 per cent kept the TV set on for three sessions in a day while 8 per cent kept the TV set on for all the four sessions in a day.

In Locality III, 7 per cent and 18 per cent of the respondents switched on the TV set for one and two sessions respectively. A majority of the respondents (75%) switched on the TV set for more than two sessions in a day.

From the data, it is inferred that respondents in Locality III consume more hours of TV than respondents in Localities I and II. It is evident that the results substantiate that TV viewing has always been greater among those in the lower socio-economic status. Also, substantiating earlier data, the present data indicate that the middle income residents watch TV for fewer hours and less persistently. We have already seen that these respondents had withdrawn their cable subscription for the sake of their children's studies. As the data indicates that respondents of Localities I and III are heavy consumers of TV, it may result in physical immobility leading to a reduction in social activity both with the outside world as well as within the family. A detailed discussion on these issues will be taken up subsequently in the next chapter.

It would be important to examine that as there are more number of channels and longer duration of telecast on CATV viewers as compared to DD, how the CATV viewers and DD viewers would

Table–3.7
Distribution of CATV Viewers and DD Viewers According to Duration of Viewing TV in the Three Localities

Duration of Viewing TV	*Locality* I	II	III	*Total*	%
One session	8 (18)	11 (21)	1 (6)	20 (45)	13.3 (30.0)
Two sessions	16 (18)	17 (18)	1 (17)	34 (53)	22.7 (35.3)
Three sessions	15 (13)	14 (11)	32 (22)	61 (46)	40.7 (30.7)
Four sessions	11 (1)	8 (-)	16 (5)	35 (6)	23.3 (4.0)
Total	50 (50)	50 (50)	50 (50)	150 (150)	100 (100)

differ in terms of the duration of viewing of TV in the three localities as well as how the duration of viewing TV would affect various dimensions of social participation.

It is interesting to note that as the number of hours of TV viewing goes up, the proportion of Cable viewers also rises. On the whole, it was observed that 13.3 per cent of the CATV viewers and 30 per cent of the DD viewers switched on the TV set for a single session in the day. About 22.7 per cent of the CATV viewers and 35.3 per cent of the DD viewers switched on the TV set for two sessions in the day while 64 per cent of the CATV viewers and 34.7 per cent of the DD viewers switched on the TV set for more than two sessions in a day.

It was inferred that majority of the DD viewers switched the TV set for a single session as compared to the Cable TV viewers. It was also indicated that majority of the CATV viewers watched TV for almost the whole day, till late night as compared to the DD viewers. Also, about 74 per cent of the Cable viewers watched TV for more than three sessions in a day. Therefore, this indicates that Cable TV viewers consumed more hours of TV as compared to DD viewers. This also means that the variety of channels and longer duration of telecast seduce viewers to increase their duration of viewing TV. This also indicates that Satellite TV may have the most profound effect on its viewers in terms of interactional patterns within as well as across families as viewers are glued to their TV sets for longer duration.

It would be interesting to compare the three localities in the light of the above inferences.

In Locality I, 16 per cent of the CATV viewers and 36 per cent of the DD viewers watched TV for a single session in a day. About 32 per cent of the CATV viewers and 36 per cent of the DD viewers watched TV for two sessions in a day. Also, about 30 per cent of the CATV viewers and 26 per cent of the DD viewers watched TV for three sessions in a day while 22 per cent of the CATV viewers and only 2 per cent of the DD viewers watched TV for almost the whole day.

In Locality II, 22 per cent of the CATV viewers and 42 per cent of the DD viewers watched TV for a single session in a day while 34 per cent of the CATV viewers and 36 per cent of the DD viewers watched TV for two sessions in a day. About 28 per cent of the CATV viewers and 22 per cent of the DD viewers watched TV for three sessions in a day while 16 per cent of the CATV viewers and none of DD viewers watched TV for all the four sessions in a day.

In Locality III, 2 per cent of the CATV viewers and 12 per cent of the DD viewers watched TV for one session in a day. Also, 2 per cent of the CATV viewers and 34 per cent of the DD viewers watched TV for two sessions in a day. Further, 64 per cent of the CATV viewers and 44 per cent of the DD viewers watched TV for three sessions in a day while 32 per cent of the CATV viewers and 10 per cent of the DD viewers watched TV for almost the whole day.

The analysis indicate that in Locality I, 48 per cent of the CATV viewers watched TV for two or less than two sessions while about 72 per cent of the DD viewers watched TV for two or less than two sessions in a day. Further, 52 per cent of the CATV viewers and only 28 per cent of the DD viewers watched TV for more than two sessions in a day.

In Locality II, majority of the DD viewers (78%) watched TV for two or less than two sessions in a day while among the CATV viewers the same proportion of respondents (78%) watched TV for two or more than two sessions in a day.

In Locality III, 96 per cent of the CATV viewers watched TV for more than two sessions in a day while 90 per cent of the DD viewers watched TV for three or less than three sessions in a day.

The data reflects that the low socio-economic group CATV respondents consume more hours of TV as compared to the respondents of high and middle socio-economic groups. It may be inferred from the above data that the viewers of Cable TV watch it for a much longer time as compared with those without a cable connection. This trend exists in all the three localities, thus suggesting a uniform association between duration of viewing and Cable television.

It would be interesting to find out then if the variables such as income, education and occupational status are related to the duration of viewing television both among CATV viewers and DD viewers. For this, bivariate tables were formed and the chi-square test was applied to test the association between income, education and occupational status with the duration of viewing TV.

Table–3.8
Distribution of CATV Viewers and DD Viewers According to Duration of Viewing TV and Income Level

Income (in Rupees) / *Duration of Viewing TV*	*0-2000*	*2001-5000*	*5001-10,000*	*10001+*	*Total*
One session	- (8)	3 (9)	17 (18)	- (10)	20 (45)
Two sessions	1 (11)	7 (14)	22 (20)	4 (8)	34 (53)
Three sessions	24 (16)	15 (12)	13 (16)	9 (2)	61 (46)
Four sessions	8 (3)	11 (2)	11 (1)	5 (-)	35 (6)
Total	33 (38)	36 (37)	63 (55)	18 (20)	150 (150)

CATV viewers $x^2_{cal} = 63.27 > x^2_{tab} = 16.919$ $p < 0.05$, d.f. = 9
DD viewers $x^2_{cal} = 16.13 < x^2_{tab} = 16.919$ $p > 0.05$, d.f. = 9

It is observed from Table 3.8 that income levels and duration of viewing were associated for CATV viewers as the calculated value of chi-square (63.27) was greater than the tabulated value (16.919). In the case of DD viewers income level was not associated with the duration of viewing TV as the calculated value of chi-square (16.13) was found to be less than the tabulated value.

It may also be inferred that low economic status CATV viewers consume more hours of television and also the high economic status CATV viewers watch TV for a lesser duration of time. This indicates an inverse association between income and viewership.

It was also observed from Table 3.9 that educational level was associated with duration of viewing TV in the case of both CATV viewers and DD viewers as the calculated value of chi-square for CATV viewers (26.57) and DD viewers (32.86) was greater than the tabulated value.

Table–3.9
Distribution of CATV Viewers and DD Viewers According to the Duration of Viewing TV and Educational Qualifications

Education / *Duration of Viewing TV*	*Below Matric*	*Matric*	*Inter-mediate*	*Graduate*	*Post-gradate*	*Total*
One session	- (6)	3 (9)	1 (-)	13 (19)	3 (11)	20 (45)
Two sessions	2 (7)	10 (15)	1 (3)	16 (19)	5 (9)	34 (53)
Three sessions	18 (12)	17 (14)	2 (4)	24 (13)	- (3)	61 (46)
Four sessions	8 (4)	9 (1)	2 (1)	10 (-)	6 (-)	35 (6)
Total	28 (29)	39 (39)	6 (8)	63 (51)	14 (23)	150 (150)

CATV viewers $x^2_{cal} = 26.57 > x^2_{tab} = 21.026$ $p < 0.05$, d.f. = 12
DD viewers $x^2_{cal} = 32.86 > x^2_{tab} = 21.026$ $p < 0.05$, d.f. = 12

From Table 3.10, it is indicated that occupational status and duration of viewing TV had an association among both CATV viewers and DD viewers as the calculated value of chi-square was found to be greater than tabulated value. It may be inferred that respondents with higher occupational prestige watched TV for a lesser duration. This means that higher prestige occupations leave respondents with lesser time to watch TV as individuals seek other avenues to achieve or satisfy their professional / occupational goals/ needs. This indicates that respondents with higher occupational status may utilize their time for social participation. It has been observed in Chapter 5 that respondents with higher occupational status choose formal organisations for social participation. This also reveals that TV viewing does not intervene in formal social participation as it is chosen voluntarily by an individual. There is a detailed discussion on these aspects in Chapter 5.

The study reveals that education and occupational status had an association with the duration of viewing TV among the CATV

Table–3.10
Distribution of CATV Viewers and DD Viewers According to the Duration of Viewing TV and Occupational Status

Duration of Viewing TV	*Occupational Prestige Category*							
	I	*II*	*III*	*IV*	*V*	*VI*	*VII*	*Total*
One session	3 (4)	9 (16)	4 (15)	3 (3)	- (3)	1 (4)	- (-)	20 (45)
Two sessions	4 (3)	18 (22)	8 (6)	4 (7)	- (3)	- (12)	- (-)	34 (53)
Three sessions	6 (3)	13 (14)	9 (6)	3 (2)	11 (9)	14 (11)	5 (1)	61 (46)
Four sessions	6 (-)	5 (1)	9 (-)	3 (-)	5 (3)	5 (1)	2 (1)	35 (6)
Total	19 (10)	45 (53)	30 (27)	13 (12)	16 (18)	20 (28)	7 (2)	150 (150)

CATV viewers $x^2_{cal} = 39.9 > x^2_{tab} = 28.869$ $p < 0.05$, d.f. = 18
DD viewers $x^2_{cal} = 42.2 > x^2_{tab} = 28.869$ $p < 0.05$, d.f. = 18

viewers. It was also indicated that income had an assoication with the duration of viewing TV among both the CATV viewers while income did not have any association with the duration of viewing TV among DD viewers. It was already observed in this chapter earlier that income was not a criterion for the non-subscription of CATV among the DD viewers, the reasons for which had already been discussed.

The earlier communication experts believed that the process of communication takes place in a social vacuum and that influence from the environment is not worth bothering about. The contributions of John W. Riley and Mathilda White Riley (1959) were an important step in a shift towards a more sociological perspective.

The research conducted by these scholars points to the role played in the communication process by primary groups and reference groups. Primary groups are distinguished by intimate relations among their members, a family being a typical example. A reference group is a group with the help of which an individual may define his attitudes, values and behaviour. He need not be a member of the group, but its norms will nevertheless guide him. Primary groups close to the individual often serve as reference groups for him as well.

The role of primary and reference groups, along with various other variables such as education, occupation gender, age etc., may be significant in inducing variations within the recipients of media. These variations often get reflected through the time people spend on watching television, the channels/programmes they choose for viewing, and the impact they receive from these. Recently, therefore, literature on communication studies lays a heavy stress on the futility of drawing generalizations and instead, looks out for different patterns of viewership among the audience.

The 'individual differences theory' postulated by De Fleur in 1970 takes into account the diversity of the audience, acknowledging that the media message contains particular stimulus attributes that have differential interactions with personality characteristics of members of the audience. In other words, different people are likely to respond differently to different stimuli.

A person's habit of selecting particular types of media content and responding to them in distinctive ways is heavily influenced by norms and other shared influences that characterize the social categories of which he or she is a member (Katz and Lazarsfeld, 1955). It follows then that people belonging to different socio-economic background may differ in their preferences for specific programmes. In the light of such assumptions, an effort is made here to analyse the association between selection of TV channels / programmes on the one hand and income, education, occupation etc. on the other.

The data from Table 3.11 indicates that among viewers of CATV, the ZEE TV channel was the most popular. In Locality I, 54 per cent of the CATV viewers preferred ZEE TV while 32 per cent preferred STAR TV. On the other hand, in Locality I, the rest of the channels had popularity among a mere 14 per cent of the CATV respondents. In Locality II, 86 per cent of CATV viewers preferred the channel ZEE TV and the rest 14 per cent preferred other channels. In Locality III, 90 per cent preferred ZEE TV and 10 per cent preferred the local

Table-3.11
Distribution of CATV Viewers According to Selection of Channel in the Three Localities

Channel	*Locality* I	II	III	*Total*	%
ZEE TV	27	43	45	115	76.7
VCR Channel	-	4	5	9	6.0
BBC	2	-	-	2	1.3
PRIME SPORTS	4	1	-	5	3.3
STAR TV	16	1	-	17	11.3
VTV	1	1	-	2	1.4
Total	50	50	50	150	100

VCR channel. On the whole, it was observed that around 77 per cent of CATV viewers preferred ZEE TV while 11.3 per cent preferred STAR TV. The remaining 9 per cent preferred other channels.

It is inferred that CATV viewers in Locality I varied in their choice of channels while respondents in Localities II and III were stereotyped in their selection of channels. It may also be inferred that as the ZEE TV channel contains a heavy dose of entertainment based programmes, respondents had a popularity with this channel. It is also indicated later in this chapter that most respondents preferred entertainment based programmes. Presently, the study lays its focus on the selection of channels by DD viewers. At the time, when the survey was conducted i.e., 1994, Doordarshan had only two operative channels.

Among the viewers of Doordarshan, the DD I channel had popularity among 63.3 per cent of the respondents while DD II was popular among 36.7 per cent of the respondents. Locality-wise, 64 per cent in Locality I, 66 per cent in Locality II and 60 per cent in Locality III preferred DD I. On the other hand, DD II had popularity with 36 per cent in Locality I, 34 per cent in Locality II and 40 per cent in Locality III. The results indicated that respondents in all the three localities preferred DD I channel to the DD II channel. The data also reflects that DD II had begun to gain popularity with some respondents. Now it also important to find out whether the selection

Table–3.12
Distribution of DD Viewers According to Selection of Channel in the Three Localities

Channel	*Locality* I	II	III	*Total*	*%*
DD I	32	33	30	95	63.3
DD II	18	17	20	55	36.7
Total	50	50	50	150	100

of channels by respondents is associated with income, education and occupation. For this, the chi-square test was applied on the following bivariate tables.

It was observed from Table 3.13 that there were many cells with non-occurence of frequencies. Therefore, the classes with frequency less than 10 were clubbed together. Hence, all other categories were clubbed together excluding the ZEE TV category to get a 2 × 4 contingency table and the Yates' correction was applied as some cells still had frequency less

Table–3.13
Distribution of CATV Viewers According to Selection of Channel and Income Level

Channel	*Income (in Rupees)* 0-2000	2001-5000	5001-10000	10001+	*Total*
ZEE TV	29	32	42	12	115
VCR	4	4	1	–	9
BBC	–	–	2	–	2
PRIME SPORTS	–	–	4	1	5
STAR TV	–	–	13	4	17
VTV	–	–	1	1	2
Total	33	36	63	18	150

$x^2_{cal} = 9.909 > x^2_{tab} = 7.815$ $p < 0.05$, d.f. = 3.

than 5. The value of chi-square was calculated and was found to be 9.909 which was greater than the tabulated value. Hence, it was concluded that the selection of channels and income levels were associated significantly.

From the Table 3.14, it was observed that the frequencies in most cells were below 5. Hence, the categories VCR, BBC, PRIME SPORTS, STAR TV and VTV were clubbed together and a 2 × 5 contingency table was formed to apply the chi-square test. The Yates' correction was applied and the chi-square value was calculated to be 14.6. The tabulated value was 9.488. Hence, it was concluded that channel selection and educational level were significantly associated in the case of CATV viewers.

Table-3.14

Distribution of CATV Viewers According to Selection of Channel and Educational Qualifications

Education Channel	*Below Matric*	*Matric*	*Inter-mediate*	*Graduate*	*Post-graduate*	*Total*
ZEE TV	25	35	5	43	7	115
VCR Channels	3	3	1	1	1	9
BBC	–	–	–	1	1	2
PRIME SPORTS	–	–	–	4	1	5
STAR TV	–	1	–	13	3	17
VTV	–	–	–	1	1	2
Total	28	39	6	63	14	150

$x^2_{cal} = 14.6 > x^2_{tab} = 9.488$ $p < 0.05$, d.f. = 4

From Table 3.15, it was observed that the cell frequencies were below 5. Hence a 2 × 7 contingency table was formed where all the other categories excluding the ZEE TV category were clubbed together.

The Yates' correction was applied and the chi-square value was calculated to be 18.24. The tabulated value was found to be 12.592. As the calculated value of chi-square was greater than the tabulated value, the two variables occupation and selection of channel were found to be associated significantly.

Table–3.15

Distribution of CATV Viewers According to Selection of Channel and Occupational Status

	Occupational Prestige Category							
Channel	*I*	*II*	*III*	*IV*	*V*	*VI*	*VII*	*Total*
ZEE TV	8	30	27	12	13	18	7	115
VCR	–	–	3	1	3	2	–	9
BBC	1	1	–	–	–	–	–	2
PRIME SPORTS	1	4	–	–	–	–	–	5
STAR TV	8	9	–	–	–	–	–	17
VTV	1	1	–	–	–	–	–	2
Total	19	45	30	13	16	20	7	150

$x^2_{cal} = 18.24 > x^2_{tab} = 12.592 \quad p < 0.05$, d.f. = 6

It was revealed that income, education and the occupational status of the Cable TV viewers were significantly associated with the selection of channels. It was also inferred earlier that the duration of viewing television among the Cable TV viewers was significantly associated with income, education and occupation. Hence, it is concluded that the duration of viewing TV and the selection of channels were significantly associated with income, education and occupational status among the Cable TV viewers. It would now be interesting to see how the DD viewers differ from the CATV viewers in this regard.

Table–3.16

Distribution of DD Viewers According to Selection of Channel and Income Level

	Income (in rupees)				
Channel	*0-2000*	*2001-5000*	*5001-10000*	*10001+*	*Total*
DD I	25	25	36	9	95
DD II	13	12	19	11	55
Total	38	37	55	20	150

$x^2_{cal} = 3.387 < x^2_{tab} = 7.815 \quad p > 0.05$, d.f. = 3

It is observed from Table 3.16 that there was no association between income levels and channel selection for DD viewers as the calculated chi-squre value (3.38) was less than the tabulated value.

It was also observed from Table 3.17 that educational qualifications were not associated with the channel selection for DD viewers as the calculated chi-square value (3.085) was less than the tabulated value.

Table-3.17
Distribution of DD Viewers According to Selection of Channel and Educational Qualifications

Education Channel	*Below matric*	*Matric*	*Inter-mediate*	*Graduate*	*Post-graduate*	*Total*
DD I	22	25	4	30	14	95
DD II	7	14	4	21	9	55
Total	29	39	8	51	23	150

$x^2_{cal} = 3.085 < x^2_{tab} = 9.488 \quad p > 0.05, \text{d.f.} = 4$

Table-3.18
Distribution of DD Viewers According to Selection of Channel and Occupational Status

Channel	*Occupational Prestige Category*							
	I	*II*	*III*	*IV*	*V*	*VI*	*VII*	*Total*
DD I	9	28	19	10	10	18	1	95
DD II	1	25	8	2	8	10	1	55
Total	10	53	27	12	18	28	2	150

$x^2_{cal} = 8.83 < x^2_{tab} = 12.592 \quad p > 0.05, \text{d.f.} = 6$

Table 3.18 indicates that there was no association between the occupational status of the respondents and channel selection for DD viewers as the calculated value of chi-square (8.83) was less than the tabulated value.

The results indicate that the income level, educational qualifications and occupational status were significantly associated with channel selection in the case of CATV viewers while the reverse was true in the case of DD viewers. This means that income, education and occupational status were not associated with the selection of channel among DD viewers mainly because Doordarshan had only two channels at the time when the survey was conducted in contrast to the variety of channels offered by the Satellite television. As the socio-economic background of the CATV viewers was associated with both the duration of viewing TV and the selection of channels, it will be important to find out what other implications this would lead to in the viewers' daily family life. This shall be discussed in the next chapter while at present the study shall lay its focus on the differences in preference of programmes held by the CATV viewers and DD viewers in the three localities as well as the association of income, education and occupation with the preference for programmes.

For the purpose of analysing the programme content on TV programmes were classified into nine mutually exclusive categories. The first category included the entertainment based programmes

Table-3.19
Distribution of Respondents According to Their Choice of Programmes in the Three Localities

	Locality				
Type of Programme	*I*	*II*	*III*	*Total*	*%*
Entertainment based	45	50	43	138	46.0
Hindi film based	10	21	42	73	24.3
Detective and horror shows	1	6	9	16	5.3
Children based	2	5	2	9	3.0
Information based	19	12	4	35	11.7
Sports based	6	1	-	7	2.3
Western based	18	2	-	20	6.7
Cookery, beauty and household tips	-	2	-	2	0.7
Miscellaneous	-	1	-	-	-
Total	100	100	100	300	100

e.g., the soap operas, family dramas, comedies and serials. The Hindi film based programmes constituted the second category. The third category included detective and horror shows. Children based programmes which included cartoons and programmes meant for children formed the fourth category. All informative programmes which included news, current affairs, general knowledge, quiz and general awareness constituted the fifth category. Programmes relating to all kinds of sports made the sixth category while western programmes, music, and serials formulated the seventh category. Programmes relating to beauty tips, cookery, life style and cultures, home and household remedies and tips formulated the eighth category. The programmes which could not be placed in any of these categories have been included in miscellaneous category.

The analysis indicated that on the whole, 46 per cent, 24.3 per cent, 5.3 per cent, 3 per cent, 11.7 per cent, 2.3 per cent, 6.7 per cent and 0.7 per cent of the respondents preferred entertainment based, Hindi film based, dectective and horror shows, children based, information based, sports based, western based, cookery, beauty and household tips and miscellaneous category programmes respectively.

In Locality I, 45 per cent, 19 per cent, 18 per cent and 10 per cent preferred entertainment based, informative programmes, western programmes and Hindi film based programmes respectively. Only 6 per cent, 2 per cent and 1 per cent preferred sports based programmes, children based programmes and dectective and horror shows respectively.

In Locality II, 50 per cent, 21 per cent, 12 per cent, 6 per cent and 5 per cent preferred entertainment based, Hindi film based, information based, detective and horror shows and children based programmes respectively. There were 2 per cent respondents in each of the categories of western based programmes and cookery, beauty and household tips based programmes respectively. Also, 1 per cent of the respondents preferred sports based and miscellanaeous category programme each respectively.

In Locality III, 43 per cent, 42 per cent, 9 per cent, 2 per cent and 4 per cent preferred entertainment based, Hindi film based, detective and horror shows, children based and informative programmes categories respectively.

It was observed that in Localities I and II the respondents were spread over in their choice of programme content in almost all categories while in Locality III the respondents were stereotyped in their choice of programme content. The data reflects that entertainment based programmes were popular among majority of the respondents. It was seen in this chapter earlier that the ZEE TV channel which contained a heavy dose of entertainment programmes was the most popular among the CATV viewers. It would now be interesting to find out how the CATV viewers and DD viewers differed in their choice of programmes in the three localities.

It was observed from the data that on the whole, 38.7 per cent of the CATV viewers and 53.3 per cent of the DD viewers preferred entertainment based programmes. In the Hindi film based programmes category there were 27.3 per cent CATV viewers and 21.4 per cent DD viewers. Further, 7.3 per cent of the CATV viewers and 3.3 per cent of the DD viewers preferred detective and horror shows. Also, 2 per cent of the CATV viewers and 4 per cent of the DD viewers preferred children based programmes. About 6 per cent of the CATV viewers and 17.3 per cent of the DD viewers preferred informative programmes. Sports based programmes were popular with 3.3 per cent of the CATV viewers and 6.7 per cent of the DD viewers. Western programmes were popular with 13.3 per cent of the CATV viewers. About 1.3 per cent and 0.7 per cent of the CATV viewers preferred cookery category and miscellaneous category programmes respectively.

Table–3.20

Distribution of CATV Viewers and DD Viewers According to their Choice of Programmes in the Three Localities

	Locality				
Type of Programme	*I*	*II*	*III*	*Total*	*%*
Entertainment based	20 (25)	25 (25)	13 (30)	58 (80)	38.7 (53.3)
Hindi film based	4 (6)	12 (9)	25 (17)	41 (32)	27.3 (21.4)
Detectives and horror shows	1 (-)	2 (4)	8 (1)	11 (5)	7.3 (3.3)

(Contd.)

Type of Programme	*Locality* I	II	III	*Total*	%
Children based	–	3	–	3	2.0
	(2)	(2)	(2)	(6)	(4.0)
Information based	3	2	4	9	6.0
	(16)	(10)	(-)	(26)	(17.3)
Sports based	4	1	–	5	3.3
	(1)	(-)	(-)	(1)	(0.7)
Western based	18	2	–	20	13.3
	(-)	(-)	(-)	(-)	(-)
Cookery, beauty and household tips	–	2	–	2	1.3
	(-)	(-)	(-)	(-)	(-)
Miscellaneous	–	1	–	1	0.7
	(-)	(-)	(-)	(-)	(-)
Total	50	50	50	150	100
	(50)	(50)	(50)	(150)	(100)

In Locality I, 40 per cent of the CATV viewers and 50 per cent of the DD viewers preferred entertainment based programmes. About 8 per cent of the CATV viewers and 12 per cent of the DD viewers preferred Hindi films based programmes. Detective and horror shows were popular among only 2 per cent of the CATV viewers while 4 per cent of the DD viewers had popularity with children based programmes. Informative programmes ware popular with 6 per cent of the CATV viewers and 32 per cent of the DD viewers. Sports based programmes were popular with 8 per cent of the CATV viewers and 2 per cent of the DD viewers. Further, 36 per cent of the CATV viewers preferred western programmes.

In Locality II, 50 per cent each among CATV viewers and DD viewers preferred entertainment programmes. About 24 per cent of the CATV viewers and 18 per cent of the DD viewers preferred Hindi films based programmes. Only 4 per cent of the CATV viewers and 8 per cent of the DD viewers preferred the dectectives and horror shows. Children based programmes were popular with 6 per cent of the CATV viewers and 4 per cent of the DD viewers. Informative programmes were popular with 4 per cent of the CATV viewers and

20 per cent of the DD viewers. About 4 per cent each among CATV viewers and DD viewers preferred western serials and cooking categories programmes respectively while 2 per cent each among CATV viewers and DD viewers preferred sports based programmes and miscellaneous category programmes respectively.

In Locality III, 26 per cent of the CATV viewers and 60 per cent of the DD viewers preferred entertainment based programmes while 50 per cent of the CATV viewers and 34 per cent of the DD viewers preferred Hindi film based programmes. About 16 per cent of the CATV viewers and 2 per cent of the DD viewers preferred detectives and horror shows. Children based programmes were popular with 4 per cent of the DD viewers while 8 per cent of the CATV viewers preferred informative programmes.

The CATV viewers and DD viewers differed to a large extent in their choice of programmes. CATV viewers were spread in their choice of programmes in all categories, while the choice of programmes of DD viewers were concentrated in three categories viz. Entertainment based Hindi film based and informative programmes. This is attributed to the fact that CATV viewers have a wider choice in selection of programmes with the availability of variety of channels.

More DD viewers preferred informative programmes than CATV viewers. This trend was also observed in Localities I and II while in Locality III more CATV viewers preferred informative programmes. Informative programmes had little popularity with CATV viewers. Sports based programmes were preferred by CATV viewers in all the three localities, while a smaller percentage of DD viewers preferred such programmes. Western programmes were preferred to large extent by CATV viewers of Locality I only. The CATV viewers of Locality II had little likeness for the western programmes.

In Localities I and II both CATV viewers and DD viewers respondents preferred entertainment based programmes whereas in Locality III more DD viewers preferred entertainment programmes. It was seen earlier that most respondents preferred channels with heavy dose of entertainment. Also, CATV viewers preferred Hindi film based programmes. The study indicates that as the quality of programmes on Doordarshan and Satellite TV differed to large extent, viewers naturally differed in their selection of programmes. The programmes on Satellite TV are designed for the urban children, urban teenagers, urban youth, urban women and urban adults while the programmes on Doordarshan are oriented towards information, education and also towards development. Hence, CATV viewers and DD viewers are expected to differ in taste for programmes.

As observed earlier, the variables income, education and occupation were associated in the case of CATV viewers and not associated in the case of DD viewers, it would be further interesting to find out if the choice of programmes by the respondents had any association with the three variables mentioned above in the three localities.

For this, the categories of programmes were reduced, i.e., some categories with no frequencies were clubbed together and then the chi-square test was applied. Three categories viz., entertainment programmes, Hindi film based programmes and all other categories categories were clubbed to form the third category. The chi-square test was applied using the Yates' correction.

The study also tested the association between the duration of viewing and choice of programmes of respondents using the chi-square test.

It is inferred from the Table 3.21 that income level and choice of programmes are associated in case of both CATV viewers and DD viewers as the calculated value of chi-square for CATV viewers (29.13) and DD viewers (13.53) was found to be greater than the tabulated value.

Table–3.21

Distribution of CATV Viewers and DD Viewers According to Choice of Programmes and Income Level

	Income (in Rupees)				
Type of Programmes	*0-2000*	*2001-5000*	*5001-10,000*	*10001+*	*Total*
Entertainment based	8 (22)	14 (22)	25 (30)	11 (6)	58 (80)
Hindi film based	20 (12)	10 (7)	10 (9)	1 (4)	41 (32)

(Contd.)

Type of Programmes	*Income (in Rupees)* 0-2000	2001-5000	5001-10,000	10001+	*Total*
Detectives & horror shows	4 (1)	5 (3)	2 (1)	– (-0)	11 (5)
Children based	– (2)	1 (2)	2 (-0)	– (2)	3 (6)
Information based	1 (1)	3 (3)	5 (14)	– (8)	9 (26)
Sports based	– (-)	– (-)	4 (1)	1 (-)	5 (1)
Western based	– (-)	– (-)	15 (-)	5 (-)	20 (-)
Cookery, beauty and household tips	– (-)	2 (-)	– (-)	– (-)	2 (-)
Miscellaneous	– (-)	1 (-)	– (-)	– (-)	1 (-)
Total	33 (38)	36 (37)	63 (55)	18 (200)	150 (150)

CATV viewers $x^2_{cal} = 29.13 > x^2_{tab} = 12.592$ $p < 0.05$, d.f. = 6
DD viewers $x^2_{cal} = 13.53 > x^2_{tab} = 12.592$ $p < 0.05$, d.f. = 6

It is also inferred from Table 3.22 that education and choice of programmes are significantly associated in the case of both CATV viewers and DD viewers as the calculated value of chi-square for CATV viewers (22.9) and DD viewers was greater than the tabulated value.

It is also inferred from Table 3.23 that occupational status and choice of programmes were associated in the case of CATV viewers and not associated in the case of DD viewers. The calculated value of chi-square (37.49) for CATV viewers was greater than the tabulated value (12.02) while the calculated value (20.9) was less than tabulated value in the case of DD viewers.

It is also inferred from Table 3.24 that duration of viewing TV and choice of programmes were associated in the case of CATV viewers and DD viewers as the chi-square calculated value for CATV viewers (15.304) and DD viewers (18.33) was greater than the tabulated value.

Table–3.22
Distribution of CATV Viewers and DD Viewers According to Choice of Programmes and Educational Qualifications

Education / *Type of Programmes*	*Below Matric*	*Matric*	*Inter-mediate*	*Graduate*	*Post-graduate*	*Total*
Entertainment based	6 (19)	16 (24)	4 (5)	28 (25)	4 (7)	58 (80)
Hindi film based	15 (7)	13 (11)	1 (–)	11 (8)	1 (6)	41 (32)
Detectives and horror shows	6 (1)	2 (1)	– (1)	2 (1)	1 (1)	11 (5)
Children based	– (1)	2 (1)	– (1)	1 (2)	1 (1)	3 (6)
Information based	1 (1)	3 (2)	– (1)	3 (15)	2 (7)	9 (26)
Sports based	– (–)	– (–)	– (–)	4 (4)	1 (1)	5 (1)
Western based	– (–)	2 (–)	– (–)	14 (–)	4 (–)	20 (–)
Cookery, Beauty and Household Tips	– (–)	1 (–)	1 (–)	– (–)	– (–)	2 (–)
Miscellaneous	– (–)	– (–)	– (–)	– (–)	1 (–)	1 (–)
Total	28 (29)	39 (39)	6 (8)	63 (51)	14 (23)	150 (150)

CATV viewers $x^2_{cal} = 22.9 > x^2_{tab} = 15.507$ $p < 0.05$, d.f. = 8
DD viewers $x^2_{cal} = 18.1 > x^2_{tab} = 15.507$p < 0.05, d.f. = 8

Table–3.23
Distribution of CATV Viewers and DD Viewers According to Choice of Programmes and Occupational Status

Type of Programmes	*Occupational Prestige Category* *I*	*II*	*III*	*IV*	*V*	*VI*	*VII*	*Total*
Entertainment based	6 (4)	22 (26)	13 (13)	7 (8)	5 (11)	3 (16)	2 (2)	58 (80)

(Contd.)

	Occupational Prestige Category							
Type of Programmes	*I*	*II*	*III*	*IV*	*V*	*VI*	*VII*	*Total*
Hindi film based	1 (-)	3 (13)	10 (3)	5 (1)	7 (6)	12 (9)	3 (-)	41 (32)
Detectives and horror shows	- (-)	2 (-)	1 (2)	- (2)	3 (-)	4 (1)	1 (-)	11 (5)
Children based	- (-)	1 (2)	2 (1)	- (1)	- (1)	- (1)	- (-)	3 (6)
Information based	1 (5)	3 (12)	1 (8)	1 (-)	1 (-)	1 (1)	1 (-)	9 (26)
Sports based	2 (1)	3 (-)	- (-)	- (-)	- (-)	- (-)	- (-)	5 (1)
Western based	9 (-)	11 (-)	- (-)	- (-)	- (-)	- (-)	- (-)	20 (-)
Cookery, beauty & household tips	- (-)	- (-)	2 (-0)	- (-)	- (-)	- (-)	- (-)	2 (-)
Miscellaneous	- (-)	- (-)	1 (-0)	- -(-)	- -(-)	- -(-)	- -(-)	1 (-)
Total	19 (10)	45 (53)	30 (27)	13 (12)	16 (18)	20 (28)	7 (2)	150 (150)

CATV viewers $x^2_{cal} = 37.49 > x^2_{tab} = 21.02$ $p < 0.05$, d.f. = 12
DD viewers $x^2_{cal} = 20.9 < x^2_{tab} = 21.02$ $p > 0.05$, d.f. = 12

Hence, it is concluded that income, education and duration of viewing TV were associated with choice of programmes in the case of both CATV viewers and DD viewers and occupational status was associated with choice of programmes in the case of CATV viewers but not in the case of DD viewers.

It is concluded that income, education and occupation were associated with the selection of channel, duration of viewing TV and the choice of programmes among CATV viewers. It is also inferred that income, education and occupation were associated significantly with the choice of programmes among DD viewers but were not associated with the selection of channels. Also, education

Table–3.24
Distribution of CATV Viewers and DD Viewers According to Choice of Programmes and Duration of Viewing TV

	Duration of Viewing (In Sessions)				
Types of Programmes	*One*	*Two*	*Three*	*Four*	*Total*
Entertainment based	6 (15)	21 (26)	22 (34)	9 (5)	58 (80)
Hindi film based	4 (11)	4 (13)	22 (7)	11 (1)	41 (32)
Detectives and horror shows	1 (1)	- (3)	7 (1)	3 (-)	11 (5)
Children based	1 (2)	- (3)	1 (1)	1 (-)	3 (6)
Information based	3 (15)	2 (8)	- (3)	4 (-)	9 (26)
Sports based	3 (1)	- (-)	- (-)	2 (-)	5 (1)
Western based	2 (-)	5 (-)	9 (-)	4 (-)	20 (-)
Cookery, beauty and household tips	- (-)	2 (-)	- (-)	- (-)	2 (-)
Miscellaneous	- (-)	- (-)	- (-)	1 (-)	1 (-)
Total	20 (45)	34 (53)	61 (46)	35 (6)	150 (150)

CATV viewers $x^2_{cal} = 15.304 > x^2_{tab} = 12.592$ $p < 0.05$, d.f. = 6
DD viewers $x^2_{cal} = 18.33 > x^2_{tab} = 12.592$ $p < 0.05$, d.f. = 6

and occupation had an association with the duration of viewing TV, while income was found to have no association with the duration of viewing TV among DD viewers. It is also observed that the duration of viewing TV and the choice of programmes were significantly associated with each other in the case of both CATV viewers and DD viewers.

It has been observed earlier in this chapter that the three localities differed in their selection of channels and programmes. It would be further interesting to see what TV does in daily family life with different patterns of selection of channels/programmes among family members. It has been observed that the duration of viewing TV has been more among the Cable TV viewers than the DD viewers indicating a positive association between duration of viewing TV and Cable TV. How the duration of viewing TV curtails social participation within the family and also how the differences in selection of channels and programmes affect family life will be the focus of the following chapter.

4
Satellite TV and Family Interaction Patterns

Generally, a family is composed of persons who are related by blood or marriage. A group may be defined as a family that is sharing the same roof, food, money, material goods or emotions. But, when the word 'family' is used we generally think of a traditional nuclear family—two parents and their dependent children; although an extended family either horizontally or vertically often stays together sharing the same roof.

The traditional family in India has undergone enormous change resulting from industrialization and urbanization among various other phenomena. There has been a decline in the quality of ties in interpersonal relationships in the traditional families. However, it is difficult to argue that family ties have weakened. The process of "nucleation" (Gupta, 1976) may separate the members seeking freedom from the patriarchal authority of the family head but the bonds are not completely broken and the Indian family cannot be called "nuclear" in the strict sense of the word (Yadava and Reddi, 1988).

Urbanization has been seen as a major cause for the breakdown of the family system in most countries, but in the Indian context this may not necessarily be true with its age old traditional, social and religious practices. One of the crucial factors however, that has changed the life styles within the urban families is the audio-visual media—mainly the television. Today, the family is seen as a vibrant unit—each family constructs its own media world. The everyday family life is enmeshed with television programmes and therefore it is important to note that this media has a definite place in family interaction patterns.

Television has invaded families to such an extent that it is structuring the daily and weekly scheme of activities of the members. Television may be used as an occasion when all family members gather yet it is often accused of weakening and separating the inter-personal and intra-personal relationships within and between families.

It is obvious that the relationship of television viewing with family interaction patterns is complex and in the absence of any significant element of participant observation of actual behaviour, beyond the interview situation, I am left with only what the respondents chose to tell me. This research in the present chapter, is focussed on comparing CATV viewers with Doordarshan viewers and their family interaction patterns within the television viewing situation.

Implications of television can be best understood by studying the family structure, power relations, the nature of social interaction within the family group and between the family and outsiders. Another important aspect of the family environment to be reviewed is the social placement of children within the family (Caplow, Bahr, Chadwick, Hill and Williamson, 1982). These patterns may not be homogeneous within different socio-economic groups and there is always a fair amount of rule breaking within the most normative socio-economic groups. Still it is possible to identify different traits of family life in different socio-economic groups and compare these specific aspects of everyday life of families in relation to the presence of television at home.

Television is embedded in such a way in family life that the programme content regulates most of the organization of time in families (Bryce, 1981; Lull, 1980). The study of television use becomes more meaningful if we understand the patterns of leisure adopted by families. TV can inhibit contacts outside the home and structure leisure time. There has been a significant reduction in participation rates of almost all forms of outdoor leisure activities with the advent of television. Although there is an overall decline in the expenditure of leisure time from 'out of home' to 'in home' activities, studies have indicated that the more affluent and highly educated families choose socializing agencies like formal organizations to spend their leisure time, moving against the indicated trend (Morley, 1988). In the US, TV stands by far first in leisure time and the third greatest consumer of time behind work and sleep. (Comstock, 1980; Condry, 1989). The present study also makes an effort to illustrate the leisure activities of the members of the families in different socio-economic groups in the context of the television viewing environment.

The central thesis being that the changing patterns of television viewing can be understood only in the overall context of family leisure activities, it is significant to point out that although television may have an addictive quality, it tends to reduce 'socializing'. Television is a primary leisure activity, a relaxable and pleasurable experience. But, it is important to point out that television is also a 'privatized' activity in comparison to other outdoor activities or outside social relations.

The appearance of TV and its meteoric rise after 1950 had a significant impact on the structuring of family life. Television has been a subject of research for nearly five decades and many varying perspectives have emerged to define the television viewing experience. Jan-Uwe Rogge (1989) in the 'Media and Everyday life' defines the media as a part of the family system, a part which is indispensable that many can no longer imagine without. Singer and Singer (1977) and Winick and Winick (1979) refer to television as a 'member of the family' indicating that TV is a significant component in the development of children. Another perspective that emerges from the survey of literature is the extent to which the families use television and families cannot be perceived as monolithic units (Ang, 1991 and Lull, 1990) but they are a different group of individuals who constantly exercise their freedom to choose what to view that emerges from the TV set. Communication researchers claim that TV has the potential to unify the audiences while Mander (1978) claims that television alienates people from reality and hypnotizes people into living in the television world.

A classic criticism of watching television is that it disrupts family communication. For some researchers TV is considered to be a negative force disrupting family life. On the other hand, there have been studies that indicate that TV can enhance communication in the family (Bryce, 1980; Lull, 1980; Messaris, 1983).

Television can enrich the possibilities of verbal and non-verbal communication when it is watched together by family members, independent of the fact that it can reduce or enhance family communication. Television can also be an excuse for talking about particular subjects or themes, avoiding deep communication or regulating conversation in families. Television viewing can also bring closeness between members if they sit together and talk about issues different from television. In his study, Barrios (1988), concluded that TV viewing can provide common ground for family interaction within and with the outside world. Narayanan's (1987) study of adults in Bombay area revealed that there were both positive and negative effects of television. While promoting passivity in people, TV at the same time increases togetherness among family members. According to some researchers a habit of silence and concentration prevails while watching TV and it can develop into a silent joint activity (Chowla, 1986). In the light of these contradictory views, it will be interesting to investigate whether TV enhances or disrupts communication between husband and wife, parents and children and between children themselves and how these types of communication differ in the three different neighbourhoods.

Television and Intra-Familial Communication

Watching television may not always be an isolated activity. It is a family activity, that involves an intermeshing of the constantly changing moods, personal priorities of each family member with the changing contents of programmes that emerge from the TV sets (Dorr, 1986). When television watching is experienced in the presence of other members, several activities and parallel processes occur around, such as eating, doing homework, playing and conversations which can enrich the TV viewing experience.

Watching television cannot be assumed as a one dimensional activity as there are differences between choices made by various kinds of viewers and different patterns of attention among viewers to the same viewing material. Also, due to different schedules and interests, watching television together may become a rare occasion in some families.

Usually people feel that more than one TV set would disrupt the communication within family members. One TV set at home compels the family members to watch it together and may make TV watching a pleasurable experience. Still people feel that they should have more than one TV set, not only to add to their status but in order to be more comfortable. Bower's research on American families (cited by Messaris 1983, p. 293) indicates that even in households with more than one TV set, family members prefer to view it in each other's company.

Since these studies implicitly indicate that intervening factors like the socio-economic status (which also determines the number of TV sets and the space available) may enhance or disrupt communication flow within families while watching TV, the present study examines which of the two perspectives is more applicable and under what circumstances.

Television and Intra-Familial Conflicts

In some cases, where families have more than one TV set, there is a possibility of isolation of family members or otherwise, according to family decision, one central TV set is watched which is placed in a social room i.e., the living room. In cases, where there is more than one TV set, family members prefer to watch TV alone or without interruptions although different family members are watching the same channel. On the other hand, where there is only one TV set switched on as a matter of central decision, there is a possibility that other sets are switched on only when a conflict arises between family members regarding the selection of channels. It is also implied that as the number of TV sets increases, there is bound to be an isolation between different segments of the family like parents (i.e., husband and wife) and children and finally the children themselves.

Apart from these factors, the power relations within the family become crucial and it is important to find out how viewing decisions are made and by whom.

It is therefore interesting to note the role played by the number of TV sets and the power relations within a household, in the conflicts within the family and how these vary in different socio-economic groups.

Rescheduling of Daily Activities

Nothing has affected the routines of families more than television and more so with Satellite television. Some people start their day by turning the TV on and listening to news or religious programmes while they are getting dressed or having breakfast. Some go directly from the bed to the TV set and therefore family organization around the TV continues all day long.

Before television entered the homes, families occupied their early evening hours with activities like listening to radio, socializing with the family and neighbours and generally going to sleep early. Family life has changed after the first TV set had been bought (Robinson, 1972; Szalai, 1972).

Family members, depending on family rules, customs and the TV setting, watch TV simultaneously with other activities such as eating, home chores, homework, listening to music or sleeping. Most families usually have dinner together, because either they have a TV set in the dining room, or they carry their food into the TV room, including bedrooms. Some families may not watch during meals, because there is no TV set near the dining table or because it may be forbidden to eat anywhere other than the dining room.

Most women watch TV while doing the domestic household chores. But this behaviour changes when interesting programmes are on the air and while watching interesting programmes viewers may not do anything else.

Most people, if asked how TV viewing affects their routines or daily lives, would say that it seldom interferes with anything important. They would be wrong if they think sleep, social interaction and reading are considered unimportant, yet they have been reduced by TV.

Johnson (1967) reported that families not only change the sleeping patterns and alter meal times because of TV, but they use it as an electronic baby sitter. Robinson (1981) reveals that activities that decrease with TV are sleep, social gatherings away from home, other leisure activities, conversations and household care. Involvement in community activities have decreased with television. Williams and Handford (1986) observed that young people's participation in community activities have dropped markedly.

Luthra and Mahajan (1993) state that families reschedule their daily chores and altering of routines is irrespective of the social background. In some cases, television may be used as companion or as a background noise and all activities happen around the set. In the back drop of these contrasting views it would be interesting to know how families alter their routines to accommodate interesting programmes and how the different socio-economic groups vary in rescheduling their activities.

Homework of children has been another major concern of researchers in the recent past. Some families require that the TV set should be turned off till all home work is done. In some other families doing homework and viewing TV at the same time is a source of conflict between the parents and children. Medrich (1979), states that the world of parentally controlled TV exists primarily in the middle and upper class families. Sheehan (1983) reported that most children watch TV while doing their home work.

TV and Power Relations within the Family

Another important aspect to be noted is the amount of time devoted by people especially the children to television viewing. Leichter *et. al* (1985) observe that despite agreements on the danger of TV viewing, the time spent on TV continues to increase. Even though parents express concern about the consumption of TV by children, nothing is done to reduce the amount of TV viewing in the household. Not only the amount of viewing but the selection of programmes is usually performed within the context of power relations, in terms of power afforded to members of the family in different roles. Men and women may differ clearly on account of their viewing habits and this is because men and women occupy particular social roles within the family. Similarly, the social placement of children within the family affects the selection of programmes and this research tends to give valuable insights into TV viewing behaviour in the family environment.

In this chapter therefore, we are going to examine the following questions:

1. What do people do during their leisure time?
2. How do they react when guests arrive while they are watching TV, in order to gauge the relationship between TV and hospitality?
3. Do they feel Cable TV has resulted into a decline in intra family interaction? If yes, how?
4. Who controls the TV set and what are its implications?

5. How varying tastes of members of a family affect the relationships within spouses, parents and children?
6. Does TV reduce or enhance conversation among family members?

Answers to these questions were sought with the help of responses, which are being presented in tabular form in the following discussion. Due to the nature of data being used and the fear of losing important insights through quantification, the analysis in the present Chapter is basically qualitative. Verbal reports of respondents constituted important source for drawing inferences.

Leisure activities were categorized into *(a)* those which made an individual relate to other/s and *(b)* those which isolate the individual. This was done in order to examine whether individuals under study spend most of leisure time in socializing or isolating activities.

It was observed that among men 28 per cent of the CATV viewers and 34 per cent of the DD viewers preferred leisure activities which relate to others while 70.7 per cent of the CATV viewers and 64.7 per cent of the DD viewers preferred leisure activities which related to their ownselves. Some men (1.3 per cent both among CATV viewers and DD viewers) said they had no time for leisure activities or there was no male head.

Table-4.1

Distribution of Leisure Activities of Men Among CATV Viewers and DD Viewers in the Three Localities

	Locality				
Type of Activity	*I*	*II*	*III*	*Total*	*%*
That which relate to other/s	30 (24)	10 (21)	2 (6)	42 (51)	28.0 (34)
That which relate to ones' ownself	20 (24)	38 (29)	48 (44)	106 (97)	70.7 (64.7)
Any other (No time for leisure No male head)	– (2)	2 (-)	– (-)	2 (2)	1.3 (1.3)
Total	50 (50)	50 (50)	50 (50)	150 (150)	100 (100)

(Figures in parentheses are the frequencies for DD viewers).

In Locality I, 60 per cent of the CATV viewers and 48 per cent of the DD viewers; in Locality II, 20 per cent of the CATV viewers and 42 per cent of the DD viewers; in Locality III, 4 per cent of the CATV viewers and 12 per cent of the DD viewers preferred activities which relate to others. About 40 per cent of the CATV viewers and 48 per cent of the DD viewers in Locality I; 76 per cent of the CATV viewers and 58 per cent of the DD viewers in Locality II and 96 per cent of the CATV viewers and 88 per cent of the DD viewers in Locality III, preferred leisure activities which relate to others.

It was inferred that among men more CATV viewers than DD viewers preferred activities that related to their ownselves.

It was also inferred that among the activities which relate to others, in the case of males, there were more CATV viewers in Locality I than DD viewers but the reverse was true in the other two localities. The data also indicated that there were more respondents in Locality III (both among CATV viewers and DD viewers) as compared to other localities who had leisure activities which related to their ownselves.

It was observed among women that 33.3 per cent of the CATV viewers and 56 per cent of the DD viewers had activities which relate to others while 66.7 per cent of the CATV viewers and 44 per cent of the DD viewers had activities which relate to their ownselves.

About 40 per cent of the CATV viewers and 56 per cent of the DD viewers in Locality I; 44 per cent CATV viewers and 46 per cent DD viewers in Locality II and 16 per cent CATV viewers and 66 per cent DD viewers in Locality III, had leisure activities which relate to others.

Further, about 60 per cent CATV viewers and 44 per cent DD viewers in Locality I; 56 per cent CATV viewers and 54 per cent DD viewers in Locality II; 84 per cent CATV viewers and 34 per cent DD viewers in Locality III preferred leisure activities which relate to their ownselves.

It was observed on the whole that among women more CATV viewers than DD viewers preferred activities which relate to their ownselves. In all the three localities more CATV viewers than DD viewers preferred activities which relate to their ownselves. More CATV viewers of Locality III preferred activities which relate to their ownselves than other localities.

Table–4.2
Distribution of Leisure Activities of Women (Lady of the Household i.e., Wife of the Respondent) Among CATV Viewers and DD Viewers in the Three Localities

	Locality				
Type of Activity	*I*	*II*	*III*	*Total*	*%*
That which relate to other/s	20 (28)	22 (23)	8 (33)	50 (84)	33.3 (56.0)
That which relate to ones' ownself	30 (22)	28 (27)	42 (17)	100 (66)	66.7 (44.0)
Any other/No time for leisure	– (-)	– (-)	– (-)	– (-)	– (-)
Total	50 (50)	50 (50)	50 (50)	150 (150)	100 (100)

It was indicated that TV a major agent of social change leads to a process of individuation in the sense that it reduces physical as well as social proximity among individuals. People may avoid each other in order to watch their favourite programmes. It was found in the proceeding data that it is the children who would mostly avoid meeting people and going for outings, in order to watch their favourite programmes on TV.

It was observed that 78 per cent of the CATV viewers and 87.3 per cent of the DD viewers among children had leisure activities which related to one's ownself while 16.7 per cent of the CATV viewers and 11.4 per cent of the DD viewers had activities which related to others.

About 26 per cent CATV viewers and 6 per cent DD viewers in Locality I; 16 per cent CATV viewers and 24 per cent DD viewers in Locality II; 8 per cent CATV viewers and 4 per cent DD viewers in Locality III, had activities which related to others while 70 per cent CATV viewers and 92 per cent DD viewers in Locality I; 72 per cent CATV viewers and 74 per cent DD viewers in Locality II; 92 per cent

Table–4.3
Distribution of Leisure Activities of Children Among CATV Viewers and DD Viewers in the Three Localities

Type of Activity	*Locality* I	II	III	*Total*	%
That which relate to other/s	13 (3)	8 (12)	4 (2)	25 (17)	16.7 (11.4)
That which relate to ones' ownself	35 (46)	36 (37)	46 (48)	117 (131)	78.0 (87.3)
No time for leisure/no kids/Infants	2 (1)	6 (1)	- (-)	8 (2)	5.3 (1.3)
Total	50 (50)	50 (50)	50 (50)	150 (150)	100 (100)

CATV viewers and 96 per cent DD viewers in Locality III, had activities which relate to ones' ownselves. In case of about 5.3 per cent CATV viewers and 1.3 per cent DD viewers, the parents said that either their children had no time for leisure or their children were infants or there were no children in the family.

It was inferred that among children majority of the respondents, both among CATV viewers and DD viewers had activities which related to ones' ownself than activities which related to others. Among activities which relate to other/s there were more CATV viewers in Locality I as compared to other localities. It is inferred from the analysis of the last few tables that men, women and children had leisure activities which related to ones' ownself. It is also observed that children emerge as a strong segment within a family in having leisure activities which lead to a weakening of intra-personal relationships within a family as well as with the outside world thus resulting in individuation. This means that with round-the-clock programmes on Satellite TV, respondents are likely to reduce physical mobility and communication outside the family. These converging factors indicate that TV is bound to curtail communication within as well as outside the family.

The respondents were also asked to comment and compare the leisure activities of their children with their own. On this aspect, most parents said that in the present days the leisure activities are indoors. "The leisure activities during our days were outdoor physical activities, creative activities, reading and we had more time to study", said a parent. But now-a-days, due to the media invasion, children are either glued to the television or play with electronic gadgets like video games. One respondent added, "TV is TB". The respondents of Locality I, pointed out that along with the electronic gadgets, swimming and parties, children enjoy no other leisure. Another respondent said, "It is TV and music all the time." "We were outdoor and they are indoors", added another respondent. Most respondents especially from Locality II observed that the present-day generation had a wide choice in choosing their leisure activities, while during their times, it was only the radio among the electronic gadgets or outdoor games. They also claimed that children had more opportunities to develop their intelligence power, they were more independent and they wanted less restrictions imposed on them. "Social life is hampered to a large extent in this generation", pointed out another respondent.

Another section of the respondents said that the work load from school these days was so much that they felt that they should allow their kids to watch a little of TV after 8 p.m., to relax. Some added, "There is no time left for leisure activities these days with the pressure of school and immense competition."

Respondents said that physical and creative activities besides reading, have been curtailed, in favour of television. They added that children had become disobedient, rash, and brutal due to television. Parents had to force them many times to study and not to watch television. They claimed that children had become irresponsible towards their academic responsibilities. One parent said, "Children are cut-off not only from the society but from fresh air which is a health hazard." The viewers of CATV said that more programmes and more channels are going to keep the children more glued to television.

Respondents of Locality III said that the present-day children were enjoying life, whereas they had to do a lot of hard work. The researcher during the survey in Locality III observed a small group of school-going children watching CATV programmes outside a shop, during school hours. The parents remarked, "We are under the impression that they are going to school but children are so fascinated by CATV that they stand on the roadside in front of any shop that has switched on to CATV channels/programmes and come back home exactly at the time when the school hours are over. And we cannot keep a check on them as we are busy with our own work."

Most mothers of Locality III added that they used to help their mothers in domestic work at home but now a days their girl child refused to do anything but watch television. They also said that the children were picking up fashions from TV and had been wasting time in front of the mirror (a respondent of Locality III). Respondents opined that times had changed and that they too were watching TV along with their children during their leisure. This reveals that respondents are seduced into watching TV programmes once the TV set is switched on.

Due to financial difficulties, one respondent in Locality III said, "We have to fulfill the desires of our children, inspite of the fact that we don't have enough to eat." This indicates that despite hardships parents relented to the demands of their children. These pointers indicate that Satellite TV is an essential part of a family – a member of the family that is indispensable.

Another section of respondents said, "We are glad that during leisure time the children are confined to their own homes with CATV, otherwise they were always in the neighbours homes or elsewhere watching CATV programmes." One respondent in Locality III interestingly remarked, "We had no TV during our times and even if it was there, our parents would have never allowed us to watch TV. We were very obedient and now-a-days we beat our children for disobedience. Television has contributed to disobedience", he added.

An effort to negate the impact of TV was also noticed. For example, one of the respondents said, "I have killed the interest of my children in television and have encouraged them to spend time on reading and playing and I have been able to succeed in this." This indicated how parents, with the help of some deliberate efforts, were able to negate the impact of television on children and their energies in other more constructive things.

Responses point that with media-invasion, the shape of leisure activities is bound to be 'individualistic' in nature. This may result in a marked drop in communication within as well as across families as viewers interact with the media. Apart from this, television has been accused of shaping in irresponsible and disobedient children. It would be also interesting to find out in what other spheres of social participation television has made dents. The following discussions reveal some interesting findings on these aspects.

Our traditional culture is known for another characteristic, i.e., hospitality. In the rural settings, the guest has always been treated as a 'God', who must be looked after well. In an urban melieu on the other hand, due to several reasons, there is a decline in such a hospitality. But does urban residence by itself result into this change? Perhaps not. Several factors may be responsible for this— one of these being the Cable television. Thus an effort was made to analyse the association between TV viewing and reaction of respondents towards the guests.

The analysis indicated that about 57.3 per cent of the Cable viewers and 51.3 per cent of the DD viewers expressed irritation when guests arrived while they were watching an interesting programme on the television. For 42.7 per cent of the Cable viewers and 48.7 per cent of the DD viewers the arrival of guests during an interesting programme did not make any difference.

In Locality I, 58 per cent of the Cable viewers and 64 per cent of the DD viewers were irritated when guests arrived while watching an interesting programme. Further, 42 per cent of the Cable viewers and 36 per cent of the DD viewers did not express irritation when guests arrived while watching an interesting programme.

In Locality II, 54 per cent of the Cable viewers and 48 per cent of the DD viewers were irritated when guests arrived while watching an interesting programme. About 46 per cent of the Cable viewers and 52 per cent of the DD viewers did not express any irritation on seeing guests while watching an interesting programme.

In Locality III, 60 per cent of the Cable viewers and 42 per cent of the DD viewers were irritated to see guests while watching an interesting programme. About 40 per cent of the Cable viewers and 58 per cent of the DD viewers indicated no irritation when guests arrived while they were watching an interesting programme.

Table-4.4
Distribution of CATV Viewers and DD Viewers According to Whether they were Irritated When Guests Arrived During an Interesting Progamme in the Three Localities

Response	*Locality*			*Total*	*%*
	I	*II*	*III*		
Irritated on Arrival of Guests	29 (32)	27 (24)	30 (21)	86 (77)	57.3 (51.3)
Not Irritated	21 (18)	23 (26)	20 (29)	64 (73)	42.7 (48.7)
Total	50 (50)	50 (50)	50 (50)	150 (150)	100 (100)

It was inferred that more CATV viewers than DD viewers were irritated when guests arrived while they were watching an interesting programme. What is significant however is that whether Cable TV or Doordarshan, in all the three localities, a greater proportion of respondents got irritated when some guests arrived while they were enjoying a programme.

The researcher further asked the respondents who got irritated, as to how they reacted when guests arrived. On the whole, it was observed that a majority of the respondents felt angry and scowled when the guests arrived. Another major section of the respondents felt upset and disturbed as their attention was diverted. A few of them even managed to ignore the guests after wishing them and continued to watch TV. Another section of respondents said that after wishing the guests, they asked them to watch the TV programme along with them. A few indicated friction between the parents and children, when the parents switched off the TV set, while entertaining the guests. A respondent in Locality II, remarked, "I feel like 'clawing' the guest when they come while I am watching an interesting programme."

It was also observed that 21.3 per cent of the CATV viewers and 12 per cent of the DD viewers felt 'disturbed' when guests arrived during an interesting programme. Some respondents indicated that the arrival of guests during an interesting programme led to friction between the parents and children. This indicates that

Table–4.5
Distribution of CATV Viewers and DD Viewers According to Type of Reactions When Guests Arrived during an Interesting Progamme in the Three Localities

Kind of Reactions	*Locality* I	II	III	*Total*	%
Get angry/scowl	12 (12)	13 (13)	8 (8)	33 (33)	22.0 (22.0)
Wish the Guest and then Watch TV	2 (6)	1 (4)	4 (3)	7 (13)	4.7 (8.7)
Feel Disturbed	13 (10)	9 (7)	10 (1)	32 (18)	21.3 (12.0)
Wish the Guest and Suggest to Watch TV	1 (4)	2 (-)	7 (9)	10 (13)	6.7 (8.7)
Friction between Family Members	1 (-)	2 (-)	1 (-)	4 (-)	2.6 (-)
No Irritations Expressed	21 (18)	23 (26)	20 (29)	64 (73)	42.7 (48.7)
Total	50 (50)	50 (50)	50 (50)	150 (150)	100 (100)

television is definitely making dents on family relationships and weakening ties both within and across families. The arrival of guests was not a pleasurable experience for many respondents. The analysis shows that in some cases the respondents asked the guests to watch TV along with them which is a clear indication of a significant reduction in communication across families. The study points towards a weakening of intra-personal and inter-personal ties as a result of television viewing.

In order to see whether television makes people avoid social visits or not, we asked the respondents whether they avoided visiting people (friends, relatives neighbours etc.) during prime time of TV (i.e., 7 p.m. to 10 p.m.). Following are the responses in the three neighbourhoods.

On the whole, it was observed that 43.3 per cent of the Cable viewers and 36 per cent of the DD viewers avoided visiting people's

Table–4.6
Distribution of CATV Viewers and DD Viewers According to Whether they Avoided Visiting People at their Homes at Prime Hours of TV in the Three Localities

Response	*Locality*				
	I	*II*	*III*	*Total*	*%*
Avoid	16	19	30	65	43.3
	(21)	(14)	(19)	(64)	(36.0)
Do not avoid	34	31	20	85	56.7
	(29)	(36)	(31)	(96)	(64.0)
Total	50	50	50	150	100
	(50)	(50)	(50)	(150)	(100)

homes during the prime hours of television. Also, 56.7 per cent of the Cable viewers and 64 per cent of the DD viewers did not consider prime hours of television as a hindering factor in visiting relatives, friends or neighbours.

In Locality I, 32 per cent of the CATV viewers and 42 per cent of the DD viewers; in Locality II, 38 per cent of the CATV viewers and 28 per cent of the DD viewers; in Locality III, 60 per cent of the CATV viewers and 38 per cent of the DD viewers avoided visiting people at prime hours of TV.

It was inferred from the data that on the whole, a majority of the Cable viewers in Locality III avoided visiting people at prime hours of TV. It may be inferred that the respondents in the lower socio-economic group were found to be more glued to TV sets. As a result they avoided going out because of their favourite programmes.

It is important to note that avoidance of social visits is not necessarily due to the fear of missing favourite programmes only. A number of respondents, especially in upper and middle income localities revealed that if they visited somebody during prime hours of TV, they generally felt unattended. Instead of getting a welcome, they had to face embarrassment since they disturbed the hosts, who were more interested in TV programmes. For the fear of being forced guests, they avoided visiting people during these hours. It was inferred that respondents did not want to socialize across families for the fear of being unwelcomed. This indicates a decline in social participation on the part of viewers due to television.

In order to find out whether there is a decline in interaction within the family due to television, the researcher sought responses on this aspect. Responses were sought to whether TV was a hindering factor or not in the time spent with the family members.

From Table 4.7 it was inferred that on the whole, 58 per cent of the Cable viewers and 39.3 per cent of the DD viewers felt that they would spend more time interacting with their family members if they did not have TV at home. About 42 per cent of the Cable viewers and 60.7 per cent of the DD viewers, thought otherwise.

Table–4.7

Distribution of CATV Viewers and DD Viewers According to Whether they Thought That They would Spend More Time Interacting with Their Family Members had they not Possessed TV in the Three Localities

	Locality				
Response	*I*	*II*	*III*	*Total*	*%*
Yes	33 (21)	20 (22)	34 (16)	87 (59)	58 (39.3)
No	17 (29)	30 (28)	16 (34)	63 (91)	42 (60.7)
Total	50 (50)	50 (50)	50 (50)	150 (150)	100 (100)

In Locality I, 66 per cent of the Cable viewers and 42 per cent of the DD viewers; in Locality II, 40 per cent of the CATV viewers and 44 per cent of the DD viewers; and in Locality III, 68 per cent of the CATV viewers and 32 per cent of the DD viewers felt that they would spend more time interacting with their family members if they did not have television at home.

Among those who felt that TV did not interfere in the time spent with the family members were 34 per cent Cable viewers and 58 per cent DD viewers in Locality I; 60 per cent CATV viewers and 56 per cent DD viewers in Locality II; and 32 per cent CATV viewers and 68 per cent DD viewers in Locality III.

The data shows that on the whole, more CATV viewers than DD viewers felt that there was a considerable decline in the time spent with family members due to television. This indicates that round-the-clock programmes through Satellite TV, leave little time for respondents to interact with their family members. It is inferred that Satellite TV is bound to curtail social participation within the family.

The results also show that in Localities I and III more CATV viewers than DD viewers felt that they would spend more time interacting with family members if they did not have television indicating an inverse association between television viewing and intra-family communication. While television reduces intra-family communication, it is also expected to reduce the physical isolation of members as they are watching television. The study substantiates the view held by Robinson (1972), Szalai (1972), Comstock (1978) and Noelle-Neumann (1981), that TV had reduced interaction among family members.

Further, television is a source which brings in physical proximity of members within a family especially in households where there is a single TV set. To find out if such a physical proximity was induced by TV, the researcher asked the respondents whether TV brought in physical closeness between family members.

It was observed that 59.3 per cent of the CATV viewers and 50 per cent of the DD viewers felt that television induced physical proximity while 40.7 per cent of the CATV viewers and 50 per cent of the DD viewers felt that television was not a factor in reducing physical isolation among family members.

In Locality I, 62 per cent of the CATV viewers and 56 per cent of the DD viewers; in Locality II, 48 per cent of the CATV viewers and an equal proportion of the DD viewers; in Locality III, 68 per cent of the CATV viewers and 46 per cent of the DD viewers felt that television brought in physical closeness between family members. From the data it was inferred that majority of the respondents in Localities I and III felt that television reduced physical isolation of family members while majority of the respondents in Locality II felt that television did not contribute to physical proximity among family members. It was also observed that on the whole, a majority of the respondents among CATV viewers felt that TV was a source which induced physical proximity among family members. It can be inferred that the variety of channels and longer duration of telecast on the Satellite TV promote physical proximity among its viewers.

Table–4.8
Distribution of CATV Viewers and DD Viewers According to Whether they Thought that TV Made All Members of Their Family Sit Together in the Three Localities

	Locality				
Response	*I*	*II*	*III*	*Total*	*%*
Yes	31 (28)	24 (24)	34 (23)	89 (75)	59.3 (50)
No	19 (22)	26 (26)	16 (27)	61 (75)	40.7 (50)
Total	50 (50)	50 (50)	50 (50)	150 (150)	100 (100)

These respondents who said that TV increased physical proximity among family members, pointed out that the meal time was always in front of the television. This made all members sit together for a longer period of time. This response was generally found among the respondents of Localities I and II. In Locality III, respondents indicated that as there was only room and one TV set, the members were physically present for a longer period of time. It may also be concluded that as the respondents of Locality III had limited space in their homes, TV was bound to increase the physical closeness among its viewers.

Among those members who said that TV did not make all members sit together, respondents in Localities I and II pointed out that as they had more than one TV set, different members had different choice of programmes and timings to watch TV. It was therefore not possible for all members to sit together. In Locality III, respondents disclosed that all family members were not free to watch programmes at a particular time. Hence, TV did not make members sit together at the same time.

From the analysis of the previous data it was observed that most respondents among CATV viewers felt that TV had reduced intra-family interaction. Further, the study also investigated whether TV had isolated family members from each other. Previous research has shown that on the one hand, TV brings in proximity between members while on the other it isolates members from each other. It would be interesting to find out whether TV had isolated family members from each other or not.

Table–4.9
Distribution of CATV Viewers and DD Viewers According to Whether they Thought that TV had Taken Family Members Away from each Other in the Three Localities

Response	Locality			Total	%
	I	*II*	*III*		
Yes	17 (14)	16 (14)	31 (10)	64 (38)	42.7 (25.3)
No	33 (36)	34 (36)	19 (40)	86 (112)	57.3 (74.7)
Total	50 (50)	50 (50)	50 (50)	150 (150)	100 (100)

The data in Table 4.9 indicates that on the whole 42.7 per cent of the CATV viewers and 25.3 per cent of the DD viewers felt that TV distanced family members while 57.3 per cent of the CATV viewers and 74.7 per cent of the DD viewers felt otherwise.

Further, 34 per cent of the CATV viewers and 28 per cent of the DD viewers in Locality I; 32 per cent of the CATV viewers and 28 per cent of the DD viewers in Locality II; and 62 per cent of the CATV viewers and 20 per cent of the DD viewers in Locality III, felt that TV had pulled family members away from each other. It was inferred that majority of the respondents in Locality III, felt that TV had isolated family members from each other. It was observed in Chapter III that the respondents of Locality III were heavy consumers of television and hence isolation of family members was bound to be felt under these circumstances and more so among the Cable viewers.

Among respondents who felt that TV had pulled family members away from each other, some disclosed that, once the TV set was switched on, members do not have the zeal to discuss the day's notes with each other, as each member is interacting with the TV. It was indicated in the discussion earlier in this chapter that the prime leisure activity of majority of the respondents was television viewing.

Both Cable viewers and DD viewers stressed that as there was no interaction between family members consequent to TV viewing, there was physical isolation as well as reduction in communication between family members. Some respondents pointed out that family members had no feelings for each other which created a gap between them.

The data clearly reflects a drop in interaction between family members due to TV viewing resulting in both physical and mental isolation. Among the respondents who said that TV was not a contributor in weakening ties between family members disclosed that TV did not make any difference to them. One respondent said, "TV or no TV, we make all the conversation that is needed and necessary at home." Some DD viewers felt that TV was not a barrier between members of the family. They added that TV had not taken them away in anyway as they communicated with each other in a normal way. They denied TV being a hinderance.

The study indicates that TV viewing results in the weakening of inter-personal and intra-personal relationships within families, with a decline in intra-family communication. Thus, it can be concluded, that although TV is a force which disrupts family life, it is indispensable. It was seen in this chapter in the begining, that respondents in Locality II were forced by their children to subscribe to Cable TV. This reveals that children have emerged as a powerful segment in the family in the television viewing environment. Another inference drawn was that children were glued to their TV sets, placing TV viewing as their prime leisure activity. It is in this context, that the present study seeks a glimpse into the social placement of children in the TV viewing situation. For this respondents were asked to give responses as to who exercised control over the television set when all the members sit together to watch programmes.

The data indicated that on a typical evening when all members of the family were together watching television, the control of TV set was in the hands of children in 58 per cent among the Cable viewers and 62 per cent among the DD viewers. Among 25.3 per cent of the CATV viewers and 20.7 per cent of the DD viewers, the control of the TV set was in the hands of male head of the household. Among 11.3 per cent of the CATV viewers and 14.7 per cent of the DD viewers said that the control of the TV set was in the hands of the lady of the household. Only 5.4 per cent of the CATV viewers and 2.6 per cent of the DD viewers said that the control of the TV set was sometimes with the parents and sometimes with children or grand parents.

Table–4.10
Distribution of CATV Viewers and DD Viewers According to who in the Family had the Control of the TV Set While Watching TV in the Three Localities

	Locality				
Which Member	*I*	*II*	*III*	*Total*	*%*
Respondent	15 (13)	7 (8)	16 (10)	38 (31)	25.3 (20.7)
Wife	4 (10)	4 (7)	9 (5)	17 (22)	11.3 (14.7)
Children	29 (26)	33 (33)	25 (34)	87 (93)	58 (62)
Sometimes parents/children	1 (1)	3 (-)	– (-)	4 (1)	2.7 (0.6)
Sometimes husband/wife	1 (-)	2 (-)	– (-)	3 (-)	2.0 (-)
Grandparents	– (-)	1 (2)	– (1)	1 (3)	0.7 (2.0)
Total	50 (50)	50 (50)	50 (50)	150 (150)	100 (100)

In Locality I, 58 per cent of the CATV viewers and 52 per cent of the DD viewers said the control of the TV set was in the hands of the children. About 30 per cent of the CATV viewers and 26 per cent of the DD viewers said the control of the TV set was in the hands of the male head of the household while 8 per cent of the CATV viewers and 20 per cent of the DD viewers said that control of the TV set was in the hands of the lady of the household. The rest i.e., 4 per cent of the CATV viewers and 2 per cent of the DD viewers said the control of the TV set was not restricted and vascillated between members.

In Locality II, 66 per cent each among both CATV viewers and DD viewers said the control of the TV set was in the hands of the children while 14 per cent of the CATV viewers and 16 per cent of the DD viewers said the control was in the hands of the male head of the household. About 8 per cent of the CATV viewers and 14 per cent of the DD viewers said the control was in the hands of the lady of the household. The rest i.e., 12 per cent of the CATV viewers and 4 per cent of the DD viewers said that the control was not restricted and varied from day-to-day.

In Locality III, 50 per cent of the CATV viewers and 68 per cent of the DD viewers said the control of the TV set was in the hands of the children while 32 per cent of the CATV viewers and 20 per cent of the DD viewers said that the control of the TV set was in the hands of the male head of the household. About 18 per cent of the CATV viewers and 10 per cent of the DD viewers said that the control was in the hands of the lady of the household. Only 2 per cent of the DD viewers said that the control of the TV set was in the hands of the grand-parents.

It is inferred from the data that in all the three localities, children had control over the television set. It was also revealed that the majority of the children of Cable viewers in Locality I exercised control over the TV set as compared to other localities as well as DD viewers. This reveals that the control over TV is exercised by children among subscribers of Cable TV.

Earlier studies have indicated that the audiences have wider choice in choosing media content as the number of channels are increasing. The increasing number of channels has persuaded many families to purchase another TV set due to differences in choice of programmes by family members (as seen in the previous chapter). Another important dimension to the increasing number of channels is the increasing conflicts between members of the family, even where there is more than a single TV set. Hence, the researcher investigated, how the respondents differed from those with and without cable connections in the three localities in this regard.

On the whole, about 57.3 per cent of the CATV viewers and only 32 per cent of the DD viewers had quarrels in the family over selection of channels. Further, 42.7 per cent of the CATV viewers and 68 per cent of the DD viewers had no quarrels at home over the selection of channels.

In Locality I, 66 per cent of the CATV viewers and 38 per cent of the DD viewers; in Locality II, 60 per cent of the CATV viewers and only 24 per cent of the DD viewers; in Locality III, 46 per cent of CATV viewers and 34 per cent of the DD viewers had quarrels over selection of programmes in the family.

Table-4.11

Distribution of CATV Viewers and DD Viewers According to Whether they had Quarrels in the Family Over Selection of Channels in the Three Localities

	Locality				
Response	*I*	*II*	*III*	*Total*	*%*
Yes	33 (19)	30 (12)	23 (17)	86 (48)	57.3 (32)
No	17 (31)	20 (38)	27 (33)	64 (102)	42.7 (68)
Total	50 (50)	50 (50)	50 (50)	150 (150)	100 (100)

It was inferred that more CATV viewers than DD viewers had quarrels over selection of programmes. In Localities I and II more CATV viewers had quarrels in their families over selection of programmes while in Locality III more CATV viewers had no quarrels at home over selection of channels. This may be attributed to the fact that respondents of Locality III were stereotyped in their selection of programmes while in the other two localities especially Locality I, respondents varied in their choice of selection of channels which was an observation made in Chapter 3.

Another important point to be noted here was that inspite of about 50 per cent of the respondents in Locality I, who had more than one TV set, they had more quarrels, over selection of channels than the other localities. This was due to the fact that only one main TV set was on for the family and only when quarrels arose the second TV set was switched on. This was observed in most families. The placement of the main TV set in the dining room or in the lobby and the subsequent sets in the bedrooms was an important point to be noted, for quarrels in the families over selection of channels in Locality I.

Another important point to be noted here, is that in Locality I, where about 50 per cent of the respondents had more than one TV set, separate family units like husband-wife unit and the children unit shared separate TV sets each. This led to quarrels between different units (i.e., between husband and wife and between children themselves) in the family and hence, there were more quarrels in Locality I as compared to other localities. This reveals a positive association between the number of TV sets and conflicts in a household.

It was also important to observe that most DD viewers did not have clashes in the family over channel selection as they had a lesser choice of channels than those with cable connections. It may be inferred that there is a positive association between the number of channels as well as conflicts. Hence, it is concluded that the variety of channels and the number of the TV sets had a positive association with conflicts. Therefore, it may be inferred that Satellite TV was a negative force in a family which usually led to disharmony among its viewers.

It is also interesting to note the frequency of quarrels over selection of channels in the three localities.

Table–4.12
Distribution of CATV Viewers and DD Viewers According to the Frequency of Quarrels Over Selection of Channels in the Three Localities

	Locality				
Frequency of Quarrels	*I*	*II*	*III*	*Total*	*%*
Often	4 (3)	11 (6)	5 (3)	20 (12)	13.3 (8)
Sometimes	27 (12)	16 (5)	16 (14)	59 (31)	39.3 (20.7)

(Contd.)

Frequency of Quarrels	*I*	*II*	*III*	*Total*	*%*
Rarely	2 (4)	3 (1)	2 (-)	7 (5)	4.7 (3.3)
Never	17 (31)	20 (38)	27 (33)	64 (102)	42.7 (68)
Total	50 (50)	50 (50)	50 (50)	150 (150)	100 (100)

In case of the frequency of quarrels, results indicated that 39.3 per cent of the CATV viewers and 20.7 per cent of the DD viewers had clashes in the family over the selection of channels only 'sometimes' while 13.3 per cent of the CATV viewers and 8 per cent of the DD viewers 'often' had quarrels in the family over selection of channels. About 4.7 per cent of the CATV viewers and 3.3 per cent of the DD viewers had quarrels over selection of channels CATV in the family only 'rarely'.

In Locality I, 8 per cent CATV viewers and 6 per cent DD viewers 'often' had quarrels while 54 per cent of the viewers and 24 per cent of the DD viewers 'sometimes' had quarrels in the family over the selection of channels. About 4 per cent of the CATV viewers and 8 per cent of the DD viewers had quarrels in the family 'rarely'.

In Locality II, 22 per cent of the CATV viewers and 12 per cent of the DD viewers 'often' had quarrels in the family while 32 per cent of the CATV viewers and 10 per cent of the DD viewers 'sometimes' had quarrels over the selection of channels. Only 6 per cent of the CATV viewers and 2 per cent of the DD viewers had quarrels over selection of channels 'rarely'.

In Locality III, 10 per cent of the CATV viewers and 6 per cent of the DD viewers 'often' had quarrels while 32 per cent of the CATV viewers and 28 per cent of the DD viewers had quarrels 'sometimes' over the selection of channels. Only 4 per cent of the CATV viewers had quarrels 'rarely' in the family.

It was inferred that in Locality II, more CATV viewers than DD viewers had more frequent quarrels in the family. Also, in Localities I and II more CATV viewers than DD viewers had quarrels 'sometimes' over the selection of channels. In Locality III, the trend was almost the same in all the categories, both among CATV viewers and DD viewers in terms of frequency of quarrels. As a majority of the CATV viewers in Locality I had high degree of frequency of quarrels, it is inferred that wide choice in the number of channels was a major contributing factor to the rising conflicts between members of the family.

It was also seen in Chapter 2 that most Cable TV viewers in Locality I, owned more than one TV set. At same time, majority of the Cable viewers in Locality I had high degree of frequency of conflicts arising over the selection of channels as compared to the other localities. This was mainly because different family units like husband and wife and children themselves shared one TV set each. This resulted in an increase in conflicts between the husband and wife or between children themselves. It can be concluded here, that an increase in the number of TV sets does not necessarily decrease conflicts. On the contrary, the increase in the number of TV sets may lead to disharmony in the family as well as physical isolation of family members.

As quarrels in the family lead to disharmony, it was important to investigate whether the relationship between husband and wife and that between children had been affected or not, due to TV viewing.

The data revealed that 47.3 per cent of CATV viewers and 28 per cent of DD viewers indicated that conflicts arising over selection of channels had affected relationships within the family. Only 10 per cent of the CATV viewers and 4 per cent of the DD viewers indicated that inspite of conflicts over selection of channels, none of the family members felt that relationships within the family had been affected.

In Locality I, 62 per cent of the CATV viewers and 26 per cent of DD viewers; in Locality II, and 42 per cent of the CATV viewers and 24 per cent of DD viewers; in Locality III, 38 per cent of the CATV viewers and 24 per cent of the DD viewers said that the relationships among the family members had been affected due to television.

It was inferred that majority of the CATV viewers of Locality I, seemed to have been affected by quarrels arising over selection of channels. In all the three localities, more CATV viewers than DD viewers felt that relationships in the family had been affected due to

Table–4.13
Distribution of CATV Viewers and DD Viewers According to Whether the Divergence in the Selection of Channels had Affected Their Relationship with their Spouse/Children in the Three Localities

Affect on Relationships	*Locality* I	II	III	*Total*	*%*
Yes	31 (13)	21 (12)	19 (17)	71 (42)	47.3 (28)
No	2 (6)	9 (-)	4 (-)	15 (6)	10.0 (4.0)
No quarrels	17 (31)	20 (38)	27 (33)	64 (102)	42.7 (68)
Total	50 (50)	50 (50)	50 (50)	150 (150)	100 (100)

quarrels over selection of channels. It may be pointed out, that the availability of variety of viewing material for subscribers of Cable TV may lead to a weakening of ties in the intra-personal relationships within the family. It can be concluded here that an increase in the number of channels and the number of TV sets tend to weaken bonds within the family thus making urbanism as a way of life more pronounced in the whole process.

It is also important to note on which segment of the family, TV had affected the most.

On probing further, the researcher asked the families as to which relationship between which members had been affected. It was found that 6 per cent of the CATV viewers and 2 per cent of the DD viewers felt that relationship between the spouse had been affected. About 6.7 per cent of the CATV viewers and 3.3 per cent of the DD viewers said the parent-children relationship had been affected while about 32 per cent of the CATV viewers and 22 per cent of the DD viewers said that the relationship between children had been affected. Also, 2.6 per cent of the Cable viewers and 0.7 per cent of the DD viewers said that the grandparent-children relationship had been affected.

Table–4.14
Distribution of CATV Viewers and DD Viewers According to Which Relationship had been Affected due to Conflicts Arising Due to Differences in the Selection of Channels in the Three Localities

Relationship Between	Locality I	II	III	Total	%
Husband-wife	3 (2)	3 (1)	3 (-)	9 (3)	6.0 (2.0)
Parents-children	4 (3)	5 (2)	1 (-)	10 (5)	6.7 (3.3)
Children themselves	21 (7)	12 (9)	15 (17)	48 (33)	32.0 (22.0)
Grandparents-children	3 (1)	1 (-)	- (-)	4 (1)	2.6 (0.7)
Total (effect on relationships)	31 (13)	21 (12)	19 (17)	71 (42)	47.3 (28.0)
No effect	2 (6)	9 (-)	4 (-)	15 (6)	10.0 (4.0)
No quarrels	17 (31)	20 (38)	27 (33)	64 (102)	42.7 (68.0)
Total	50 (50)	50 (50)	50 (50)	150 (150)	100 (100)

In Locality I, 42 per cent of the CATV viewers and 14 per cent of the DD viewers; in Locality II, 24 per cent of the CATV viewers and 18 per cent of the DD viewers; in Locality III, 30 per cent of the CATV viewers and 34 per cent of the DD viewers said that the relationships between children had been affected.

In Locality I, 6 per cent of CATV viewers and 4 per cent of DD viewers; in Locality II, 6 per cent of CATV viewers and 2 per cent of DD viewers; in Locality III, only 6 per cent of CATV viewers felt that the husband-wife relationship had been affected due to conflicts arising over the selection of channels. Further, 8 per cent of the CATV viewers and 6 per cent of the DD viewers in Locality I; 10 per cent of the CATV viewers and 4 per cent of the DD viewers in Locality II; and 2 per cent of DD viewers in Locality III, felt that parent-children relationship had been affected due to conflicts arising over the selection of channels.

There were 6 per cent CATV viewers and 2 per cent DD viewers in Locality I; and 2 per cent CATV viewers in Locality II, who said that the grandparents-children relationship had been affected due to conflicts arising over the selection of channels.

It was observed that in all the three localities more CATV viewers than DD viewers said that intra-familial relationships had been affected. In all three localities the trend was the same in all the relationship categories. In Localities I and II, more CATV viewers than DD viewers indicated that the relationship between their children had been affected whereas in Locality III, more DD viewers said that the relationship between children had been affected. However, whether Cable TV or Doordarshan it was important to note that the relationship between children themselves was affected due to conflicts arising over the selection the channels in all the three localities. The findings indicate that TV had made a maximum dent on children in all the three neighbourhoods. Therefore, a separate chapter i.e. Chapter 6 has been fully devoted to study the impact of TV on children. There were some interesting revelations by the lady of the household regarding intra-familial relationships. Most of them said that they were upset at their husband's behaviour in controlling the TV channels. This resulted in some friction between the husband and wife and the frustration was shown in other quarrels.

In cases, where children quarrelled, the parents had to intervene and stop them from beating each other. In cases, where the children were grown up, the female child usually succumbed to her brother's choice. The parents had decided to purchase another TV set at frequent instances of quarrels between the family members. In some instances where the parents and children had different choices in the selection of channels, majority of the parents relented to their childrens' choice of programmes to avoid the 'heat' in the room.

Some respondents, (in Locality II) indicated that when there were quarrels between children themselves, the parents usually switched off the TV set. In a few cases, the parents intervened to settle for a compromise between their children before reswitching the TV set. Most parent expressed irritation at their childrens' behaviour. In case of the conjugal relationship usually the female counterpart willingly allowed her husband to switch on to the channel of his choice. But in one case, the lady (female counterpart) remarked, "I don't speak to my husband for a couple of hours after he takes control of the TV set against my choice." In another interesting case, a male child aged 11 years, had quarrels of severe intensity with his grandmother everyday that, it made the parents purchase another TV set so that they could 'live in peace'. In another case, the parents disclosed, "We were better off with only one DD channel. We don't need another as it has led to disharmony in the family."

Among some respondents of Locality III, parents said that they did not interfere in the quarrels between their children and only when it was absolutely necessary, did they switch off the TV set. These revelations by the respondents point towards a weakening of intra-familial relationships. It is also observed that conflicts arising over the selection of channels may persuade people to purchase another TV set, if the resources are available. This may further lead to physical isolation within the family members. At same time, it is also important to note that the increase in the number of TV sets may not necessarily decrease the clashes—only the segmental nature (i.e., quarrels may occur only between husband-wife and between children themselves, an observation made earlier among the respondents of Locality I) of conflicts may take a different shape.

Earlier studies have indicated that television viewing leads to a joint silent activity. In the previous chapter, survey of literature had indicated that men preferred to watch TV without any interruption, rather attentively and in a silent environment thus reducing intra-family communication. Therefore, the study investigates how family members react when a member speaks while an interesting programme is on.

The researcher questioned the subjects as to how they reacted when someone spoke during an interesting programme. To this, 74.7 per cent of the CATV viewers and 56 per cent of the DD viewers said that they asked the person to 'shut up' while 22.7 per cent of the CATV viewers and 41.3 per cent of the DD viewers said they were indifferent to such interferences. Another 2.6 per cent of the

CATV viewers and 2.7 per cent of the DD viewers said that they made non-verbal expressions like making faces, scowling or showing eyes angrily at the interruptor.

Table–4.15
Distribution of CATV Viewers and DD Viewers According to Their Reaction when Someone Spoke During an Interesting Progamme in the Three Localities

Kind of Reactions	*Locality* *I*	*II*	*III*	*Total*	*%*
Shut him/her up	33 (34)	44 (35)	35 (15)	112 (84)	74.7 (56.0)
Indifferent	17 (16)	3 (11)	14 (35)	34 (62)	22.7 (41.3)
Any other	– (-)	3 (4)	1 (-)	4 (4)	2.6 (2.7)
Total	50 (50)	50 (50)	50 (50)	150 (150)	100 (100)

In Locality I, 66 per cent of the CATV viewers and 68 per cent of the DD viewers; in Locality II, 88 per cent of the CATV viewers and 70 per cent of the DD viewers; in Locality III; 70 per cent of the CATV viewers and 30 per cent of the DD viewers said that they asked the person to 'shut up' when they spoke while an interesting programme was on.

An indifferent attitude was observed among 34 per cent CATV viewers and 32 per cent DD viewers in Locality I, 6 per cent CATV viewers and 22 per cent DD viewers in Locality II and 28 per cent CATV viewers and 70 per cent DD viewers in Locality III. Further, only 2 per cent of the CATV viewers in Locality III, reacted non-verbally (showing facial expressions like scowling and rounding up of eyes etc.) when somebody spoke during an interesting programme.

It was observed from the data that in all the three localities majority of the respondents except the DD viewers in Locality III, asked the person, who interrupted to 'shut-up' while watching an interesting programme. More DD viewers than CATV viewers were indifferent when a person spoke while an interesting programme was on in Localities II and III. This signifies the fact that viewing of a programme of one's choice often would lead to closure of a conversation/communication among the family members. The time they spend together would thus be spent on silently watching the TV, with an intolerance for any kind of interruption, thus cutting down the intra-family communication.

It was interesting to find out as to how family members reacted when the male head of the household or children switched on the TV set as soon as they came back from office and/or school and/or college.

The data indicates that an equal number of family members (i.e., male head of the household and children) both among CATV viewers and DD viewers (46%) switched on the television set as soon as they came back from school or college or the office. An equal number of respondents (54%) among CATV viewers and DD viewers replied in the negative.

In Locality I, 32 per cent of CATV viewers and 34 per cent of DD viewers; in Locality II, 26 per cent each among CATV viewers and DD viewers; in Locality III, 54 per cent CATV viewers and 52 per cent of the DD viewers had members in the family who switched on the television set as soon as they were back from school or college or the office.

Table–4.16
Distribution of CATV Viewers and DD Viewers According to Whether their Spouse/Children Switched on the TV Set as Soon as they Came Back from Office/School/College in the Three Localities

	Locality				
Response	*I*	*II*	*III*	*Total*	*%*
Switched on the TV set	16 (17)	26 (26)	27 (26)	69 (69)	46 (46)
Did not switch on the TV set	34 (33)	24 (24)	23 (24)	81 (81)	54 (54)
Total	50 (50)	50 (50)	50 (50)	150 (150)	100 (100)

*(These questions were posed to the wife of the respondent).

In Locality I, 68 per cent of the CATV viewers and 66 per cent of the DD viewers; in Locality II, 48 per cent each among CATV viewers and DD viewers and in Locality III, 46 per cent of the CATV viewers and 48 per cent of the DD viewers said that none of the family members switched on the TV set as soon as they came back from school or college or the office.

It may be inferred here that TV was a magnetic force in some households. Respondents were attracted by it, as soon as they entered their homes after attending office/school/college. It was also observed that majority of the respondents of Locality II and Locality III as compared to those of Locality I, switched on the television sets as soon as they entered their homes. It will also be interesting to find out which member in the family switched on the TV set as soon as they entered their homes after their respective day's schedules.

Table–4.17

Distribution of CATV Viewers and DD Viewers According to Which Member in the Family Switched on the TV Set as Soon as they Came Back From Office/School/College in the Three Localities

	Locality				
Which Member	*I*	*II*	*III*	*Total*	*%*
Male head of the household	3 (5)	9 (5)	1 (-)	13 (10)	8.7 (6.7)
Children	11 (8)	11 (19)	25 (26)	47 (53)	31.3 (35.3)
Both father and Children	2 (4)	6 (2)	1 (-)	9 (6)	6 (4)
Don't Switch on the TV set	34 (33)	24 (24)	23 (24)	81 (81)	54.0 (54.0)
Total	50 (50)	50 (50)	50 (50)	150 (150)	100 (100)

The data indicated that the male head of the household switched on the TV set as soon as he came back from office among 8.7 per cent of CATV viewers and 6.7 per cent of the DD viewers. The children switched on the TV set among 31.3 per cent of CATV viewers and

35.3 per cent of DD viewers as soon as they came back from school or college. In cases, where both the male head of the household and children came home and switched on the TV set, there were 6 per cent of CATV viewers and 4 per cent DD viewers.

In Locality I, 6 per cent of CATV viewers and 10 per cent of DD viewers; in Locality II, 18 per cent of CATV viewers and 10 per cent of DD viewers; in Locality III, 2 per cent of CATV viewers the male head of the household switched on the TV set as soon as he came back from office.

In Locality I, 22 per cent of the CATV viewers and 16 per cent of the DD viewers; in Locality II, 22 per cent of the CATV viewers and 38 per cent of the DD viewers; in Locality III, 50 per cent of the CATV viewers and 52 per cent of the DD viewers, the children switched on the TV set as soon as they came back from school or college.

In Locality II, about 12 per cent of the CATV viewers and 4 per cent of the DD viewers indicated that both the male head of the household as well as children switched on the TV set as soon as they came back from office or school/college.

It was observed that majority of the children of Locality III switched on the TV set as soon as they came back from school or college. On the whole also, in all the three localities, the children switched on the TV set as soon as they came back from school or college. This means that children instead of interacting with members of the family as soon as they came back from school or college interacted with the TV thus indicating a further decline in intra-familial communication. It was seen in the previous discussions in this chapter that quarrels were the maximum between children themselves over the selection of channels. All these converging factors indicate that the maximum impact of Satellite TV was felt on children.

The reactions of other family members towards the act of switching on the TV set by any member, as soon as they come from office or school were sought from respondents, which varied from family to family. Although, the reactions were almost uniform in the three localities, the environment of the family was an important factor to be considered in the analysis.

The parents in general were fed up of telling their kids to stop switching on the TV set, but in vain. They were angry at the behaviour of their kids, and inspite of shouting at them the kids did not relent. One respondent added, "There is no option left, we have to live with it as there is nothing that can stop them. The kids don't listen to us, and we feel upset about it." Another respondent added, "Initially we used to mind it but now we have got used to it. Scolding them has no effect." Children disobeyed their parents' instructions in most cases. In another interesting case, the father of kids wanted to break the TV set and a couple of times, he had also removed the cable wires. Another respondent said, "Where is the question of switching on the TV set when they come from school or office? It is on all the time." In some cases, the parents did not mind their kids switching on the TV set, once they were back from school. Another parent added, "There is no point in getting furious, and scolding them everyday. If they don't do it on one particular day, (due to shouting) they repeat it the next day." In very few cases, the parents managed to convince their kids, not to do so. In one case, the lady of the household added, "Once the kids switch on the TV set, I too start watching along with them." In quite a few cases, the parents were happy that their children remained indoors and that was the reason they did not object to their switching on the TV set.

It was observed the lady of the household felt ignored by her husband and was upset on this account. One lady said, "More importance is given to the TV and its programmes than to the wife." The indifferent behaviour of the husband towards the wife, all attributed to TV made the lady of the household upset.

While the interview was being conducted, a lady of the household cried bitterly in the presence of the researcher and said that her life had become miserable. She also commented that her husband used the television to ignore her and she cried almost everyday and skipped her meals. She further revealed that she and her husband were not on talking terms. In contrast, another section of the respondents said that they were happy that their husbands were busy with the television and that they were much relieved from the bossing around of their husbands. There were also cases where the lady of the household did not react in either positive or negative way when their husbands switched on the TV set as soon as they came back from office. The word "irritated" was most commonly used by the lady of the household when her husband switched on the TV set as soon as they came from office.

The study indicated that viewing of Satellite TV led to a breakdown of intra-familial communication as well as relationships. The parents expressed unhappiness with their children and the lady of the household was upset with her husband on account of TV viewing. These pointers indicate an instability in the family environment. The present study, therefore substantiates the theoretical perspective which indicates TV was a negative force as well as an agent which reduces social activity.

There are also some other factors which indicate that viewing of TV leads to a further closure of the communication in families. These are taken up in the following discussion.

Reaction of the respondents were sought when family members avoided important household discussions and outings for the sake of watching television.

The data shows that 34.7 per cent of the CATV viewers and 29.3 per cent of the DD viewers had members in the family who avoided important household issues for discussion while watching television.

Table–4.18

Distribution of CATV Viewers and DD Viewers According to Whether Their Spouse/Children Avoided any Important Household Issue for Discussion for the Sake of Watching TV in the Three Localities

	Locality				
Response	*I*	*II*	*III*	*Total*	*%*
Avoid important Discussions	11 (10)	16 (16)	25 (18)	52 (44)	34.7 (29.3)
Do not avoid	39 (40)	34 (34)	25 (32)	98 (106)	65.3 (70.7)
Total	50 (50)	50 (50)	50 (50)	150 (150)	100 (100)

Among those who avoided important household issue for discussion for the sake of watching television, were 22 per cent CATV viewers and 20 per cent DD viewers in Locality I; 32 per cent each among CATV viewers and DD viewers in Locality II and 50 per cent CATV viewers and 36 per cent DD viewers in Locality III.

The data indicated that more CATV viewers on the whole avoided important household issue for discussion for the sake of watching television than compared to the other localities. This clearly indicates the closure of communication within the family. It may also be inferred that the viewers of Cable TV feel its impact more deeply than their Doordarshan counterparts. The number of channels, the variety of programmes and round-the-clock transmission of programmes have contributed to the decline in intra-familial communication.

As observed earlier in the present chapter that children have emerged as a powerful unit within the family in the context of TV viewing, it would be interesting to find out which segment of the family avoided important household discussion and outings for the sake of watching TV.

Table–4.19
Distribution of CATV Viewers and DD Viewers According to Which Member in the Family Avoided Important Household Issue for Discussion for the Sake of Watching TV in the Three Localities

	Locality				
Which Member	*I*	*II*	*III*	*Total*	*%*
Male head of the houshold	6 (6)	6 (6)	4 (1)	16 (13)	10.7 (8.7)
Children	5 (2)	6 (8)	19 (17)	30 (27)	20.0 (18.0)
Both father and children	– (2)	4 (2)	2 (–)	6 (4)	4.0 (2.7)
Don't avoid discussions	39 (40)	34 (34)	25 (32)	98 (106)	65.3 (70.6)
Total	50 (50)	50 (50)	50 (50)	150 (150)	100 (100)

The above table indicates that among 10.7 per cent CATV viewers and 8.7 per cent DD viewers, the male head of the household avoided important household issues for discussion. Further, among

20 per cent CATV viewers and 18 per cent DD viewers children avoided important household issues for discussion while watching TV.

In Locality I, 12 per cent each of both the CATV viewers and DD viewers; in Locality II, 12 per cent each among the CATV viewers and DD viewers; in Locality III, 8 per cent of CATV viewers and 2 per cent of DD viewers, the male head of the household avoided important household issue for discussion while watching television.

Further, in Locality I, 10 per cent of CATV viewers and 4 per cent of DD viewers; in Locality II, 12 per cent of CATV viewers and 16 per cent of DD viewers; in Locality III, 38 per cent of CATV viewers and 34 per cent of DD viewers, the children avoided any important household issue for discussion for the sake of watching TV.

It was inferred from the data, that among CATV viewers the male head of the household avoided important household issue for disucssion while watching TV. It was also observed that the children of Locality III, avoided important household issues for discussion both among CATV viewers and DD viewers as compared to other localities. On the whole also, both among CATV viewers and DD viewers it was observed that children avoided important household issue for discussion while watching TV.

Reactions of Family Members When Members Avoided any Important Household Discussion While Watching TV

In all the three localities the reactions of respondents were uniform, when any member of the family avoided important household issue for discussion while watching TV. Generally, there was a tendency to postpone the matter to be discussed after the programme, conveying this message either angrily or ignoring the member who wanted to discuss any important household matter. The lady of the household was irritated as well as upset in most cases and termed TV as 'nuisance' at home. One lady interestingly remarked, "We have reconciled to the bad fate due to television." "We have no option left," said another lady of the household.

On the parent-child relationship front, it was observed that the parents seemed very angry at their children's behaviour as they were glued to the television all the time. One respondent said, "I feel like taking off the cable connection, everytime my children tend to disobey or not listen to me." As a result of disobedience, some parents switched off the TV set." A male respondent added, "My wife is always grumbling at me, but she doesn't understand that after a tired day at the office, I feel the need to relax and sit in front of the TV set."

The study reflected a tendency on the part of the respondents to close communication/conversation in families. The attraction of children and the male head of the household towards TV led to unpleasant situations within the family. While the male head of the household justified his TV viewing behaviour, it was not possible for the lady of the household to adjust to the situation. These indicators point towards a negative effect of TV on the conjugal unit as well as on the parent-child relationship. As seen from the previous table that it was mostly the children who avoided important household issues for discussion for the sake of watching TV, it would be further important to see whether TV reduced social activity outside home.

Table–4.20
Distribution of CATV Viewers and DD Viewers According to Whether they Avoided Outings for the Sake of Watching TV in the Three Localities

	Locality				
Response	*I*	*II*	*III*	*Total*	*%*
Yes	8 (20)	14 (10)	22 (16)	44 (46)	29.3 (30.7)
No	42 (30)	36 (40)	28 (34)	106 (104)	70.7 (69.3)
Total	50 (50)	50 (50)	50 (50)	150 (150)	100 (100)

The data indicates that 29.3 per cent of the CATV viewers and 30.7 per cent of the DD viewers avoided outings for the sake of watching television. About 70.7 per cent of the CATV viewers and 69.3 per cent of the DD viewers said that TV did not matter to them where outings were concerned.

In Locality I, 16 per cent of CATV viewers and 40 per cent of DD viewers; in Locality II, 28 per cent of CATV viewers and 20 per cent of DD viewers; in Locality III, 44 per cent of CATV viewers and 32 per cent of DD viewers avoided outings for the sake of watching TV.

It was inferred that a majority of the respondents of Locality III avoided outings for the sake of watching television. It was observed in Chapter III that these respondents had been viewing TV for longer durations as compared to the other localities. It was also observed from the data that whether it was Cable TV or Doordarshan, respondents avoided social activities outside their homes. It can be concluded that on the one hand Satellite TV reduces intra-familial communication while on the other hand, it weakens inter-familial relationships. This means as the duration of viewing rises there is a proportionate decrease in communication across families. The loss of physical mobility as a result of watching TV leads to a loss of social participation across families.

On the whole, in about 6 per cent of CATV viewers and 10.7 per cent of DD viewers, the male head of the household avoided outings for the sake of watching TV. Further, 20 per cent of CATV viewers and 17.3 per cent of DD viewers indicated that children avoided outings in favour of watching TV.

Further, about 10 per cent of CATV viewers and 12 per cent of DD viewers in Locality I; 12 per cent each among both CATV viewers and DD viewers in Locality II and 38 per cent of CATV viewers and 28 per cent of DD viewers in Locality III, said that their children avoided going out in favour of watching TV.

It was inferred that on the whole, children avoided social activities outside their homes in favour of watching TV. It was also observed that majority of the children who avoided outings to watch TV belonged to Locality III. It may be inferred again that whether the issue was to avoid communication within or across families, the children were the most prominent segment of families to be affected in the process. It was inferred that the respondents of Locality III, felt the impact of Satellite TV on almost every dimension of social participation.

Reactions of Family Members When Someone in the Family Avoided Outings

In cases, where the children refused to accompany their parents for outings, most parents added that they left their children behind

Table–4.21
Distribution of CATV Viewers and DD Viewers According to Which Member in the Family Avoided Outings for the Sake of Watching TV in the Three Localities

Which Member	*Locality* I	II	III	*Total*	*%*
Male head of the household	1 (12)	5 (2)	3 (2)	9 (16)	6 (10.7)
Children	5 (6)	6 (6)	19 (14)	30 (26)	20 (17.3)
Both father & children	2 (2)	3 (2)	– (–)	5 (4)	3.3 (2.7)
Don't avoid outings	42 (30)	36 (40)	28 (34)	106 (104)	70.7 (69.3)
Total	50 (50)	50 (50)	50 (50)	150 (150)	100 (100)

and continued on their planned outing. Parents claimed that inspite of regularly shouting at the kids, they refused to move from their seats. Some parents switched off the TV set and and forced their reluctant children to join them on the outings. A lady of the household said, "Neither my husband nor my children are ready for an outing in favour of the television, and this is the very reason for which I hate TV." Another lady added that she felt hurt at her husbands' attitude and did not speak to him for the whole day for spoiling or delaying the very idea of an outing. Most of the ladies said that they were hurt and upset at their husbands' attitude and felt that they were being ignored, all due to television.

These responses indicate that viewers were cut-off from social activities across the families. The study stands to substantiate its earlier findings that Satellite TV is a catalytic agent in promoting individuation as well as isolation within the family and with the outside world.

Another important observation to be made here is that while children were fascinated by TV, the lady of the household felt that TV was a source of nuisance, and a hindering factor in strengthening relationships with their husbands as well as children.

It was seen in the preceeding data, that TV promotes a habit of silence reducing intra-family communication. Investigating further, the researcher asked the respondents whether TV on the whole had reduced or enhanced communication.

Table–4.22
Distribution of CATV Viewers and DD Viewers According to Whether TV had Facilitated or Reduced Communication Between Family Members in the Three Localities

	Locality				
Response	*I*	*II*	*III*	*Total*	*%*
Facilitated discussion	6	3	–	9	6.0
	(9)	(3)	(1)	(13)	(8.7)
Reduced conversation	29	22	31	82	54.7
	(30)	(12)	(20)	(62)	(41.3)
No change	15	24	19	58	38.6
	(10)	(30)	(29)	(69)	(46)
Can't say	–	1	–	1	0.7
	(1)	(5)	(-)	(6)	(4)
Total	50	50	50	150	100
	(50)	(50)	(50)	(150)	(100)

About 54.7 per cent of the CATV viewers and 41.3 per cent of the DD viewers said that television had reduced conversation between married couples as well as between parents and children; while only 6 per cent of CATV viewers and 8.7 per cent of DD viewers said that TV facilitated discussion as a subject of interaction between married couples as well as between parents and children. About 38.6 per cent of the CATV viewers and 46 per cent of the DD viewers said there was no change while about 0.7 per cent CATV viewers and 4 per cent DD viewers said that they could not say anything in this regard.

In Locality I, 12 per cent of CATV viewers and 18 per cent of DD viewers; in Locality II, 6 per cent each among CATV viewers and DD viewers and in Locality III, 2 per cent of the DD viewers said that television facilitated discussion as a subject of interaction between members of the family.

About 58 per cent of CATV viewers and 60 per cent of DD viewers in Locality I; 44 per cent of CATV viewers and 24 per cent of DD viewers in Locality II; and 62 per cent of CATV viewers and 40 per cent of DD viewers in Locality III said that television had reduced the conversation between married couples as well as between parents and children.

It was inferred that a majority of the respondents felt that TV had reduced the conversation between couples and/or between parents and children. A majority of the CATV viewers as compared to DD viewers felt that TV had reduced the conversation between couples on the one hand, and between parents and children on the other. This is attributed to the fact that TV viewing material was available round-the-clock for CATV viewers with a number of channels to choose from; while DD viewers were restricted by the limited telecast hours and the availability of lesser choice of channels. The study substantiates the earlier findings of this chapter that Satellite TV had reduced intra-family communication.

As observed earlier, TV had affected many dimensions in the family environment. Therefore, it is significant to find out from the respondents if TV had affected their family interaction patterns and if so, in which way.

Table–4.23
Distribution of CATV Viewers and DD Viewers According to Whether TV had Affected their Family Interaction Patterns in the Three Localities

	Locality				
Response	*I*	*II*	*III*	*Total*	*%*
Yes	39 (28)	22 (17)	28 (17)	89 (62)	59.3 (41.3)
No	11 (22)	28 (33)	22 (33)	61 (88)	40.7 (58.7)
Total	50 (50)	50 (50)	50 (50)	150 (150)	100 (100)

It was observed that 59.3 per cent of the CATV viewers and 41.3 per cent of the DD viewers felt that TV had affected family interaction patterns while 40.7 per cent of the CATV viewers and 58.7 per cent of the DD viewers felt that TV did not interfere in their family interaction patterns.

In Locality I, 78 per cent of the CATV viewers and 56 per cent of the DD viewers; in Locality II, 44 per cent of the CATV viewers and 34 per cent of the DD viewers; and 56 per cent of the CATV viewers and 34 per cent of the DD viewers in Locality III, felt that TV had affected their family interaction patterns.

It was inferred that more CATV viewers of Locality I felt that TV had affected their family interaction patterns as compared to other localities. Also, most respondents of Locality I felt that TV had affected their family interaction patterns both among CATV viewers and DD viewers as compared to other localities. On the whole, majority of the respondents said that TV had affected family interaction patterns.

The family interaction patterns of the respondents were affected in many dimensions. Most respondents claimed that family interaction between members was reduced to a considerable extent. Another segment of the respondents said that TV had shaped their life styles and members in the family had begun to imitate the life styles and mannerisms of TV stars and models.

A few respondents said that there was improved and increased conversation as well as communication in the family had become 'healthy' due to television. Some respondents on the other hand, said that TV was a continuous background noise at home and all activities whether it was reading a newspaper or a book or doing home work or domestic work or getting dressed up, or having meals, all of these were done in front of the switched on television. One respondent added, "It is ages since we ate on the dining table. Our table manners have been hit by the idiot box." Many respondents said that they had shifted the television from the drawing room to the dinning room.

Another respondent said, "The parent and child communication is being reduced largely due to television. Also, the children don't communicate among themselves and this is setting up an unhealthy trend." Another section of respondents said, "Television is improving our general knowledge and hence our quality of discussion on current issues is also improving."

It can be concluded that apart from reducing communication within the family, TV had also shaped the styles of communication in many households. There was a healthy change in the type of communication/conversation among a few respondents. Another important restructuring in families due to the arrival of TV sets into their homes was a change in style of eating habits. When the first TV arrived in homes, the viewers usually placed it in the drawing room or the lobby to add to their status. But, gradually with the passage of time TV has become a member of the family with a shift in its placement into bedrooms or the dinning room. It is important to note that in many households respondents did not eat on the dinning table if there was no TV in that room. It was also observed that majority of the respondents had their meals/dinner while watching TV further reducing communication within families. It was also observed that on the one hand, a few respondents favoured TV saying that it enhanced their general knowledge while some other criticised it terming it as an 'idiot box'. Despite these variations, it was concluded that TV was often accused by majority of the respondents at every stage, of weakening the intra-personal and inter-personal relationships within the families. Finally, it can be concluded here, that this study rejects the perspective which states that TV enhances intra-family communication. Instead, perspective which states that TV disrupts communication in families has been substantiated by our findings.

With the advent of TV, there has been a major rescheduling of daily activities at home. Now, with the CATV and round-the-clock TV it would be interesting to find out how respondents have rescheduled their daily chores for watching their favourite programmes.

It was observed that 41.3 per cent of the CATV viewers and 29.3 per cent of the DD viewers had rescheduled their daily chores for watching television. About 58.7 per cent of the CATV viewers and 70.7 per cent of the DD viewers said that they had not rescheduled their daily activities for watching TV.

About 30 per cent of CATV viewers and 28 per cent of DD viewers in Locality I; 40 per cent of CATV viewers and 32 per cent of DD viewers in Locality II and 54 per cent of CATV viewers and 28 per cent of DD viewers in Locality III, had rescheduled their daily chores for watching television.

Table–4.24
Distribution of CATV Viewers and DD Viewers According to Whether they Rescheduled Their Daily Chores for Watching TV in the Three Localities

	Locality				
Response	*I*	*II*	*III*	*Total*	*%*
Yes	15 (14)	20 (16)	27 (14)	62 (44)	41.3 (29.3)
No	35 (36)	30 (34)	23 (36)	88 (106)	58.7 (70.7)
Total	50 (50)	50 (50)	50 (50)	150 (150)	100 (100)

It was inferred that majority of the CATV viewers of Locality III had rescheduled their daily chores for watching television as compared to other localities. Among DD viewers, more respondents of Locality II had rescheduled their daily chores for watching TV as compared to other localities. On the whole, among those whose had rescheduled their daily chores, there were more CATV viewers than DD viewers.

Respondents who said that they had rescheduled their daily chores to watch TV, pointed out that the lady of the household completed her kitchen work, especially cooking early and in some cases the food was laid early on the dining table so that they would watch TV programmes without any disturbance and interruptions. Some respondents added that children completed their homework early so that they could sit in front of the television without being nagged by the parents. Most respondents added that they had their meals, especially dinner while watching television. Some men added that they finished their pending jobs both at home and outside early to be back to watch TV. Some respondents added that they ate their dinner a little earlier than usual if they had to watch an interesting programme. One respondent said, "We have not rescheduled our daily chores, but television has rescheduled us and has shaped our routines."

Another major inference drawn in the study was that television had ushered in revolutionary changes in many households – it has weakened ties both within the family as well as with the outside world; it has reduced intra-family communication; it has rescheduled the daily and weekly scheme of activities of family members. On the other hand, TV has improved the quality of conversation in some households, enhanced general awareness and knowledge and also altered the eating habits. It can be concluded that TV had both the negative and positive effects. The negative factors outscored the positive aspects on all dimensions of social participation. Hence, we can infer that Satellite TV had made a significant impact on social participation within as well as across families.

With the increasing number of channels the amount of consumption of TV is bound to increase. It is in this context, the researcher asked the respondents if they would like to change their TV viewing duration.

On questioning the respondents if they would like to change their duration of watching television, it was observed that 95.3 per cent of the CATV viewers and 97.3 per cent of the DD viewers said that they would like to continue their viewing hours. A small and equal proportion of both CATV viewers and DD viewers (1.3%) wanted to increase their viewing hours while about 3.4 per cent of the CATV viewers and 1.4 per cent of the DD viewers said that they would like to decrease their duration of watching TV. It was inferred that majority of the respondents wanted to continue the same duration of viewing TV.

Table-4.25

Distribution of CATV Viewers and DD Viewers According to their Desire to Change their Duration of Viewing TV in the Three Localities

	Locality				
Response	*I*	*II*	*III*	*Total*	*%*
Increase the viewing hours	– (2)	2 (-)	– (-)	2 (2)	1.3 (1.3)
Decrease the viewing hours	1 (1)	4 (-)	– (1)	5 (2)	3.4 (1.4)
Continue the same	49 (47)	44 (50)	50 (49)	143 (146)	95.3 (97.3)
Total	50 (50)	50 (50)	50 (50)	150 (150)	100 (100)

Reasons assigned for continuing the same duration of viewing of television were that their routine was set. One respondent added, "Watching television has become a habit, an addiction. It is not possible to decrease the viewing hours even if we want to." Another respondent added, "What will we do if we don't watch television, it is indispensable now." Another respondent said, "Nobody is going to listen to us for decreasing the viewing hours, so there is no point in asking the kids or any other family member to reduce the viewing hours." Another respondent said, "Now we cannot disturb our routine."

Among respondents who wanted to increase the viewing hours said that they wanted to increase and gain more knowlege, enjoy more leisure and entertainment and relaxation at home.

Among those who wanted to decrease the viewing hours most of the respondents said that they wanted their children to study. Most respondents said that, "TV is a colossal waste of time." A few others added that TV is a health hazard and affecting the eye sight of their children.

Despite an agreement by parents on the dangers of excessive TV viewing, respondents did not want to change their viewing duration. There was an adamancy on the part of the respondents to change the viewing duration. Earlier research in this field reveals that there is a gradual increase in the time spent on TV viewing. The study substantiates the findings of Leichter and her associates (1985) that inspite of the dangers of TV viewing, viewers continue to increase their viewing duration. This means that as the viewing duration increases with the constant increase in the number of channels on Satellite TV, communication will occur rarely in families. This will further lead to gradual decline in social participation within the family as well as with the outside world.

This chapter gives a deep insight on the impact of Satellite TV on various dimensions of social participation within the family. The following inferences were made :

1. The prime leisure activity of majority of the respondents was TV viewing—an activity which leads to a process of individuation. Social activities outside home were displaced in pursuit of TV viewing by majority of the children.

2. The arrival of guests during prime hours of TV was not a pleasurable experience for many respondents. The study indicated a significant decline in inter-personal relationships across families. The analysis indicated a negative relationship between TV viewing and hospitality. The increasing number of channels on Satellite TV resulted in a reduction in intra-familial communication. The respondents revealed that for the fear of being forced guests they avoided visiting people at their home during prime hours of TV. Also, as the TV viewing duration increased consequent to the increase in the number of channels, there was a decrease in inter-family communication. The increase in duration of viewing TV led to a further decrease in physical mobility resulting in decline in inter-familial communication.
3. The study suggested that on the onehand, TV increased physical closeness and proximity (especially among the viewers of Locality III) while on the other hand TV weakened ties among family members. Further, it was inferred that TV promoted passivity among family members. Hence, it can be inferred the TV was a catalytic agent in weakening bonds within and across families.
4. The children exercised maximum control over the TV set in all the three localities, the study suggested. Also, the study indicated a positive association between conflicts and the number of TV sets on the one hand and with the number of channels on the other. The frequency of quarrels were maximum between children themselves. The viewers of Satellite TV disclosed that there was a weakening of ties among family members. Also, it had contributed to disharmony in the husband-wife as well parent-child relationships. Physical isolation was increasing in families with the increasing rise in the number of channels and the number of TV sets in a household.
5. Family interaction within the family declined considerably in most households. Family members disclosed that they did not want any interruptions while watching interesting programmes on TV. They also avoided important household issues for discussion as well as outings in favour of watching TV. It was also concluded that children

avoided social interaction within as well as across families. Respondents had rescheduled their activities to watch TV programmes and were adamant on reducing their duration of viewing TV.

It can be concluded that present study substantiates the perspective that TV curtails intra-family communication suggesting a decline in informal social participation within the families. It would now be interesting to find out the impact of TV on the other dimensions of social participation i.e., formal participation as well as an informal participation across families. The following chapter richly illustrates these aspects.

5

Satellite TV and Social Participation: An Analysis

Data presented in the preceeding chapters underlined the viewing patterns of the upper, middle and low socio-economic groups under study. That CATV viewers differ from the DD viewers in terms of the programmes they select for viewing, was also confirmed. An important finding in the chapter concerned the fact that on the whole, subscribers of CATV view television for more time as compared to the DD viewers. The impact of TV—whether DD or the Cable, on social life within the families was evident since the respondents and their children often felt upset whenever some guests arrived, disturbing them in an interesting TV programme. Such observations in a way hint at a possibility—that TV, especially the Cable TV, by restricting the physical mobility of its viewers, would reduce the social participation of people across the families too. In other words, being glued to TV sets during most of the day, inter-familial ties with neighbours, relatives, friends etc., would normally decline. The present chapter undertakes an appraisal of this hypothesis. The question posed in this chapter is—Does TV viewing (especially the cable) in any way affect patterns of social participation among city dwellers? If it does, in what ways?

Emphasis in this chapter will be upon the patterns of social participation across families. The reason being that the impact of TV viewing on intra-familial interaction has already been examined in the last chapter. Here, an attempt will be made to study the extent to which Cable TV has restricted or boosted social participation across the families.

Socially, an individual may participate at two levels-viz. 'formal' and 'informal'. These concepts have already been defined in Chapter I (pp. 21-22). While human beings have always been interacting socially in the informal groups such as neighbourhood, relatives etc., such informal social participation characterized the traditional agrarian societies to a large extent (Chandra, 1977). With the rise of cities, while the realm of such informal participation gets minimized, there is an increased participation among urbanites in the organizations or groups which are 'formal' in nature (Wirth, 1938; Chandra, 1977; Gill and Dhawan, 1992). For this reason, formal social participation has been considered as an indicator of urban way of life. Simple observation would indicate a preponderance of formal organizations ranging from sports, religion, business to entertainment—which may be completely unknown or less known in a rural set up. This however does not mean a total disappearance of the informal participation. No known society infact—rural or urban, can survive without the primary, informal groupings. But the fact remains that more urban dwellers participate at formal level—in organizations into which they seek membership voluntarily, to which they may or may not be making financial contribution and which lays down formal rules of conduct and behaviour.

The growing participation in formal organizations in cities can be traced back to the expansion in the 'instrumental' roles as compared to the 'expressive' especially in the modern urban melieu. An individual, in order to satisfy specific goals/needs would seek membership into particular organizations. These interests may vary from purely professional to those concerning entertainment. Our findings so far have indicated a substantial impact of TV viewing on intra-familial relationships. It would be pertinent now to examine whether television, mainly the Cable TV, has curtailed formal social participation of city dwellers or not. Besides this, an effort will also be made to study the impact of Cable TV on informal social participation outside the family.

One of the striking features of Industrial Revolution has been the massive increase in urban dwellings. Urbanisation has been usually defined on the basis of demographic changes viz. migration to the urban areas and concentration of migrants in cities. As a result, of such a demographic transformations, many cultural and social changes have also occured which include a decline in the social significance of family, reduction of contact with neighbours, an increase in the family mobility and weakening of ties with the kinsmen. The old traditions and agrarian ways of life have often been discarded in preference to urban life styles.

The emergence of new sets of values and behaviour patterns among the city dwellers increased the curiosity of the western scholars witnessing such changes in a large scale. One of the most important contributions in this field has been *Urbanism as Way of Life* by Wirth (1938). The propositions put forth by the western thinkers are characterized by a different socio-cultural and historical background and their applicability to the Indian situation has proved problematic. The experience of the less developed countries has been significantly different from that of the developed nations (Anderson, 1960).

Since urbanisation began first in Europe, due to the Industrial Revolution, the entire emphasis of the scholars remained on the 'city'. As a result, various sociologists explained the processes of ecological and socio-economic changes where the 'city' was projected mainly as an 'ecological' unit with peculiar features. The frameworks developed by Durkheim (1933), Tonnies (1940) and Maine (1961) provided important dichotomous charaterizations of societies undergoing change. The rural-urban dichotomy which was later modified as the folk-urban continnum gained popularity since it seemed to explain the process of social change in the western societies (Redfield, 1947).

Urbanisation is not a single unitary, universally similar process but assumes different forms depending on the socio-economic and cultural conditions. Wirth (1938) explained the socio-cultural characteristics of the city dwellers with the help of the folk-urban continuum and made a distinction between urbanisation and urbanism. He differentiated between urbanism and urbanisation by considering the former as that complex of traits which makes up the characteristic mode of life in cities and urbanisation as a process of development and extension of these factors. Wirth put forth three conditions, a large size, greater density and heterogeneity of the population that led to the emergence of secondary, segmental and artifical social relationships among urban dwellers.

The distinctive features of the urban mode of life are the substitution of primary by secondary contacts and the weakening bonds of kinship. As a consequence, social ties within the family may weaken in the face of an increasing individualization. For Wirth, the process of urbanisation is essentially a process of disorganisation with the development of impersonality, superficiality, anonymity and transitoriness in personal relations leading an individual to be indifferent, calculating and rational in behaviour.

Contradicting Wirth's observation of high degree of anonymity and isolation, in a study of the Mexico city, Lewis (1965) concluded that the urban way of life varied with the socio-economic status. He also added that the affluent are more urbanized than the poor. Later, Gans (1968) argued that there is a lack of uniformity within the urban dwellers with respect to the way of life, depending on the socio-economic status.

In the backdrop of these observations, it is interesting to note how urbanisation influences the social life and interactional patterns. One must however, remember that there are many intervening variables that shape urban social life and any generalization must be based on a careful observation of smaller social segments of urban settlements rather than the city as a whole.

Consequent to the replacement of primary contacts with the secondary ones, an individual seeks membership informal organisations to satisfy his psychological needs. Formal participation thus has been considered as an indicator of urbanism since membership in such organisations pre-supposes a voluntary choice on the part of the members. People enter into different kinds of networks and these tend to cut across the traditional boundaries of ascriptive groups (Sharma, 1975). The displacement of persons from their native places limits one's ties of kinship and other ascriptive networks.

Consequently, the bases of social organisation may undergo a transformation. There is a shift from informal social participation to formal participation based on intervening variables like education occupation and income. There seems to be a positive association between formal participation and economic, educational and occupational status (Chandra, 1977; Pasricha, 1988; Gill, 1991).

Confirming this, Gill and Dhawan (1992) report that there was a weakening of traditional social networks towards a strengthening of formal social participation in the upper income groups. On the other hand, the lower income group respondents in the same study were found to be maintaining strong ties at the informal level, i.e., kinsmen, neighbours etc.

Studies conducted in the urban context especially for understanding the rural-urban differences in family structure and caste system (Kapadia, 1956; Kolenda, 1967 and Kurian, 1976) have made little contribution in analysing the factors influencing social interaction outside the family i.e., with relatives, friends and neighbours. Another drawback is the non-applicability of the western models in understanding the Indian situation (Kapadia, 1956; Epestein, 1962; Lambert, 1962; Rao, 1970; Chandra, 1977; Gill and Dhawan, 1992). While urban residence has normally been treated as an independent variable inducing social and cultural change, not much attention has been focussed upon the factors which often intervene in the process. Studies in the Indian context have indicated on the one hand a reduced communication among urban dwellers, while on the other, they point towards a restreng thening of social ties within as well as across families. Such contradictory results occur mainly due to the fact that urban residence does not exercise its impact on social interaction in a vacuum. There are various intervening factors which get more pronounced in the urban melieu – thus producing different results. We therefore need to conduct micro-level studies to examine the conditions under which patterns of social participation among city dwellers undergo a change both within as well as outside the family. The present study is an endeavour exactly in this direction.

Among the factors which have revolutionized interpersonal relations is television viewing especially the Satellite TV, which makes the viewers glued to the TV set, making both a physical and mental impact. The impact of TV on social interaction and social networks has been discussed by various scholars mainly in the western societies. Relevant inferences of these have been discussed in the preceeding chapter. Review indicates that while TV viewing consistently for many hours may disrupt intra-familial ties, not many studies have been attempted to analyse the impact of TV on social interaction outside the family i.e., with relatives, friends and neighbours.

While more people of the upper socio-economic groups in a city participate in formal organisations as has been suggested by various empirical studies, whether TV viewing impacts such social participation or not, is yet to be examined. Therefore, in this chapter, an attempt has been made to illustrate the nature and degree of formal and informal participation besides studying the extent to which television viewing boosts or disrupts social participation.

Data regarding the formal social participation shall be presented first and subsequently the findings concerning informal participation will be presented.

The researcher segmented the data to identify the number of households who were members of any formal organisation. Even if a single member or more than one person of a family unit held membership of any formal organisation, it was considered that one household was a member of an organisation. The data indicated that in one household, more than one person had membership in different organisations. Also, if the same person held membership in more than one formal organisation, it was considered that one household held a membership of formal organisation as indicated in Table 5.1.

Table–5.1
Distribution of Respondents According to Membership of any Formal Organisation in the Three Localities

	Locality			
Type of Respondents	*I*	*II*	*III*	*Total*
CATV Viewers	30	6	2	38
DD viewers	33	3	1	37
Total Members	63	9	3	75
Non-Members	37	91	97	225
Total	100	100	100	300

It was observed that in Locality I, about 63 per cent of respondents were members of some formal organisation. In Locality II, only 9 per cent while in Locality III, 3 per cent of the respondents were members of any formal organisations.

Among CATV viewers, it was observed that 30 per cent in Locality I, 6 per cent in Locality II and about 2 per cent in Locality III were members of atleast some formal organisations. Among DD viewers, 33 per cent in Locality I, 6 per cent in Locality II and about 1 per cent in Locality III were members of formal organisations. On the whole, about 12.7 per cent of CATV viewers and 12.3 per cent of DD viewers were members of formal organisations. Among the total respondents, 25 per cent were members of formal organisations. The data indicated that a majority of the respondents in Locality I, were members of formal organisations. There was not much difference between CATV viewers and DD viewers regarding memberships in formal organisations, in all the three localities. However, in Locality III, the number of families who were members of formal organisations was less than that in Localities I and II. Substantiating the earlier studies, our data reflects a positive association between formal participation and socio-economic status, since very few respondents from middle and low income localities were members of formal organisations.

Table–5.2
Distribution of Member Respondents According to Income in the Three Localities

	Locality			
Income (in Rupees)	*I*	*II*	*III*	*Total*
up to 2000	– (–)	– (–)	– (–)	– (–)
2001-5000	– (–)	1 (–)	2 (1)	3 (1)
5001-10,000	20 (19)	4 (3)	– (–)	24 (22)
10001+	10 (14)	1 (–)	– (–)	11 (14)
Total Members	30 (33)	6 (3)	2 (1)	38 (37)

(Figures in parentheses are the frequencies for DD viewers).

Data indicates that out of the total respondents who were members of a formal organisation, more than 75 per cent had an income above Rs. 5000 a month. In fact, out of 75 members, 63 belonged to the upper income locality, i.e., Locality I; nine belonged to the middle income Locality I i.e., Locality II and three belonged to the low income Locality I i.e., Locality III.

In Locality I, 60 per cent of the CATV viewers and 66 per cent of the DD viewers who were members had an income above Rs. 5000 a month. In Locality II, 10 per cent of the CATV viewers and 6 per cent of the DD viewers who were members had an income above Rs. 5000 a month. In Locality III, 4 per cent of the CATV viewers and 2 per cent of the DD viewers who were members had an income between Rs. 2001-5000 a month.

The data indicates that a majority of the members of formal organisations had an income above Rs. 5000 a month. Also, there was no variation between CATV viewers and DD viewers among the members of formal organisations in terms of income in the three localities. It was inferred that majority of the members in Locality I had an income of Rs. 5001-10000 a month among both CATV viewers and DD viewers.

Data from Table 5.3 indicates that out of the total respondents who were members of a formal organisation, about 90 per cent were either graduates or post-graduates. In fact, out of a total of 75 members, there were 67 members who were either graduates or post-graduates. Also, out of these 67 members, 60 members belonged to Locality I and seven members belonged to Locality II. In Locality III, two out of a total of three respondents who were members had their education qualification upto matric level.

The results indicate that most of the respondents who were members of some formal organisation, were graduates. Cable viewers and DD viewers did not differ in terms of educational qualifications among members of formal organisations. This indicates that formal participation has a positive association with education as well as with economic status.

It was observed from Table 5.4 that out of the total respondents who were members of a formal organisation, 25 per cent belonged to occupational prestige Category I, 65.3 per cent to occupational prestige Category II and 5.3 per cent to occupational prestige Category III.

Table–5.3
Distribution of Member Respondents According to Education in the Three Localities

Educational Qualification	*Locality* I	II	III	*Total*
Below matric	–	1	1	2
	(–)	(–)	(–)	(–)
Matric	3	–	1	4
	(–)	(–)	(1)	(1)
Intermediate	4	1	–	1
	(–)	(–)	(–)	(–)
Graduation	20	4	–	24
	(21)	(2)	(–)	(23)
Post-graduation	7	–	–	7
	(12)	(1)	(–)	(13)
Total members	30	6	2	38
	(33)	(3)	(1)	(37)

In Locality I, 84 per cent of the respondents who were members of a formal organisation belonged to either occupational prestige Category I or occupational prestige Category II. In Locality II, 12 per cent of the respondents who were members of a formal organisation belonged to either occupational prestige Category II or occupational prestige Category III.

There were no considerable differences between CATV viewers and DD viewers among the members of a formal organisation in terms of occupational status. The data suggested that members of formal organisations belonged to high occupational prestige categories. This means that an individual seeks voluntary membership informal organisations to achieve specific occupational goals/needs as some high prestige occupations usually require that an individual widens his social parameters. Therefore, it is inferred that occupational status has a positive association with formal participation. It is concluded that formal participation is positively associated with income, education and occupational status. The present study substianties the earlier findings of Chandra (1977), Pasricha (1988), Gill (1991) and Gill and Dhawan

(1992) that there is a positive association between formal participation and economic status.

Table–5.4
Distribution of Member Respondents According to Occupation in the Three Localities

Occupational Prestige	*Locality* I	II	III	*Total*
Prestige Category I	11 (8)	– (–)	– (–)	11 (8)
Prestige Category II	19 (25)	3 (2)	– (–)	22 (27)
Prestige Category III	– (–)	3 (1)	– (–)	3 (1)
Prestige Category IV	– (–)	– (–)	1 (–)	1 (–)
Prestige Category V	– (–)	– (–)	1 (1)	1 (1)
Prestige Category VI	– (–)	– (–)	– (–)	– (–)
Prestige Category VII	– (–)	– (–)	– (–)	– (–)
Total Members	30 (33)	6 (3)	2 (1)	38 (37)

Among the families who held membership in formal organisations, it was observed that members of the family i.e., the male head, the lady of the household and children owned separate memberships in formal organisations. The total number of families who held memberships were 75 but the number of individual memberships in families of the respondents accounted to 101. Therefore, the data shall be presented further on the total number of individual memberships and not on family memberships.

Data in Table 5.5 indicates that out of a total of 101 memberships in formal organisations, 69 memberships were held by the male head of the household i.e., nearly 68 per cent memberships were held by the male head of the household. About 18.8 per cent of the memberships were held by the lady of the household while 12.8 per cent of the memberships were held by the male child (son) of the household.

Table-5.5
Distribution of Members of Formal Organisations According to Which Member in the Family held Membership in Formal Organisations in the Three Localities

Member	Locality I	II	III	Total
Male head of the household	29 (28)	7 (3)	1 (1)	37 (32)
Lady of the household	8 (7)	3 (-)	1 (-)	12 (7)
Son	7 (5)	1 (-)	- (-)	8 (5)
Total	44 (40)	11 (3)	2 (1)	57 (44)

It was also indicated that in Locality III, one out of a total of three memberships, were held by the lady of the household while in Locality II, three out of a total of 14 memberships were held by the lady of the household. In Locality I, 15 out of a total of 84 memberships were held by the lady of the household. It was further observed that on the whole, in Locality I, about 14.2 per cent of the total memberships of Locality I, were held by the male child of the household. In all the three localities, the female child (daughter) did not hold any independent membership in formal organisations. Data also indicates that on the whole, 56.4 per cent of the total memberships were held by CATV viewers while 43.6 per cent of the total memberships were held by DD viewers.

It was inferred that in all the three localities, the male head held membership in formal organisations and there was no considerable difference between CATV viewers and DD viewers.

From Table 5.6, it was observed that a majority (58%) of the respondents, both among CATV viewers and DD viewers, chose

Table–5.6
Distribution of Membership According to the Nature of Organisation Both Among CATV Viewers and DD Viewers in the Three Localities

Nature of the Organisation	*Locality* I	II	III	*Total*
Religious	–	1	–	1
	(1)	(-)	(-)	(1)
Political	–	–	–	–
	(-)	(-)	(-)	(-)
Entertainment	26	6	–	32
	(25)	(2)	(-)	(27)
Sports	14	2	–	16
	(10)	(1)	(1)	(12)
Welfare	2	–	1	3
	(1)	()	(-)	(1)
Recreational	1	1	1	3
	(1)	(-)	(-)	(1)
Any other	1	1	–	2
	(2)	(-)	(-)	(2)
Total	44	11	2	57
	(40)	(3)	(1)	(44)

membership in organisations which were entertainment based in nature. About 38 per cent of the total respondents preferred sports organisations, while a meagre 4 per cent each chose welfare and recreational organisations respectively for formal social participation. Further, 2 per cent of the respondents chose religious organisations for social participation. Among CATV viewers, 56 per cent held memberships in entertainment based organisations while 28 per cent preferred sports organisations for social participation.

Among DD viewers, 61 per cent preferred entertainment based organisations, while 27 per cent chose sports organisations for formal social participation. However, in Locality I, among CATV viewers about 59 per cent and about 63 per cent among DD viewers preferred entertainment based organisations. Around 38 per cent among CATV viewers in Locality I and 25 per cent among DD viewers preferred sports organisations for formal social participation. In Locality II, among CATV viewers, around 55 per cent preferred entertainment based organisations, while 18 per cent preferred sports organisations. Among DD viewers in the same locality, 67 per cent preferred entertainment based organisations while 33 per cent preferred sports organisations. In Locality III, among CATV viewers, 50 per cent each preferred welfare and recreational organisations. The only DD viewer who held membership in formal organisations in Locality III, preferred sports based organisation for social participation.

The data indicates that in localities I and II, respondents preferred membership in entertainment based organisations while in Locality III the respondents preferred sports, welfare and recreation based formal organisations. The data also indicates that majority of the respondents of Localities I and II sought membership in formal organisations which were entertainment or sports based in nature. It was seen in the preceeding data that these respondents had a high occupational status and therefore to satisfy their specific goals/needs they sought memberships into particular type of organisations.

It was important to find out the duration for which members held memberships in some formal organisations. For this, four categories were made out ranging from less than 5 years to above 15 years. These were:

(i) less than 5 years,
(ii) 5+ to 10 years,
(iii) 10+ to 15 years, and
(iv) above 15 years.

The data indicated that on the whole, 33.6 per cent of the total memberships in some formal organisation were held for less than 5 years; 39.6 per cent were held between 5-10 years; 12.8 per cent were held between 10-15 years and 13.8 per cent of the memberships were held for more than 15 years. In Locality I, 29.8 per cent of the total memberships of Locality I were held for less than 5 years; 41.7 per cent of the total memberships were held for 5-10 years; 14.2 per cent each of the total memberships were held for 10-15 years and above 15 years respectively.

Table–5.7
Distribution of Members of Formal Organisations According to Duration of Membership in Formal Organisations in the Three Localities (Data Collected During 1994)

	Locality			
Duration (in Years)	*I*	*II*	*III*	*Total*
Less than 5	14 (12)	1 (1)	1 (-)	22 (12)
5 + to 10	15 (20)	3 (1)	– (1)	18 (22)
10 + to 15	9 (3)	– (1)	– (-)	9 (4)
Above 15	6 (6)	1 (-)	1 (-)	8 (6)
Total	44 (40)	11 (3)	2 (1)	57 (44)

It was observed in Chapter 2 of the present study that the mean duration of stay (in years) in Chandigarh of respondents in Locality I was 19.4 years. It may be inferred here that majority of the respondents of Locality I were holding these memberships in formal organisation for atleast 10 years. In Localities II and III, majority of the respondents held memberships for less than 10 years. There was only one respondent in Locality III who held membership in a formal organisation for more than 15 years.

It was inferred that majority of the members held membership in formal organisations for 5-10 years. Also, there were a greater number of DD viewers than CATV viewers who held membership for the same duration. It was further interesting to find out the nature of formal participation of the members of formal organisations.

Data in Table 5.8 indicates that on the whole, 80.7 per cent of the CATV viewers and 75 per cent of the DD viewers who were members of formal organisations were consumers of services only. There were no respondents who contributed money only, both among CATV viewers and DD viewers. About 15.7 per cent of the

CATV viewers and 20.5 per cent of the DD viewers contributed money and participated actively in formal organisations. Also, 3.5 per cent of the CATV viewers and 4.5 per cent of the DD viewers were office holding respondents.

Table–5.8
Distribution of Members of Formal Organisations According to the Nature of Formal Participation in the Three Localities

Nature of Formal Participation	*Locality* I	II	III	*Total*
Only Consumers of Services	37 (29)	8 (3)	1 (1)	46 (33)
Contribute money only	– (-)	– (-)	– (-)	– (-)
Contribute money and Participate Actively	6 (9)	3 (-)	– (-)	9 (9)
Office-holding	1 (2)	– (-)	1 (-)	2 (2)
Total	44 (40)	11 (3)	2 (1)	57 (44)

The data indicated that in Locality I, 78.5 per cent of the members were consumers of services only. The data also revealed that 17.8 per cent of the members of formal organisations in Locality I, contributed money as well as participated actively in these organisations while only 3.5 per cent were office holding members.

This means that once a person sought voluntary membership in formal organisations, he definitely availed its services. It was seen here that none of the respondents contributed money only. They availed the services of the organisation if they paid for its memberships. The data revealed that on the whole out of a total of 101 memberships, 79 of them i.e., 78 per cent were consumers of services only.

In Locality II, 78.5 per cent were consumers of services only, in formal organisations. About 21.4 per cent of the members contributed money and participated actively in formal organisations. There were no office-holding members in Locality II.

In Locality III, two out of a total of three members, were consumers of services while one member was an office-holding respondent.

The data revealed that majority of the respondents were consumers of services in formal organisations. Further, there were more CATV viewers than DD viewers who were consumers of services while there were more DD viewers than CATV viewers who contributed money as well as participated actively in formal organisations.

The data suggested that TV—whether it was Cable TV or Doordarshan, it did not make any difference in the type of participation in formal organisations. The inference drawn here is that television did not intervene in formal social participation as this type of participation is a paid form of social participation. It is also interesting to find out at what level i.e., neighbourhood, city or national level, the respondents participated in formal organisations.

From Table 5.9, it is observed that on the whole, 13.8 per cent of the members participated at the neighbourhood level only while a majority of the members i.e., 86 per cent participated at the city level in formal organisations. The data also indicated that in Locality I, about 15.4 per cent of its total members participated in the formal organisations at the neighbourhood level only.

Table-5.9

Distribution of Members of Formal Organisations According to the Area of Operation of Membership in Formal Organisations in the Three Localities

	Locality			
Area of Operation	*I*	*II*	*III*	*Total*
Neighbourhood only	7 (6)	- (-)	1 (-)	8 (6)
City wide	37 (34)	11 (3)	1 (1)	49 (38)
Total	44 (40)	11 (3)	2 (1)	57 (44)

Further, 70.2 per cent of the members in Locality I participated at the city level in formal organisations. There were no respondents who participated at the national and international level in formal organisations in all the three localities. In Locality II, there were no respondents who participated in formal organisations at the neighbourhood level. All the respondents in this locality participated at the city level. In Locality III, two out of a total of three participated at the city level while one respondent participated at the neighbourhood level in formal organisations.

The results show that the level of participation was the highest at the city level among members of formal organisations. The data indicates that a few respondents in Locality I participated at the neighbourhood level. This was so because the sectors included in Locality I, had formal organisations within the neighbourhood area itself. In Locality II, the formal organisations in the neighbourhood area were non-operative. It may be observed that the members of Locality I had a high degree of mobility and hence participated at the city level also in formal organisations. Since there is a high degree of mobility among the upper socio-economic strata, it is easier for them to participate across greater distances and more frequently in formal organisations. These aspects shall be discussed in the following Table 5.10:

Table–5.10

Distribution of Members of Formal Organisations According to Frequency of Visits to Formal Organisations in the Three Localities

	Locality			
Frequency of Visits	*I*	*II*	*III*	*Total*
Once a month	7 (3)	1 (1)	– (-)	8 (4)
Fortnighty	3 (6)	5 (1)	– (-)	8 (7)
Weekly	14 (10)	5 (-)	1 (-)	20 (10)
Almost everyday	20 (21)	– (1)	1 (1)	21 (23)
Total	44 (40)	11 (3)	2 (1)	57 (44)

On the whole, 11.9 per cent of the members visited formal organisations once a month while about 14.8 per cent of the members visited formal organisations fortnightly. Also, 29.7 per cent of the members participated in formal organisations once in a week. Further, a majority of the members i.e., 43.5 per cent visited formal organisations almost everyday. The analysis also indicated that in Locality I, abôut 11.9 per cent of the members visited formal organisations once a month while about 10.7 per cent of them visited formal organisations fortnightly. Further, 28.6 per cent of the members visited formal organisations once a week. A majority of the members i.e., 48.8 per cent visited formal organisations almost everyday. In Locality II, 57 per cent of its members visited formal organisations either once a month or fortnightly. Further, 35.7 per cent of the members of Locality II visited formal organisations once a week. In Locality III, two out of a total three members visited formal organisations almost everyday.

It was observed that on the whole, majority of the respondent visited formal organisations almost everyday.

The analysis also indicated that majority of the members of Locality I had a high degree of formal participation. They were visiting formal organisations atleast once a week or almost daily. The study also indicated that the degree of formal participation of members of Locality I was high as they had resources for a high degree of mobility. It was also observed earlier in this chapter that, majority of the respondents who were members of formal organisations, had a monthly income of above Rs. 5000 a month indicating a positive association between economic status and the degree of formal participation. It would be further interesting to find out the type of activities the members involved themselves in formal organisations. For this four categories were made out to assess the nature of the type of activities. They were:

(i) Dining/boozing/playing cards and tambola.
(ii) Sports and games.
(iii) Welfare.
(iv) Miscellaneous—which included economics, business, trade etc.

It was observed that 73.8 per cent of the total members participated in formal organisations for dining or playing cards and tambola or boozing while 27.7 per cent participated in formal organisations for sports and games. Only 4.9 per cent and 5.9 per cent of the members were involved in welfare and miscellaneous activities respectively.

Table–5.11

Distribution of Members of Formal Organisations According to the Type of Activity in Formal Organisations in the Three Localities

	Locality			
Type of Activity	*I*	*II*	*III*	*Total*
Dinning/boozing/playing tambola and cards	26 (25)	8 (2)	1 (-)	35 (27)
Sports	14 (10)	2 (1)	– (1)	16 (12)
Welfare	2 (2)	– (-)	1 (-)	3 (2)
Miscellaneous	2 (3)	1 (1)	1 (1)	3 (3)
Total	(40) 44	(3) 11	2 (1)	57 (44)

In Locality I, 67.8 per cent of the members participated for entertainment based activities like playing cards and tambola, dining and boozing while 28.5 per cent were involved in sports and games. Further, 4.7 per cent and 5.9 per cent were interested in welfare and miscellaneous activities. In Locality II, 71.4 per cent of the members participated for entertainment based activities while 21.4 per cent preferred sports activities in formal organisations. In Locality III, one member each participated for entertainment, sports and welfare activities respectively in formal organisations.

It was inferred that majority of the respondents participated in formal organisations for dining or boozing or playing cards and tambola. It was also inferred that sports was another important activity for which members participated in formal organisations. As formal participation was oriented towards entertainment based activities by majority of the members, it may be inferred that these members preferred out-of-home entertainment activities. A particular need was being gratified by its members by joining formal organisations.

It was therefore important to find out whether TV intervened in the formal participation of respondents. As the following discussion relates to formal participation across families, the data shall be presented on the number of families and not on individual memberships from now onwards.

Table–5.12

Distribution of Member Respondents According to Whether TV had an Effect on Their Participation in Formal Organisations in the Three Localities

	Locality			
Response	*I*	*II*	*III*	*Total*
Affected	11 (7)	1 (-)	1 (1)	13 (8)
Not affected	19 (26)	5 (3)	1 (-)	25 (29)
Total	30 (33)	6 (3)	2 (1)	38 (37)

On the whole, 28 per cent of the total members said that TV had affected their degree of social participation in formal organisations, while 72 per cent disclosed that TV did not intervene in their formal social participation. In Locality I, 28.5 per cent; in Locality II, 11.1 per cent and in Locality III, 66.6 per cent said that TV intervened in their social participation in formal organisations.

It may be inferred that majority of the members felt that TV did not affect social participation at the formal level. The data in this chapter had earlier suggested that TV did not disrupt formal participation. In this type of participation an individual seeks voluntary membership and it is a paid form of social participation. Therefore, it can be concluded that Satellite TV did not intervene in formal social participation. It is therefore, interesting to find out if Satellite TV had an impact on social participation at the informal level across families. It is seen in the preceeding chapter that Satellite TV had an impact on many dimensions of social participation in the family viewing situation. If such an impact is exercised by Satellite TV or not on informal social participation i.e., with relatives, friends and neighbours are important questions. The answers to these questions will be taken up in following discussions. But, before that, the study gives a glimpse of the type of effect TV had among members who said that TV had intervened in their formal social participation.

Table–5.13
Distribution of Member Respondents According to the Type of Effect TV had on Their Participation in Formal Organisations in the Three Localities

	Locality			
Type of Effect	*I*	*II*	*III*	*Total*
Spend less time	9 (5)	1 (-)	1 (1)	11 (6)
Spend more time	2 (2)	– (-)	– (-)	2 (2)
Withdrawn membership	– (-)	– (-)	– (-)	– (-)
No effect	19 (26)	5 (3)	1 (-)	25 (29)
Total	30 (33)	6 (3)	2 (1)	38 (37)

On the whole, 22.6 per cent of the members said that they had started spending lesser time in formal organisations while 5.3 per cent said that they had started spending more time in formal organisations. There was no respondent who withdrew his membership in formal organisations for the sake of watching TV. In Locality I, 22.2 per cent of the members said that they started spending lesser time in formal organisations, while 6.3 per cent of the members said that they had started spending more time in formal organisations. Also, in Locality II, one respondent said that he had started spending lesser time in formal organisations. In Locality III, two out of a total of three members said that they had started spending lesser time in formal organisations.

It may be inferred here that on the one hand, there were members who had started spending less time in formal organisations in favour of watching TV, while on the other hand, there were also respondents who had started spending more time in these organisations. It may be inferred that some respondents wanted to watch TV as less as possible and therefore started spending more time in formal organisations, as there was an increase in the duration of transmission with the advent of Cable TV, they were fed up of the 'idiot box'.

Reasons assigned by majority of the respondents for TV not intervening in their formal participation were they did not have much interest in TV nor did they place television viewing as an important daily activity. Respondents also stated that they were left with little time to watch TV after participating in social organisations almost daily. One respondent said, "We are not TV addicts." Another added, "As it is we have no time to watch television, so the question of it intervening in any kind of social participation does not arise."

It was observed in the preceeding data of the present chapter that majority of the respondents had a high degree of formal participation. They had been visiting formal organisations frequently—almost daily. There is a clear indication from the responses that TV did not intervene in the process of formal social participation.

Table-5.14
Distribution of Member Respondents According to Whether They Aspired to be Members of Additional Formal Organisations in the Three Localities

	Locality			
Response	*I*	*II*	*III*	*Total*
Yes	2 (1)	2 (2)	- (-)	4 (3)
No	28 (32)	4 (1)	2 (1)	34 (34)
Total Members	30 (33)	6 (3)	2 (1)	38 (37)

On the whole, 9.3 per cent of the members aspired to become members of more formal organisations while about 90.7 per cent of the members indicated that they were not interested in joining additional formal organisations for social participation.

Among those respondents who aspired to be members of more formal organisations listed out that they wanted to involve themselves in additional welfare and sports activities. They also wanted to have more social activity and develop social contacts outside their neighbourhood area.

Also, the members who did not want to be members of any more formal organisations said that, the present social activity was enough for them and they had little or no time in their busy routine/ schedule.

Table-5.15
Distribution of Non-Member Respondents According to Whether they Aspired to be Members of any Formal Organisation in the Three Localities

	Locality			
Response	*I*	*II*	*III*	*Total*
Yes	–	6	–	6
	(2)	(1)	(-)	(3)
No	20	38	48	106
	(15)	(46)	(49)	(110)
Total non-members	20	44	48	112
	(17)	(47)	(49)	(113)

On the whole, about 4 per cent of the non-members aspired to be members of formal organisations. Also, majority of the non-members i.e., 96 per cent did not want to be members of any formal organisations. Among non-members, the respondents of Locality II showed a keen interest in joining formal organisations. About 8 per cent wanted to join formal organisations but there were some intervening factors which dissuaded them from formal social participation.

Among non-members, the reasons listed out for aspiring to be members of any formal group or organisation was to have social activity outside their homes.

Those who did not want to be members of any formal organisation listed out plethora of reasons and they differed from one locality to the other. In Locality I, the reason assigned was that they did not have any time for social activity or they were too old for club activities. In Locality II, the reasons ranged from the death of a spouse, to a divorce, being too old, lack of interest in such activities, no time, presumption that they don't belong to such a status, being financially tight, new arrivals to Chandigarh, reluctance of the older members (parents of the male head of the household) to let them join formal organisations for social activities.

However in Locality III, most non-members did not understand the concept, while others said that they felt shy from such activities. A few mentioned that they were not educated to know about clubs and that they did not belong to that strata of the society and their financial status did not permit them. Some added that they were not interested in 'such' activities.

It was observed that among members most respondents did not aspire be members of additional formal organisations while among non-members, most respondents did not want to be members of any formal organisation.

Viewing of Satellite Television and Informal Participation

It has been inferred from the data that Satellite TV did not intervene in the process of formal social participation. We had seen in the previous chapter that family interaction patterns had been restructured mainly due to the advent of Satellite TV. One dimension of informal social participation i.e., interaction within the family revealed that Satellite TV had curtailed communication within families as well as weakened ties within family members. The study also revealed a lack of hospitality on the part of viewers. The inter-familial relationships were found to have suffered within the city dwellers as respondents avoided social visits across families for the fear of being unwanted guests especially during interesting programmes on the Cable network. Whether such an impact is exercised by Satellite TV on patterns of informal social participation i.e., with relatives, friends and neighbours among city dwellers is a pertinent question. The following discussion illustrates the patterns of informal social participation of the residents of the city of Chandigarh. Two dimensions, namely: *(i)* degree of informal participation and *(ii)* nature of informal participation were taken into consideration while analysing informal social participation. These concepts have already been defined in Chapter 1.

Degree of Informal Participation

To measure the degree of informal participation, an index was constructed. The degree of informal participation was measured in terms of the frequency of contacts with the neighbours, friends and relatives.

The respondents were questioned as to how frequently in a month they visited their relatives, friends and neighbours. The responses posed were *(i)* often (once a week), *(ii)* sometimes (once in a fornight), *(iii)* rarely (once a month or later than that), and *(iv)* never. The respondents were given scores to the responses in a descending order, 'often' was given score 3, 'sometimes' was given score 2, 'rarely' was given score 1 and 'never' was scored zero. The individual scores for relatives, friends and neighbours were added and it was found that the highest score an individual had was nine and the lowest score was zero. (The scores of an individual ranged from 0 to 9). These were divided into 3 categories viz. 0-5, 6-7 and 8-9 and according to the Quartiles Q_1 and Q_3, they were designated as low, medium and high levels of degree of informal participation. Those respondents who did not have either relatives or friends outside the neighbourhood area or in the city of Chandigarh were not included while measuring the degree of informal participation.

Informal Participation in Locality III (Ram Darbar)

The respondents of Locality III were not included while measuring the degree of informal participation. During the data analysis, it was observed that about 90 per cent of the respondents in Locality III i.e., Ram Darbar did not have friends or relatives outside their neighbourhood area. There is a qualitative difference in the characteristics of social participation of the residents of Ram Darbar from other two localities. While the respondents of Locality I preferred informal participation strongly with relatives and friends, respondents of Locality III preferred to have social interaction within the neighbourhood area only. This is also attributed to the fact that most relatives of the residents of Locality III resided in the neighbourhood area. Another factor is the housing patterns of Locality III; the closely knit housing pattern induces community living, resulting in intimate neighbourhood ties.

The closely knit neighbourhood relations provide the maximum social and psychological security to the residents of Locality III. It was also observed that the residents of Ram Darbar shared their family problems as well as important family events (like festivals) with each other indicating strong neighbourhood ties. It was observed that the close neighbourhood ties were indicated by a high degree of interaction and intimacy between neighbours in the low socio-economic group.

Another significant point to be noted is that the population in Ram Darbar consists of migrants from neighbouring states who invite their relatives to settle down in the locality. Consequently, all the relatives of the residents of the Ram Darbar locality were their neighbours and friends too. The residents of Ram Darbar did not have social participation at the informal level independently from relatives and friends outside the neighbourhood area.

A similar observation was made by Gill and Dhawan in 1991 while studying the traditional and non-traditional bases of social organisation in a low income group locality of Chandigarh.

Table–5.16
Distribution of CATV Viewers and DD Viewers According to the Degree of Informal Participation

	Locality		
Degree of Informal Participation	*I*	*II*	*Total*
Low	8 (11)	9 (15)	17 (26)
Medium	25 (16)	26 (16)	51 (32)
High	12 (14)	8 (7)	20 (21)
Total	45 (41)	43 (38)	88 (79)
No relatives and/or friends	5 (9)	7 (12)	12 (21)
Total	50 (50)	50 (50)	100 (100)

The data indicated that there were some respondents in Localities I and II, who did not have relatives and or friends in Chandigarh. Only those respondents who had relatives and friends in Chandigarh were included while measuring the level of informal participation, as a composite index was used. It was observed that a total of 33 respondents in both Localities I and II did not have either relatives or friends in Chandigarh. Therefore, the following data shall be presented on the number of families (167) who had both relatives and friends outside their neighbourhood area in the city of Chandigarh.

Data indicates that 25.7 per cent of the total respondents had low degree of informal participation; 49.7 per cent had medium degree of informal participation and 24.5 per cent had high degree of informal participation.

The data also indicated that in Locality I, 17.7 per cent of the CATV viewers and 26.8 per cent of the DD viewers had low level of informal participation while 55.5 per cent of the CATV viewers and 39 per cent of the DD viewers had medium level of informal participation. Further, 24.7 per cent of the CATV viewers and 34 per cent of the DD viewers had high level of informal participation.

In Locality II, 20.9 per cent of the CATV viewers and 39.4 per cent of the DD viewers had low level of informal partcipation while 60.4 per cent of the CATV viewers and 42.1 per cent of the DD viewers had medium level of informal participation. Also, 18.6 per cent of the CATV viewers and 18.4 per cent of the DD viewers had high level of informal participation.

It was inferred that majority of the respondents had either low or medium degree of informal participation. A total of only 42 respondents out of 167 respondents indicated a high degree of informal participation. It was also observed that majority of the CATV viewers in Localities I and II indicated medium degree of informal participation. Data reflects that majority of the respondents had lower degrees of informal participation i.e., with relatives, friends and neighbours, making urbanism as a way life more pronounced. On the one hand, low degree of informal participation is a characteristic of urban city dwellers, while on the other Satellite TV, may reduce the degree of informal participation as viewers are glued to television.

It was also observed in Chapter 4 that respondents and their children often felt irritated and upset whenever guests arrived during interesting programmes. Such an indication suggests that not only the restriction of physical mobility reduces informal participation but respondents avoided social visits across families as well during prime hours of TV further reducing the degree of informal participation. Whether TV intervenes in the degree of informal social participation or whether these are characteristics of city dwellers is yet to be seen. But before that it would be interesting to not whether the level of informal participation is associated with the variables such as income, education and occupation. For this purposes bi-variate tables were formulated and the chi-square test was applied to test the association between the demographic variables and level of informal participation.

It is inferred from Table 5.17 that income level and the degree of informal participation were significantly associated in the case of CATV viewers but the reverse was true in the case of DD viewers. It may be pointed out that majority of the respondents had a medium degree of informal participation. Income is also a criterion for the degree of physical mobility i.e., degree of informal participation outside the neighbourhood area and across greater distances. The study had indicated that as a result of viewing round-the-clock TV programmes, there was a considerable decline in the physical mobility of the viewers. This means that income as well as Satellite TV have an association with the degree of informal participation. The study stands to substantiate this view point. Further, discussion reveals whether education has an association with Satellite TV or not.

Table–5.17

Distribution of CATV Viewers and DD Viewers According to the Degree of Informal Participation and Income

	Degree of Informal Participation			
Income (In Rupees)	*Low*	*Medium*	*High*	*Total*
Upto Rs. 2000	–	–	–	–
	(2)	(–)	(–)	(2)
2001-5000	4	10	2	16
	(6)	(10)	(1)	(17)

(Contd.)

Income (in Rupees)	*Low*	*Medium*	*High*	*Total*
5001-10000	11 (14)	33 (16)	12 (12)	56 (42)
10001+	2 (4)	8 (6)	6 (8)	16 (18)
Total	17 (26)	51 (32)	20 (21)	88 (79)

CATV viewers $x^2_{cal} = 28.76 > x^2_{tab} = 12.592$ $p < 0.05$, d.f. = 6
DD viewers $x^2_{cal} = 8.92 < x^2_{tab} = 12.592$ $p > 0.05$, d.f. = 6.

It is also inferred from Table 5.18 that the educational level was not associated with the degree of informal participation in the case of CATV viewers but was significantly associated in the case of DD viewers.

Table–5.18
Distribution of CATV Viewers and DD Viewers According to the Degree of Informal Participation and Education

	Degree of Informal Participation			
Educational Qualification	*Low*	*Medium*	*High*	*Total*
Below matric	1 (3)	3 (–)	– (–)	4 (3)
Matric	2 (3)	10 (9)	2 (1)	14 (13)
Intermediate	5 (3)	3 (2)	1 (–)	9 (5)
Graduate	9 (15)	28 (13)	14 (10)	51 (38)
Post-graduate	– (2)	7 (8)	3 (10)	10 (20)
Total	17 (26)	51 (32)	20 (21)	88 (79)

CATV viewers $x^2_{cal} = 13.502 < x^2_{tab} = 15.507$ $p > 0.05$, d.f. = 8
DD viewers $x^2_{cal} = 21.54 > x^2_{tab} = 15.507$ $p < 0.05$, d.f. = 8.

We had observed in the previous discussion of the present chapter that socio-economic status was associated with formal participation. Also, as informal participation is marked by social interaction across relatives, friends and neighbours, and the findings in Chapter 3 suggested that highly educated DD viewers watched TV for a lesser duration of time (due to lesser availability of viewing content) it can be concluded that the degree of informal participation was associated with the educational level among DD viewers.

Table–5.19

Distribution of CATV Viewers and DD Viewers According to the Degree of Informal Participation and Occupational Status

	Degree of Informal Participation			
Occupational Prestige	*Low*	*Medium*	*High*	*Total*
Prestige Category I	3 (4)	8 (1)	4 (6)	15 (11)
Prestige Category II	7 (10)	24 (18)	11 (15)	42 (43)
Prestige Category III	5 (10)	15 (6)	5 (-)	25 (16)
Prestige Category IV	2 (1)	4 (7)	– (-)	6 (8)
Prestige Category V	– (-)	– (-)	– (-)	– (-)
Prestige Category VI	– (1)	– (-)	– (-)	– (1)
Prestige Category VII	– (-)	– (-)	– (-)	– (-)
Total	17 (26)	51 (32)	20 (21)	88 (79)

CATV viewers $x^2_{cal} = 3.118 < x^2_{tab} = 21.026$ $p > 0.05$, d.f. = 12
DD viewers $x^2_{cal} = 27.35 > x^2_{tab} = 21.026$ $p < 0.05$, d.f. = 12.

It is inferred from the above table that the occupational status and the degree of informal participation were not associated in the case of CATV viewers but were associated in the case of DD viewers. Data presented in Tables 5.17, 5.18 and 5.19 indicate that there is no consistent relationship between degree of informal participation on the one hand, and income, education and occupation on the other. This trend leads us to the conclusion that unlike formal participation which has a definite relationship with income, education and occupation, the patterns of informal participation do not have any consistent association with these variables.

We had seen from the responses in the preceeding data that there was a high degree of formal participation among members of formal organisations. The study also indicates that by and large there was a medium degree of informal participation among respondents. Whether TV exercises a uniform effect on both dimensions of social participation i.e., formal and informal participation will be revealed in the subsequent discussions.

Table–5.20

Distribution of Respondents According to the Degree of Formal Participation and Duration of Viewing TV

	Degree of Informal Participation				
Duration of Viewing TV	*Once a Month*	*Fort-nightly*	*Weekly*	*Almost Daily*	*Total*
One session	3	3	8	5	19
Two sessions	5	7	6	13	31
Three sessions	1	3	6	10	20
Four sessions	2	–	2	1	5
Total	11	13	22	29	75

$x^2_{cal} = 9.2049 < x^2_{tab} = 16.919$ $p > 0.05$, d.f. = 9.

It was inferred that the duration of viewing and the degree of formal participation of the respondents were not associated with each other. We had observed in the earlier discussion that formal participation was a paid form of social participation where an individual seeks voluntary membership into formal organisations. Therefore, the process of formal social participation which is a charactertic of urbanites, is not intervened by the duration of viewing TV. From Table 5.20, there is a clear indication that the duration of viewing TV is not associated with formal social participation.

Table–5.21

Distribution of CATV Viewers and DD Viewers According to the Degree of Formal Participation and Duration of Viewing TV

	Degree of Informal Participation				
Duration of Viewing TV	*Once a Month*	*Fort-nightly*	*Weekly*	*Almost Daily*	*Total*
One session	1 (2)	– (3)	4 (4)	3 (2)	8 (11)
Two sessions	4 (1)	5 (2)	4 (2)	5 (8)	18 (13)
Three sessions	– (1)	2 (1)	3 (3)	2 (8)	7 (13)
Four sessions	2 (-)	– (-)	2 (-)	1 (-)	5 (-)
Total	7 (4)	7 (6)	13 (9)	11 (18)	38 (37)

CATV viewers $x^2_{cal} = 8.3616 < x^2_{tab} = 16.919$ p > 0.05, d.f. = 9

DD viewers $x^2_{cal} = 6.2717 < x^2_{tab} = 16.919$ p > 0.05, d.f. = 9.

It was inferred that the duration of viewing TV and the degree of formal participation were not associated in the case of both CATV viewers and DD viewers. As observed earlier study suggested that TV– whether it was Cable TV or Doordarshan did not restrict the degree of formal social participation. Whether TV curtails the degree of informal participation will be revealed in the next Table.

It is inferred from the above Table that the duration of viewing of the respondents was not associated with the degree of informal participation. It is also inferred that duration of viewing TV did not restrict informal participation. It is important to point out that prime hours of TV kept respondents away from visiting relatives, friends and neighbours. Therefore, respondents may choose convenient times to participate in social activity across relatives, friends and neighbours. Also, their duration of viewing TV is not restricted by the degree of informal participation i.e., with relatives, friends and neighbours. Hence, it may be inferred that low levels of degree of informal participation are signified by emergence of new behavioural patterns due to demographic transformations as a result of urbanisation and not due to TV.

Table–5.22
Distribution of Respondents According to the Degree of Informal Participation and the Duration of Viewing TV

	Degree of Informal Participation			
Duration of Viewing TV	*Low*	*Medium*	*High*	*Total*
One session	13	22	13	48
Two sessions	20	29	13	62
Three sessions	6	21	13	40
Four sessions	4	11	2	17
Total	43	83	41	167

$x^2_{cal} = 6.4758 < x^2_{tab} = 12.592$ $p > 0.05$, d.f. = 6.

Table–5.23
Distribution of CATV Viewers and DD Viewers According to the Degree of Informal Participation and the Duration of Viewing TV

	Degree of Informal Participation			
Duration of Viewing TV	*Low*	*Medium*	*High*	*Total*
One session	1 (12)	14 (8)	3 (10)	18 (30)
Two sessions	9 (11)	13 (16)	7 (6)	27 (33)
Three sessions	3 (3)	13 (8)	8 (5)	24 (16)
Four sessions	4 (-)	11 (-)	2 (-)	17 (-)
Total	17 (26)	51 (32)	20 (21)	88 (79)

CATV viewers $x^2_{cal} = 8.81 < x^2_{tab} = 12.592$ $p > 0.05$, d.f. = 6
DD viewers $x^2_{cal} = 5.24 < x^2_{tab} = 12.592$ $p > 0.05$, d.f. = 6.

It is inferred from Table 5.22 that the duration of viewing of the respondents was not associated with the degree of informal participation in the case of both CATV viewers and DD viewers. This means that round – the-clock transmission on Satellite TV and limited channels of Doordarshan were not associated with the degree of informal participation which was medium level in the case of majority of the respodents. Therefore, the degree of informal participation of respondents could be attributed to the characteristics of urban dwellers and not due to TV. The weakening of ties is a distinctive feature of city dwellers and the impact of TV is not felt on informal participation of the respondents. It is concluded that the duration of viewing television had no association with the degree of informal participation, but these were a characteristics of the urban ways of life. Therefore, the hypothesis posed in this Chapter that TV viewing would affect formal and informal participation has been rejected by the study. However, we also attempted some qualitative analysis to probe into the relationship between TV viewing and imformal participation. But before that it would be further interesting to find out the levels of intimacy of ties of respondents across relatives, friends and neighbours.

"Nature" of Informal Participation

The nature of informal participation with relatives, friends and neighbours was measured in terms of casualness, outings, and intimacy of visits. An index was developed to measure the nature of informal participation in terms of intensity of ties. The respondent was asked to identify his nature of contact with relatives, friends and neighbours separately. To measure the nature of ties among neighbours, questions different from those pertaining to relatives and friends were posed to the respondents (for details see Appendix A). A score ranging from 3 to 0 in each of the questions according to the levels of intimacy were assigned to the individual.

It was observed that the highest composite score i.e., comprising relatives, friends and neighbours an individual could get was 12 and the lowest score he could get was 0. (The actual scores of an individual ranged from 12 to 2). These were divided into three categories viz. 0-4, 5-7 and 8-12 (according to Quartiles Q_1 and Q_3)

and they were designated as low, medium and high levels of intimacy of nature of contact with relatives, friends and neighbours.

Table-5.24
Distribution of CATV Viewers and DD Viewers According to the Nature of Contact (in Terms of Level of Intimacy)

	Locality		
Level Intimacy	*I*	*II*	*Total*
Low	13 (9)	13 (19)	26 (28)
Medium	26 (25)	22 (15)	48 (40)
High	6 (7)	8 (4)	14 (11)
Total (respondents with relatives and friends)	45 (41)	43 (38)	88 (79)
No relatives and/or friends	5 (9)	7 (12)	12 (21)
Total	50 (50)	50 (50)	100 (100)

Data reflects that on the whole, 32.3 per cent had low level of intimacy while 52.7 per cent of the respondents had medium level of intimacy with relatives, friends and neighbours. Further, 15.1 per cent of the respondents had a high level of intimacy with relatives, friends and neighbours. In Locality I, 25.5 per cent of the respondents had low level of intimacy while 59.3 per cent of the respondents had medium level of intimacy with relatives friends and neighbours. Also, about 15 per cent of the respondents had high level of intimacy with relatives, friends and neighbours. In Locality II, 30.9 per cent of the respondents had low level of intimacy and 52.1 per cent of the respondents had medium level of intimacy. Also, 16.9 per cent of the respondents had high level of intimacy with relatives, friends and neighbours.

The results suggest that majority of the respondents had medium level of intimacy with relatives, friends and neighbours. Majority of the respondents in the both localities had lower levels of intimacy which suggests that weakening of ties are the urban characteristics of city dwellers. It was also observed that both Cable TV viewers and DD viewers majority had low levels of intimacy across relatives, friends and neighbours. This means that TV is not a major factor in a decline in the levels of intimacy of respondents but these are the features of the urban mode of life. The study substantiates the findings of Chandra, 1977 and Gill and Dhawan, 1992, that there were weakening bonds of kinship across informal social networks and a strengthening of formal social participation in upper income groups.

The respondents were also specifically asked by the researcher whether television had restricted their relations with kinsmen and friends in any way. The responses indicated that by and large respondents felt that TV did not intervene in the relationship between kinsmen and friends. Data discussed so for in this chapter leads us to the conclusion that TV was not associated with both formal and informal participation. This finding was quite intriguing because during my field work experience, there were enough indications that physical immobility caused by television especially the Cable, had restricted informal social interaction. Further, as the low income groups were found to be maintaining strong ties with their kinsmen and neighbours, it was important to find out whether TV exercised any impact on the neighbourhood relations.

The data in Table 5.25 indicated that on the whole, 18.7 per cent of the CATV viewers and 7.3 per cent of the DD viewer felt that TV had not restricted neighbourhood relations while 14 per cent of the CATV viewers and 20.7 per cent of the DD viewers felt that TV had restricted neighbourhood relations to some extent. About 66.7 per cent of the CATV viewers and 68 per cent of the DD viewers felt that TV had definitely restricted neighbourhood relations. Further, 0.67 per cent of the CATV viewers and 4 per cent of the DD viewers felt that they couldn't say or did not know it TV had restricted neighbourhood relations.

In Locality I, 24 per cent of the CATV viewers and 4 per cent of the DD viewers felt that TV had not restricted neighbourhood relations while 18 per cent of the CATV viewers and 14 per cent of the DD viewers felt that TV had restricted neighbourhood relations to some extent. Further, 58 per cent of the CATV viewers and 82 per

Table–5.25
Distribution of CATV Viewers and DD Viewers According to Whether People are Glued to the TV Sets Thus Restricting Neighbourhood Relations in the Three Localities

Response	*Locality* I	II	III	*Total*	*%*
Not at all	12 (2)	16 (7)	– (2)	28 (11)	18.7 (7.3)
To some extent	9 (7)	8 (8)	4 (16)	21 (31)	14.0 (20.7)
Definitely yes	29 (41)	25 (29)	46 (32)	100 (102)	66.7 (68.0)
Can't say and Don't know	– (-)	1 (6)	– (-)	1 (6)	0.6 (4.0)
Total	50 (50)	50 (50)	50 (50)	150 (150)	100 (100)

cent of the DD viewers felt that TV had definitely restricted neighbourhood relations.

In Locality II, 32 per cent of the CATV viewers and 14 per cent of the DD viewers felt TV had not restricted neighbourhood relations while 16 per cent each of the CATV viewers and DD viewers felt that TV had restricted neighbourhood relations to some extent. Also, 50 per cent of the CATV viewers and 58 per cent of the DD viewers said that TV had definitely restricted neighbourhood relations.

Further, in Locality III, about 8 per cent of the CATV viewers and 32 per cent of the DD viewers felt that TV had restricted neighbourhood relations to some extent while 92 per cent of the CATV viewers and 64 per cent of the DD viewers felt that TV had definitely restricted neighbourhood relations.

It was observed that majority of the respondents both among CATV and DD viewers felt that TV had restricted neighbourhood relations. As there were more DD viewers who felt that TV had restricted neighbourhood relations, this can be attributed to the fact that they were justifying their non-subcription to Cable TV. Further, the CATV viewers were giving a general response as the question did not pertain to themselves only. Majority of Cable TV viewers in Locality III felt that was decline in neighbourhood relations as they had very strong and intimate ties with their neighbours. (The neighbourhood relations of the residents of Locality III have been already discussed in this chapter.) The study further reveals that low income respondents who had been maintaining strong neighbourhood ties felt that TV had intervened in their neighbourhood relations. This was because there was an increase in the number of channels as well as a qualitative difference in the programmes of Cable TV as compared to those of Doordarshan. As a result, there was a decline in physical mobility as viewers are glued to the TV, watching programmes. It was seen in Chapter 3 of the present study that the respondents of Locality III were heavy consumers of TV content. Hence, it is inferred that TV—especially the Cable TV had definitely made an impact on the neighbourhood relations. The quantitative analysis proved to be futile while the qualitative analysis revealed rich responses which were fruitful for the study. Respondents were not able to give fabricated responses when they were specifically asked by the researcher if TV had intervened in their informal participation across families. We experienced a loss of vital information through to the quantitative analysis. The study suggests that Satellite TV had definitely exercised its impact on informal social participation. To further substantiate this, the researcher asked the subjects if they missed TV programmes to visit their relatives, friends or neighbours. This factual question assumes significance as we have already seen in Chapter 3 that Cable TV viewers had longer duration of viewing TV which restricted physical mobility. The findings of Chapter 4 also, had suggested that there was a loss of physical mobility as well as a weakening of inter-familial relationship as respondents avoided social visits and expressed unhappiness over the arrival of guests during interesting programmes. As a direct question was posed, the respondents were unable to manipulate their responses.

The data from Table 5.26 indicated that on the whole 48.7 per cent of the CATV viewers and 46.7 per cent of the DD viewers never missed TV programmes for the sake of visiting relatives, friends and/or neighbours. About 51.3 per cent of the CATV viewers and 53.3 per cent of the DD viewers felt otherwise.

In Locality I, 44 per cent of CATV viewers and 56 per cent of DD viewers never missed TV programmes for the sake of visiting relatives, friends and/or neighbours while 56 per cent of CATV viewers and 44 per cent of DD viewers missed TV programmes for the sake of visiting relatives, friends and/or neighbours.

Table–5.26

Distribution of CATV Viewers and DD Viewers According to Whether They Missed TV Programmes for the Sake of Visiting Relatives, Friends or Neighbours in the Three Localities

	Locality				
Response	*I*	*II*	*III*	*Total*	*%*
Never missed	22 (28)	17 (19)	34 (23)	73 (70)	48.7 (46.7)
Missed	28 (22)	339310	16 (27)	77 (80)	51.3 (53.3)
Total	50 (50)	50 (50)	50 (50)	150 (150)	100 (100)

In Locality II, 34 per cent of CATV viewers and 38 per cent of DD viewers never missed TV programmes for the sake of visiting relatives, friends and/or relatives while 66 per cent of CATV viewers and 62 per cent of the DD viewers felt otherwise.

In Locality III, 68 per cent of CATV viewers and 46 per cent of DD viewers never missed TV programmes for visiting relatives, friends and/or neighbours while 32 per cent of CATV viewers and 54 per cent of DD viewers felt otherwise.

The data indicated that nearly half the respondents both among CATV viewers and DD viewers never wanted to miss TV programmes for visiting relatives, friends and/or neighbours. It was also observed that majority of the respondents of Locality III never wanted to miss TV programmes as compared to respondents of other localities.

This means that nearly half of the total respondents preferred to watch TV instead of visting relatives, friends and neighbours. They were glued to the TV sets thus restricting informal participation. Earlier data indicates that informal participation had not been affected by Satellite TV. However, when respondents were specifically asked whether they avoided visiting kinsmen, friends and neighbours, nearly half the total respondents admitted that they preferred to watch their favourite programmes on television instead of visiting their relatives, friends and neighbours. This means that television had definitely made an impact on social participation. The main drawback of the quantative analysis is that it does not reveal specific responses. The qualitative analysis on the other hand suggested that Satellite TV had intervened in the process of informal social participation. We had seen from the previous data that respondents had rescheduled their daily activities to watch their favourite programmes on television. It may also be pointed out that respondents had rescheduled their daily activities to watch TV programmes as well as socialize across families. This substantiates the findings of Chapter 4 that respondents had rescheduled their activities. It may be important to suggest findings of Chapter 4 that respondents avoided social visits across families as well as 'ignored' guests at home while watching TV. These findings suggest that interesting programmes on TV seduce their viewers into watching them instead of socializing across relatives, friends and neighbours. It can be concluded that Satellite TV exercised an impact on the informal participation.

The data indicates that on the whole, among 38 per cent of the CATV viewers and 37.3 per cent of the DD viewers it was the children who never wanted to miss TV programmes for the sake of visiting relatives, friends and/or neighbours while among 3.3 per cent of CATV viewers and 2 per cent of DD viewers the male head of the household never wanted to miss TV programmes for the sake of visiting relatives, friends and neighbours. Further, 4.7 per cent each among CATV and DD viewers, the lady of the household never wanted to miss TV programmes while in 1.3 per cent each among CATV and DD viewers the couple together never wanted to miss TV programmes. Among 0.7 per cent each among CATV viewers and DD viewers the male head of the household and the children together and also the same proportion of respondents (0.7%) among the wife and children together never wanted to miss TV programmes for the sake of visiting relatives, friends and neighbours.

Among 44 per cent CATV viewers and 40 per cent DD viewers, in Locality I; 22 per cent CATV viewers and 30 per cent DD viewers in Locality II; 48 per cent CATV viewers and 42 per cent DD viewers in Locality III; the children never wanted to miss TV programmes for the sake of visiting relatives, friends and neighbours.

Table–5.27
Distribution of CATV Viewers and DD Viewers According to Which Member in the Family Never Wanted to Miss TV Programmes for the Sake of Visiting Relatives, Friends and Neighbours

	Locatlity				
Which Member	*I*	*II*	*III*	*Total*	*%*
Children	22 (20)	11 (15)	24 (21)	57 (56)	38.0 (37.3)
Male head	– (2)	2 (1)	3 (–)	5 (3)	3.3 (2.0)
Wife	– (4)	2 (3)	5 (–)	7 (7)	4.7 (4.7)
Couple together	– (1)	1 (–)	1 (1)	2 (2)	1.3 (1.3)
Fathers and kids	– (1)	1 (–)	– (–)	1 (1)	0.7 (0.7)
Wife and kids	– (–)	– (–)	1 (1)	1 (1)	0.7 (0.7)
Total (never missed)	22 (28)	17 (19)	34 (23)	73 (70)	48.7 (46.7)
Others	28 (22)	33 (31)	16 (27)	77 (80)	51.3 (53.3)
Total	50 (50)	50 (50)	50 (50)	150 (150)	100 (100)

Among 4 per cent DD viewers in Locality I; 4 per cent CATV viewers and 2 per cent DD viewers in Locality II, and 6 per cent CATV viewers in Locality III, the male head of the household never wanted to miss TV programmes. Further, about 8 per cent DD viewers in Locality I; 4 per cent CATV viewers and 6 per cent DD viewers in Locality II; and 10 per cent CATV viewers in Locality III; the lady of the household never wanted to miss TV programmes for the sake of visiting relatives, friends and neighbours.

Among 2 per cent of DD viewers in Locality I, 2 per cent of CATV viewers in Locality II and 2 per cent each among CATV and DD viewers in Locality III, the couple together never wanted to miss TV programmes while among 2 per cent DD viewers in Locality II, the male head of the household and children together never wanted to miss TV programmes for the sake of visiting relatives, friends and neighbours. Also, among 2 per cent each among CATV viewers and DD viewers the lady of the household and children together never wanted to miss TV programmes for the sake of visiting relatives, friends and neighbours.

The results indicated that both among CATV viewers and DD viewers, the children never wanted to miss TV programmes for the sake of visiting relatives, friends and neighbours. This further substantiates the findings of Chapter 4 that whether the issue was to avoid important household issue for discussion, or outings, the children emerged as a prominent segment within a family where TV had exercised the maximum effect.

In this chapter the following conclusions are drawn:

1. Formal participation was positively associated with income, education and occupational status. Majority of the members of formal organisations belonged to Locality I. Memberships in majority of the families were held by the male head of the household.
2. Respondents sought membership in entertainment based formal organisations for dining/playing cards and tambola as well as sports activities. The nature of formal social participation was that respondents were consumers of services only. The participation of majority of the respondents was at the city level and majority of the memberships were held for 5-10 years.
3. The degree of formal participation was frequent—almost daily among majority of the members. Television did not affect the formal participation of members on both dimensions—degree and nature.
4. The informal participation of the respondents of Localities I and II were at a medium level on both dimensions—degree as well as nature. The respondents of Locality III had very strong neighbourhood ties, the study suggested. The quantitative analysis revealed that the degree of informal

participation was not associated with the duration of viewing TV both among CATV viewers and DD viewers in the upper and middle income localities. Also, there was no consistent association between income, education and occupation with the degree of informal participation both among CATV viewers and DD viewers. Further, the low levels of degree and nature of informal participation were characteristics of urban dwellers in Localities I and II. However, the qualitative analysis revealed that majority of the respondents felt that TV had restricted neighbourhood relations. Also, nearly half the respondents did not want to miss TV programmes for visiting relatives, friends and neighbours thus indicating that TV contributed to a decline in inter-familial relationships. Further, children avoided visiting relatives, friends and neighbours in favour of watching TV programmes.

The analysis in this chapter has revealed that different trends followed out of quantitative and qualitative investigation of the data. While responses analysed through the use of the index indicated that informal participation had little relationship with TV viewing, indirect questioning of respondents elicited altogether different trends. These responses clearly indicated that television had certainly curtailed their outdoor activities especially in relation to their visits to relatives, neighbours and friends. But the fact remains that this had happened more among the younger generation.

It is indicated that Satellite TV did not exercise a uniform effect on social participation. It had affected interaction patterns across families but did not exercise any effect on patterns of formal participation. Further, Satellite TV had definitely restricted neighbourhood relations in all the three income groups. It was also inferred that informal participation was affected by Satellite TV in the sense that they avoided social visits across families during prime hours of TV as well as did not want guests at home. This means that Satellite TV had made an impact on dimensions of informal participation. Children emerged as a powerful segment within the family unit in terms of control of TV set as well as the pursuit of TV viewing as a prime leisure activity resulting in a decline in social participation both within and across families. In the light of these inferences, it is important to see how television affects children especially with the western media creeping into Indian homes. The next chapter proposes answers to this question.

6

Impact of Satellite TV on Children: An Appraisal of Viewers' Perceptions

Television has transformed the socio-cultural landscape of most countries around the world in the last couple of decades. In almost every nook and corner of the globe, it has become an integral part of daily life for the young and the old, rich and the poor and also for the urban and rural populations.

With the spread of television far and wide, it has become the medium that has been the subject of research in both developed and developing countries. The social messages of television are so ubiquitous and yet so complex that the role they play in the lives of viewers, especially the children, is not fully understood. It is the very nature of this ubiquity and power of this medium, especially in the lives of children, that has caused so much concern over the last three decades.

Children today are born into television homes. Although, children of every generation have always been faced with changes taking place around them, the media explosion today presents special challenges because television is playing a crucial role in the definition of their adult roles.

Early television research on children focussed on the issues of violence, advertising and gender stereotyping and a little later, on the attention, comprehension and behaviour to the different forms of television content. Little empirical research has been conducted on the media imperialism thesis.

Satellite television brings into homes not only the popular culture and western value systems but it is also encouraging the young people to envy and seek to join the alien culture they are viewing (Schiller, 1976; Lee, 1980). American media products undermine the indigeneous culture of a less developed society. Programmes from America and Western European countries are much cheaper for third-world countries to buy than produce and some critics are worried that America and Western European cultural, social and political values and ideologies will drive out supposedly the traditional cultural values (Berger, 1992). This thesis is known as the "cultural imperialism."

Some critical theorists believe that American media will destroy regional and local cultures and lead to domination of American ideologies and a loss of cultural identity by people in other cultures. Massing (1986) in a study concluded that viewers in different countries view popular culture differently. It is in this context, that the present chapter seeks to explore the impact of western media through the Satellite TV as perceived by the audience in the Indian situation.

Creating and sustaining values in society is a task that is left to the family and educational systems (Unnikrishnan and Bajpai, 1996). How parents influence their children in maintaining the Indian value system and whether or not parents mediate the television viewing behaviour will be the focus of this chapter.

The general phenomenon of parent-child interaction is related to the parent's mediation of the child's television behaviour. A child's internalization of moral values is strongly influenced by parental disciplinary practices and internalized control of their children's social behaviour (Hoffman and Saltzstein, 1967).

In a society that has become more diversified, the parent-child relationship has been greatly affected. The import of western technologies and products inevitably influences the young people who seek more freedom; wanting to be treated as individuals to make their own decisions. They are less willing to follow parental rules or obey them unquestioningly. Consequently, parents also have less control over their children and further, more children are less tied to their parents as they were a decade ago (Greenberg, Ku and Li, 1992).

In Chapter 4 of the present study, it was observed that parents had been having lesser and lesser control on their children especially in dissuading them from watching television. That parents are unable to assert their authority on their children, was one of the important indications in the present study, in the earlier chapters. The present study substantiates the findings of earlier research by Greenberg, Ku and Li (1992) in the same context.

Parental mediation of their children's media experiences is influenced by several factors. In the changing parent-child relationship, parents may enforce no rules about TV viewing or may not be able to enforce the rules made by them. In this dynamic context, communication patterns between parents and their children are changing. Communication is less frequent and less authoritative.

Studies have indicated that the traditional family is weakening in terms of the hold of parents on their offspring and that the youth want what they perceive as a more western mode of family interaction, marked by greater independence in personal decisions. It is in the backdrop of these observations that this chapter examines whether parents monitor, mediate or regulate their children's viewing patterns on the one hand and on the other, it compares viewers of CATV and Doordarshan in terms of their perceptions of the impact of western culture.

Nearly four decades ago, research in this field indicated that interaction rarely occurred in British families during television viewing (Himmelweit, Oppenheim and Vince, 1958). Similar results were observed in American television households with only about 20 per cent of their parents mediating their children's TV viewing (Schramm, Lyle and Parker, 1961). Another study indicated that actual viewing prohibitions are seldom practiced in families (Mohr, 1976) while another indicated that such mediation takes the non-restrictive form of co-viewing in families.

Most research conducted in Asian countries does not contradict this pattern. Feng (1976) and Wu (1989) reported in their respective studies that families had no specific rules about their children's television viewing. Parents pay no attention to their children's television watching (Han, 1986) while the Research Group on Adolescence and Television (1984) in China observed that there were rules about the duration for which children could watch television. In Japan, Mitsuya (1988) in his study suggested that parents did not allow their children to watch television until late at night and that as the number of rules increased the amount of viewing decreased.

The amount of time devoted by children to watching TV has been a major concern in the literature about the impact of TV all over the world. Related to this, Leichter and her associates (1985) observe that despite the agreements on the danger of TV viewing, the time spent on TV continues to increase. In a study in Venezuela, Barrios (1988) indicated that only one father expressed concern about the consumption of TV by children. No one else in his sample of families said or did anything to reduce the amount of TV viewing in the household. The study also indicated that most parents expressed no worries on the habits concerning TV such as doing homework or eating meals while watching TV.

There are other intervening variables to be considered in the parental monitoring of childrens' TV viewing. Apart from the socio-economic status, there may be other variables to be considered in the parental monitoring of TV. Parental involvement in regulating their children's television viewing has been found to decline with age (Greenberg and Dominick, 1969; Lyle and Hoffman, 1972; Mc Leod, Atkin and Chaffee, 1972). Parents are more likely to regulate viewing patterns for girls than for boys (Feng, 1976; Gross and Walsh, 1980).

Some studies report that there is a greater mediation by parents in the higher socio-economic groups (Himmelweit and Swift, 1976) whereas another study failed to show such differences (Gross and Walsh, 1980). It is also indicated that larger families are not likely to control television viewing of children; having more children poses greater difficulty in supervising viewing among siblings. It would be interesting to find out in the present study, how the three localities differ in regulating their children's TV viewing behaviour.

The data on parental involvement in regulating TV shall be presented first and the impact of western media and culture as perceived by the respondents shall be presented subsequently.

The data indicated that on the whole, 52.7 per cent of the CATV viewers and 50.7 per cent of the DD viewers reported that they regulated TV for their children. Further, 31.3 per cent of the CATV viewers and 42 per cent of the DD viewers did not monitor TV for

Table-6.1
Distribution of CATV Viewers and DD Viewers According to Whether Parents Regulated TV for Their Children in the Three Localities

	Locality				
Regulate TV	*I*	*II*	*III*	*Total*	*%*
Yes	28 (27)	24 (23)	27 (26)	79 (76)	52.7 (50.7)
No	14 (20)	22 (24)	11 (19)	47 (63)	31.3 (42.0)
No child is studying	6 (2)	– (2)	12 (5)	18 (9)	12.0 (6.0)
No kids	2 (1)	4 (1)	– (-)	6 (2)	4.0 (1.3)
Total	50 (50)	50 (50)	50 (50)	150 (150)	100 (100)

(Figures in parentheses are the frequencies for DD viewers).

their children. For 16 per cent of the CATV viewers and 7.3 per cent of the DD viewers this question was not applicable as they had no child who was studying or were issueless parents.

In Locality I, 56 per cent of CATV viewers and 54 per cent of the DD viewers; in Locality II, 48 per cent of the CATV viewers and 46 per cent of the DD viewers; in Locality III, 54 per cent of the CATV viewers and 52 per cent of the DD viewers said that they regulated TV for their children. On the other hand, 28 per cent CATV viewers and 40 per cent DD viewers in Locality I; 44 per cent CATV viewers and 48 per cent DD viewers in Locality II and 22 per cent CATV viewers and 38 per cent DD viewers in Locality III, did not regulate TV for their children.

It was inferred that a greater number of CATV viewers reported that they monitored the TV viewing habits of their children as compared to DD viewers. It was also indicated from the data that more CATV viewers from Locality I regulated TV for their children. It was also indicated that in all the three localities a majority of the DD viewers did not regulate TV viewing habits of their children. It may be due to the fact that DD viewers do not feel much need for this as there are limited programmes on DD. On the other hand, the transmission through the Cable continues throughout the day and night. It is, therefore is understandable that more Cable TV viewers were regulating TV viewing of their children. Whether this regulation was effective or not, is an altogether different question, which will be examined later in this chapter. Data indicates that there is a greater mediation in the high and the low socio-economic groups. It is important to refer to the findings in Chapter 3, where majority of the respondents of Locality II had withdrawn Cable TV connections for their childrens' studies. Also, the findings in Chapter 3 and Chapter 4 indicate that parents were unable to exercise control over their children, especially in the TV viewing situation. That parents regulated TV among majority of the cases – as the study suggests, is therefore contradictory to the earlier findings of the study.

Proceeding with the analysis therefore, the researcher asked those regulating TV viewing of children as to how they monitored TV for their children. The data indicated that in case of a small proportion among our respondents i.e., 7.3 per cent each among CATV viewers and DD viewers, parents switched on the TV set only at a particular time. About 21.4 per cent of the CATV viewers and 22 per cent of the DD viewers allowed their children to watch TV for a fixed period of time. Also, 23.3 per cent of the CATV viewers and 21.4 per cent of the DD viewers allowed their children to switch on their TV set only at a particular time and also allowed them to watch TV for a fixed period of time.

In Locality I, 4 per cent of the CATV viewers switched on the TV set only at a particular time for their children while 24 per cent of the Cable viewers and 12 per cent of the DD viewers allowed their children to watch for a fixed period of time. Also, 28 per cent of the CATV viewers and 42 per cent of the DD viewers switched on the TV set only at a particular time as well as also allowed them to watch it only for a fixed period of time.

In Locality II, 18 per cent of the CATV viewers and 20 per cent of the DD viewers switched on the TV set only at a particular time while 18 per cent of the CATV viewers and 14 per cent of the DD viewers allowed them to watch TV only for a fixed period of time. Further, 12 per cent each among CATV viewers and DD viewers

Table–6.2
Distribution of CATV Viewers and DD Viewers According to the Type of TV Regulation for their Children in the Three Localities

Regulate	*Locality*				
	I	*II*	*III*	*Total*	*%*
Switch TV at a particular time	2 (–)	9 (10)	– (1)	11 (11)	7.3 (7.3)
Switch to channel they prefer	– (–)	– (–)	– (–)	– (–)	– (–)
Allow to watch for fixed period of time	12 (6)	9 (7)	11 (20)	32 (33)	21.4 (22.4)
Both 1 and 3	14 (21)	6 (6)	15 (5)	35 (32)	23.3 (21.4)
Both 2 and 3	– (–)	– (–)	1 (–)	1 (–)	0.7 (–)
Don't regulate TV	14 (20)	22 (24)	11 (19)	47 (63)	31.3 (42.0)
No child is studying	6 (2)	– (2)	12 (5)	18 (9)	12.0 (6.0)
No kids	2 (1)	4 (1)	– (–)	6 (2)	4.0 (1.3)
Total	50 (50)	50 (50)	50 (50)	150 (150)	100 (100)

switched on the TV set only at a particular time for their children as well as allowed them to watch it only for a fixed period of time.

In Locality III, 2 per cent of the DD viewers switched on the TV set only at a particular time while 22 per cent of the CATV viewers and 40 per cent of the DD viewers allowed their children to watch TV for a fixed period of time. Also, 30 per cent of the CATV viewers and 10 per cent of the DD viewers switched on the TV set only at a particular time as well as allowed them to watch it for a fixed period of time.

The results indicated that majority of the respondents both among CATV viewers and DD viewers said to be regulating TV in such a way that they switched on the TV set only at a particular time as well as allowed them to watch it for a fixed period of time. Most DD viewers allowed their children to watch TV only for a fixed period of time while among CATV viewers, the parents switched the TV set at a particular time as well as allowed them to watch it for a fixed period of time.

In Locality I, majority of the respondents switched on the TV set only at a particular time and also allowed their children to watch it for a fixed period of time while in Locality II, most CATV viewers preferred the same pattern. Further, among DD viewers parents allowed their children to watch TV for only a fixed period of time. In Locality III, the trend was the same among CATV and DD viewers in almost all the categories. It is interesting to note here that responses in preceeding tables were found to be exaggerated. On further probing the researcher found some inconsistencies in the responses of parents. Although the data presented so far indicates an efficient monitoring of TV viewing of children by parents in all the three localities, this was mainly found inoperative at the practical level. In order to test the effectiveness of parents' regulations over TV viewing, an effort was made to compare the academic performance of children whose viewing patterns were regulated and those who watched TV without any such regulations.

The analysis indicated that 52 per cent of the CATV viewers and 50.7 per cent of the DD viewers reported that there was a deterioration in the academic performance of their children. Further, 30 per cent of the CATV viewers and 39.3 per cent of the DD viewers said that there was no change in the academic performance of their children. Only 0.7 per cent of CATV viewers and 1.3 per cent of the DD viewers said that there was an improvement in the academic performance of their children while about 1.3 per cent each among both CATV viewers and DD viewers said that they were uncertain about the academic performance of their children.

In Locality I, 52 per cent of the CATV viewers and 34 per cent of the DD viewers said that there was deterioration in the academic performance of their children while 2 per cent each among CATV viewers and DD viewers said that there was improvement in the academic performance of their children. About 28 per cent among CATV viewers and 58 per cent among DD viewers said that there was no change in the academic performance of their children.

Table–6.3
Distribution of CATV Viewers and DD Viewers According to the Perceived Impact of TV on the Academic Performance of Their Children in the Three Localities

Academic Performance	*Locality* I	II	III	*Total*	*%*
Deterioration	26 (17)	29 (33)	23 (26)	78 (76)	52.0 (50.7)
Improvement	1 (1)	– (1)	– (-)	1 (2)	0.7 (1.3)
No change	14 (29)	16 (11)	15 (19)	45 (59)	30.0 (39.3)
Uncertain	1 (-)	1 (2)	– (-)	2 (2)	1.3 (1.3)
Any other	8 (3)	4 (3)	12 (5)	24 (11)	16.0 (7.4)
Total	50 (50)	50 (50)	50 (50)	150 (150)	100 (100)

(Any other: No child is studying and/or no children).

In Locality II, 58 per cent of the CATV viewers and 66 per cent of the DD viewers said that there was deterioration in the academic performance of their children while 32 per cent CATV viewers and 22 per cent DD viewers felt that there was no change in the academic performance of their children. Further, only 2 per cent of the DD viewers felt that there was improvement in the academic performance of then children.

In Locality III, 46 per cent of the CATV viewers and 52 per cent DD viewers reported deterioration in the academic performance while 30 per cent CATV viewers and 38 per cent DD viewers indicated that there was no change in the academic performance of their children.

It was inferred that on the whole, the respondents felt that there was a deterioration in the academic performance of their children due to TV. In Locality I, majority of the CATV viewers felt there was deterioration in the academic performance of their children while in the same locality, majority of the DD viewers stated stability in the academic performance of their children. In the other two localities, majority of the DD viewers felt that there was deterioration in the academic performance of their children due to TV. It would also be interesting to see the perceived impact of TV among regulators and non-regulators of TV on the academic performances of children.

The study suggested that due to TV—whether Cable or Doordarshan, among majority of the respondents admitted that there was a deterioration in the academic performance of their children.

Table–6.4

Distribution of CATV Viewers and DD Viewers (Among Regulators of TV) According to the Percieved Impact of TV on the Academic Performance of their Children in the Three Localities

Academic Performance	*Locality* *I*	*II*	*III*	*Total*	*%*
Deterioration	22 (13)	18 (18)	20 (23)	60 (54)	40.0 (36.0)
Improvement	– (1)	– (1)	– (-)	– (2)	– (1.3)
No change	6 (13)	6 (4)	7 (3)	19 (20)	12.7 (13.4)
Uncertain	– (-)	– (-)	– (-)	– (-)	– (-)
Total Regulators	28 (27)	24 (23)	27 (26)	79 (76)	52.7 (50.7)
Non-regulators and other categories	22 (23)	26 (27)	23 (24)	71 (74)	47.3 (49.3)
Total	50 (50)	50 (50)	50 (50)	150 (150)	100 (100)

Among the respondents who regulated TV for their children, 40 per cent of the CATV viewers and 36 per cent of the DD viewers indicated a deterioration in the academic performance of their children, while 12.7 per cent of the CATV viewers and 13.4 per cent of the DD viewers felt that there was no change in the academic performance of their children. Only 1.3 per cent of the DD viewers felt that there was an improvement in the academic performance of their children.

In Locality I, 44 per cent of the CATV viewers and 26 per cent of the DD viewers said that there had been a deterioration in the academic performance while 12 per cent of the CATV viewers and 26 per cent of the DD viewers felt that there was no change in the academic performance of their children. Only 2 per cent of the DD viewers felt that there was an improvement in the academic performance of their children.

In Locality II, 36 per cent each among both CATV viewers and DD viewers felt that there had been a deterioration in the academic performance of their children while 12 per cent of the CATV viewers and 8 per cent of the DD viewers did not feel so. Only 2 per cent of the DD viewers among those regulating TV viewing felt that there was an improvement in the academic performance of their children.

In Locality III, 40 per cent of the CATV viewers and 46 per cent of the DD viewers said that there had been a deterioration in the academic performance of their children due to TV while 14 per cent of the CATV viewers and 6 per cent of the DD viewers felt that there was no change in the academic performance of their children among the regulators of TV.

On the whole, the data indicates that, even among the regulators of TV, a greater number of CATV viewers felt there was deterioration in the academic performance. In Locality I, there were more CATV viewers who felt that there was deterioration in the academic performance of their children as compared to DD viewers and CATV viewers in other localities. It may be recalled that respondents in Locality I earlier had indicated a higher parental-mediation in the TV viewing patterns of their children. Inspite of regulation therefore, it was found that their children came down in their academic performance.

In Locality III, majority of the DD viewers felt that there was deterioration in the academic performance of their children. Hence, it may be inferred that earlier responses indicating TV regulation by parents was an exaggeration—an observation which will be verified later in this chapter.

Among the non-regulators of TV, 12 per cent of the CATV viewers and 14.7 per cent of the DD viewers felt that there was deterioration in the academic performance of their children while 17.3 per cent of the CATV viewers and 26 per cent of the DD viewers felt that there was no change in the academic performance of their children. Only 0.7 per cent of the CATV viewers felt that there was an improvement in the academic performance of their children.

In Locality I, 8 per cent each among CATV and DD viewers felt that there was deterioration in the academic performance while 16 per cent of the CATV viewers and 32 per cent of the DD viewers felt that there was no change in the academic performance of their children.

Table–6.5
Distribution of CATV Viewers and DD Viewers (Among Non-Regulators of TV) According to the Perceived Impact of TV on the Academic Performance of Their Children in the Three Localities

	Locality				
Academic Performance	*I*	*II*	*III*	*Total*	*%*
Deterioration	4 (4)	11 (15)	3 (3)	18 (22)	12.0 (14.7)
Improvement	1 (-)	– (-)	– (-)	1 (-)	0.7 (-)
No change	8 (16)	10 (7)	8 (16)	26 (39)	17.3 (26.0)
Uncertain	1 (-)	1 (2)	– (-)	2 (2)	1.3 (1.3)
Total non-regulators	14 (20)	22 (24)	11 (19)	47 (63)	31.3 (42.0)
Regulators	28 (27)	24 (23)	27 (26)	7.9 (76)	52.7 (50.7)
Not relevant	8 (3)	4 (3)	12 (5)	24 (11)	16.0 (7.3)
Total	50 (50)	50 (50)	50 (50)	150 (150)	100 (100)

In Locality II, 22 per cent of the CATV viewers and 30 per cent of the DD viewers felt that there was deterioration in the academic performance of their children while 20 per cent of the CATV viewers and 14 per cent of the DD viewers felt that there was no change in the academic performance of their children.

In Locality III, 6 per cent each among CATV and DD viewers felt that there was deterioration in the academic performance of their children while 16 per cent of the CATV viewers and 32 per cent of the DD viewers felt that there was no change in the academic performance of their children.

It was inferred that most non-regulators of TV felt that there was no change in the academic performance of their children. Also, more DD viewers felt that there was stability in the academic performance of their children. Hence, it may be inferred that respondents who regulated TV for their children, experienced a deterioration in the academic performance while non-regulators indicated stability in the academic performance of their children. This indicates that parental mediation in the TV viewing patterns of their children was found to be ineffective as majority of the regulators reported a deterioration in the academic performance of their children. These findings may be explained with the help of earlier studies discussed in the beginning of this chapter, signifying the ineffectiveness of regulation of TV viewing by parents (Mohr, 1976).

Table–6.6
Distribution of CATV Viewers and DD Viewers According to Whether TV Made an Impact on Extra-Curricular Activities, Dress Sense, Life Style, Music and Creativity Among Children in the Three Localities

	Locality				
Response	*I*	*II*	*III*	*Total*	*%*
Effected	33 (24)	36 (10)	39 (22)	108 (56)	72.0 (37.3)
Not effected	15 (25)	10 (39)	11 (28)	36 (92)	24.0 (61.4)
Not relevant	2 (1)	4 (1)	– (–)	6 (2)	4.0 (1.3)
Total	50 (50)	50 (50)	50 (50)	150 (150)	100 (100)

The analysis indicates that 72 per cent of the CATV viewers and 37.3 per cent of the DD viewers said that various types of activities like extra-curricular activities, dress sense, life style, taste of music, creativity etc. among children had been affected by TV. Further, 24 per cent of the CATV viewers and 61.4 per cent of the DD viewers said that such an impact was not observed among their children.

About 66 per cent of the CATV viewers and 48 per cent of the DD viewers in Locality I; 72 per cent of the CATV viewers and 20 per cent of the DD viewers in Locality II, 78 per cent of the CATV viewers and 44 per cent of the DD viewers said that various activities like extra-curricular activities, dress sense, life styles, music and creativity had been affected by TV. About 30 per cent of the CATV viewers and 50 per cent of the DD viewers in Locality I, 20 per cent of the CATV viewers and 78 per cent of the DD viewers in Locality II, 22 per cent of the CATV viewers and 56 per cent of the DD viewers in Locality III replied in the negative on the impact of TV on various activities.

It was inferred that majority of the CATV viewers felt that their children were affected by TV especially in their extra-curricular activities, dress sense, life style, taste of music and creativity. Majority of the CATV viewers of Locality III were affected by TV as compared to the other localities in this context and majority of the DD viewers of Locality III did not indicate any effect of TV on such activities. The study indicates that viewers of Satellite TV were affected both by the western media as well as in terms of decline in the outdoor activities of children. As there is a qualitative difference in the content of Satellite TV and Doordarshan, viewers of Satellite TV felt that extra-curricular activities, dress sense, taste of music and life style of their children had undergone a sea-change. Also, the western channels according to them bring in Indian homes the western value system and life style which were found to be influencing children especially among the viewers of Satellite TV. Further, the 24 hours transmission by the Satellite TV had curtailed the extra-curricular activities like sports, reading etc. It may be recalled that findings in Chapter 4 indicated that majority of the children due to an execssive TV viewing had given up outdoor activities as well as other constructive leisure activities. Hence, it is suggested that the western media is definitely making an impact on the children in Indian homes. The observation that TV had influenced the children on these dimensions did not differ much among the three localities.

Most respondents complained that their children had given up all outdoor activities, especially outdoor games and spent most of their leisure time in front of the TV. A small section of the respondents also said that their children had developed more interest in sports activities only to be watched on TV and not otherwise.

Regarding dress sense, most respondents said that their children wanted to dress up like the TV models and ape the western dress sense. They also said that their children pressurised them to purchase the western dresses, especially jeans and miniskirts even against their wishes.

Some respondents on the other hand reiterated that the western life style had widened the horizons of the youth and influenced their cultural outlook. There was a sea-change in the life styles of their children—their values were totally western and they had developed "cold" attitudes. They also lived in a fantasy world—a world of TV. Parents also complained that there was lack of original ideas and thus TV had blocked creative power of children. "All ideas were being picked up from TV," they asserted.

On the music scene, one parent said, "It is music on the lips and hips." Others said, VTV is lowering the taste of music and children are forgetting our culture." They also lamented that children were imitating vulgar dances and poses and they are all the time interested in western music, especially the heavy metal rock music. These responses clearly confirmed that TV viewing by children was hardly under any control of the parents. On the contrary, parents had got sick of the "idiot box" which had contributed significantly to the generation gap. Inspite of all these reactions, it is important to find out whether parents desired to change the TV viewing patterns of their children or not.

The results indicated that 44.7 per cent of the CATV viewers and 50 per cent of the DD viewers wanted their children to reduce the viewing duration while 40.7 per cent of the CATV viewers and 36.7 per cent of the DD viewers wanted their children to continue

Table–6.7
Distribution of CATV Viewers and DD Viewers According to their Desire to Change the Duration of Viewing TV of their Children in the Three Localities

Viewing Duration	*Locality* I	II	III	*Total*	%
Increase	– (-)	– (-)	– (-)	– (-)	–
Reduce	19 (26)	21 (24)	27 (25)	67 (75)	44.7 (50.0)
Continue the same	26 (13)	19 (23)	16 (19)	61 (55)	40.7 (36.7)
Abstain totally	3 (10)	6 (2)	7 (6)	16 (18)	10.6 (12.0)
No kids	2 (1)	4 (1)	– (-)	6 (2)	4.0 (1.3)
Total	50 (50)	50 (50)	50 (50)	150 (150)	100 (100)

the same duration of viewing. Only 10.6 per cent of the CATV viewers and 12 per cent of the DD viewers wanted their children to abstain from viewing TV totally. There were no respondents who wanted that their children should increase the viewing duration.

It was also observed that 38 per cent of the CATV viewers and 52 per cent of the DD viewers in Locality I; 42 per cent of the CATV viewers and 48 per cent of the DD viewers in Locality II; 54 per cent of the CATV viewers and 50 per cent of the DD viewers in Locality III, wanted their children to reduce the viewing duration.

Further, 52 per cent of the CATV viewers and 26 per cent of the DD viewers in Locality I; 38 per cent of the CATV viewers and 46 per cent of the DD viewers in Locality II; 32 per cent of the CATV viewers and 38 per cent of the DD viewers in Locality III, wanted their children to continue the same viewing duration.

Only about 6 per cent of CATV viewers and 20 per cent of DD viewers in Locality I; 12 per cent of the CATV viewers and 4 per cent of the DD viewers in Locality II; 14 per cent of the CATV viewers and 12 per cent of the DD viewers in Locality III wanted their children to abstain from viewing TV totally.

It was inferred that most respondents wanted their children to reduce the viewing duration of TV. The data indicated that even among DD viewers majority of the parents wanted that their children should reduce the duration of viewing TV. The data also suggests that majority of the respondents in Localities II and III wanted that their children should reduce the viewing duration while the respondents of Locality I (especially the CATV viewers) wanted their children to continue the same viewing duration. After being exposed to serious complaints of parents against viewing behaviour of children, it was astonishing to find that many of them were still desirous of continuing with the same viewing pattern. However, such a trend may be attributed to their inability to exercise any kind of control over their children. Parents stated that it was hardly a question of their choice, reducing the viewing hours of TV for their children was just not possible. What they were more worried about was that this duration should not increase further. The situation was therefore found to be out of the parents' control in most of the cases.

The analysis indicated that 36.7 per cent of CATV viewers and 40.7 per cent of DD viewers felt that TV had exercised a deep influence on the relationship between their children and their friends while 22 per cent CATV viewers and 34.7 per cent DD viewers did not think so. Further, 37.3 per cent of the CATV viewers and 23.3 per cent of the DD viewers said that they did not know if TV had any impact on the relationship between their children and their friends.

In Locality I, 36 per cent of CATV viewers and 28 per cent of DD viewers said that TV had definitely made an effect on the relationship between their children and their friends while 20 per cent of CATV viewers and 36 per cent of DD viewers replied in the negative. About 40 per cent of CATV viewers and 34 per cent of DD viewers said that they did not know if TV had an effect on the relationship between their children and their friends.

In Locality II, 42 per cent of CATV viewers and 40 per cent of DD viewers said that TV had an effect on the relationship between their children and their friends while 38 per cent of CATV viewers

Table–6.8
Distribution of CATV Viewers and DD Viewers According to Whether TV had Affected the Relationship Between the their Children and their Friends in the Three Localities

Response	*Locality* I	II	III	*Total*	%
Affected	18 (14)	21 (20)	16 (27)	16 (61)	36.7 (40.7)
Not affected	10 (18)	19 (14)	4 (20)	33 (52)	22.0 (34.7)
Don't know	20 (17)	6 (15)	30 (3)	56 (35)	37.3 (23.3)
No kids	2 (1)	4 (1)	– (-)	6 (2)	4.0 (1.3)
Total	50 (50)	50 (50)	50 (50)	150 (150)	100 (100)

and 28 per cent of DD viewers thought otherwise. About 12 per cent of CATV viewers and 30 per cent of DD viewers said that they did not know if TV had an effect on the relationship between their children and their friends.

In Locality III, 32 per cent of CATV viewers and 54 per cent of DD viewers felt that TV had an effect on the relationship between their children and their friends while 8 per cent CATV viewers and 40 per cent of DD viewers said that TV had no effect on the relationship between their children and their friends. About 60 per cent of CATV viewers and 6 per cent of DD viewers said that they did not know if TV had made an impact on the relationship between their children and their friends.

It was inferred that on the whole, more CATV viewers said they did not know whether TV had made an impact on the relationship between their children and their friends while more DD viewers felt that TV had made an effect on the relationship between their children and their friends. In Localities I and III more CATV viewers said they did not know if TV had an effect on the relationship between their children and their friends. While in Locality II, the reverse was observed. More DD viewers in Locality III felt that TV had made an impact on the relationship between their children and their friends while more CATV viewers in Localities I and II felt that TV had made an impact on the relationship between their children and their friends.

Majority of the respondents said that their children often disscussed only TV programmes with their friends. The respondents said that their children made telephonic conversation with their friends and the topic of discussion was—TV serials, films, songs and film stars. One respondent said, "Children are discussing everything that they see on TV with their friends. They hardly discuss their academics with their friends." It was also found that children discussed the vulgar scenes and obscenity exhibited on the western channels as well as Hindi channels with their friends. They questioned their friends about sex in many cases, responses revealed. One respondent disclosed, "I was shocked to overhear my son talking over the telephone with his friend, discussing as to what should be the ideal size of the female body." "It is terrible", he said. Another respondent said, "Children exchange nude photographs and pictures of girls among their friends." According to these parents, all this was happening due to TV alone. On the other hand, parents found that their children avoided their friends whenever they visited their homes. It was also observed that children asked their friends to watch TV with them or said that they were 'busy.' Children did not want to participate in outdoor activities, sports and games and instead preferred to watch TV programmes. It may be inferred here that on the one hand TV curtailed social interaction and social activities of chidlren, while on the other, the western channels provoked the curiosity of children towards sex which was the hot topic of discussion among their friends.

On the whole, about 64.7 per cent of CATV viewers and 66.7 per cent of DD viewers felt that in the behaviour of their children was different from the way they had behaved with their parents. 31.3 per cent of CATV viewers and 32 per cent of DD viewers however, felt otherwise.

About 70 per cent CATV viewers and 64 per cent DD viewers in Locality I; 54 per cent CATV viewers and 58 per cent DD viewers in Locality II; 70 per cent CATV viewers and 78 per cent DD viewers in

Table–6.9
Distribution of CATV Viewers and DD Viewers According to Whether there was any Difference Between the Behaviour of their Children and Their Own Behaviour as Children Towards their Parents in the Three Localities

Response	*Locality* I	II	III	*Total*	%
Yes	35 (32)	27 (29)	35 (39)	97 (100)	64.7 (66.7)
No	13 (17)	19 (20)	15 (11)	47 (48)	31.3 (32.0)
Not applicable	2 (1)	4 (1)	– (-)	6 (2)	4.0 (1.3)
Total	50 (50)	50 (50)	50 (50)	150 (150)	100 (100)

Locality III said that there was definitely a difference between the present behaviour of their children as compared to their behaviour towards their parents.

Majority of the respondents felt that their children behaved very differently as compared to their own behaviour towards their parents.

In Locality I, more CATV viewers than DD viewers and in Localities II and III more DD viewers than CATV viewers felt that there was a difference between the behaviour of their children and their own behaviour as children towards their parents.

Most parents expressed their anguish over the disobedience, disrespect, back answering, rude and rash behaviour of their children towards them while most of them recalled that they respected their parents and never spoke harsh or rude words in their presence. It is important to point out that majority of the children were influenced by the western media. Parents had indicated that their children were adopting the western value system as well as the western life style. Consequent to the exposure to western channels, according to respondents the behaviour of children among Satellite TV viewers (especially in Locality I) was disrespectful towards their parents as well the generation gap had

Table-6.10
Distribution of CATV Viewers and DD Viewers According to on Whether there was a Generation Gap Between Themselves and Their Children in the Three Localities

Response	Locality I	II	III	Total	%
There is a generation gap	11 (20)	21 (15)	31 (18)	31 (53)	42.0 (35.3)
There is no generation gap	37 (29)	25 (34)	19 (32)	81 (95)	54.0 (63.4)
Not applicable	2 (1)	4 (1)	- (-)	6 (2)	4.0 (1.3)
Total	50 (50)	50 (50)	50 (50)	150 (150)	100 (100)

widened between parents and children. Whether TV has been generating common issues for discussion between parents and children—thus bridging the communication gap, or it has widened it, was a pertinent question to be taken up at this juncture. Hence, the respondents were asked whether they thought TV viewing by their children had increased the generation gap between them and their children or not. They were first asked whether they perceived any such gap and if yes, whether they attributed it to television.

On the whole, 42 per cent of the CATV viewers and 35.3 per cent DD viewers admitted that there was a generation gap between them and their children while 54 per cent CATV viewers and 63.4 per DD viewers felt otherwise.

About 22 per cent CATV viewers and 40 per cent DD viewers in Locality I; 42 per cent CATV viewers and 30 per cent DD viewers in Locality II and 62 per cent CATV viewers and 36 per cent DD viewers felt that there was a generation gap between them and their children. About 74 per cent of CATV viewers and 58 per cent DD viewers in Locality I; 50 per cent CATV viewers and 68 per cent DD viewers in Locality II and 38 per cent CATV viewers and 64 per cent DD viewers felt that there was no generation gap between them and their children.

It was inferred that a majority of the respondents felt that there was no generation gap between them and their children. Among those who said that there was a generation gap between them and their children, majority were CATV viewers. It was also inferred that majority of the CATV viewers in Locality III and the DD viewers in Locality I felt there was a generation gap between them and their children. Earlier responses especially in the context of the influence of western channels of Satellite TV had indicated that parents were agitated about the western value system and life style creeping into Indian homes. At the same time, majority of the respondents indicated that there was no generation gap between parents and children. The responses seemed inconsistent as previous data indicates that parents were extremely concerned about the adoption of different value system and life style by their children.

Among those responsents who said that there was a generation gap between them and their children, about 36.7 per cent of the CATV viewers and 32 per cent of the DD viewers attributed this to TV. About 63.3 per cent of the CATV viewers and 68 per cent of the DD viewers either felt that there was no generation gap between them and their children or they attributed the generation gap to other factors.

About 18 per cent of the CATV viewers and 34 per cent of DD viewers in Locality I, 36 per cent CATV viewers and 26 per cent DD viewers in Locality II and 56 per cent CATV viewers and 36 per cent

Table–6.11
Distribution of CATV Viewers and DD Viewers (Among those who Felt there was a Generation Gap Between Themselves and Their Children) According to Whether they Attributed the Generation Gap to TV in the Three Localities

	Locality				
Response	*I*	*II*	*III*	*Total*	*%*
Generation gap due to TV	9 (17)	18 (13)	28 (18)	55 (48)	36.7 (32.0)
Others	41 (33)	32 (37)	22 (32)	95 (102)	63.3 (68.0)
Total	50 (50)	50 (50)	50 (50)	150 (150)	100 (100)

DD viewers in Locality III attributed the generation gap between them and their children to television.

Most respondents did not attribute the growing generation gap to TV. Most of them either felt that there was no generation gap between them and their children or commented that generation gap was a universal phenomenon and could not be attributed to TV only. Majority of the DD viewers in Locality I and majority of the CATV viewers in Locality III attributed the generation gap to TV. Also, more CATV viewers than DD viewers attributed the generation gap to TV. From this, it can be inferred that Satellite TV contributed in widening the generation gap between parents and children. The viewers of Doordarshan were by and large exposed to the indigeneous culture while viewers of Satellite TV were increasingly being exposed to the alien culture. The study suggested that viewers of Cable TV attributed the generation gap to television as there was a qualitative difference in the programmes of Satellite TV and Doordarshan. The programmes of Satellite TV are targeted towards the urban masses while Doordarshan programmes are usually oriented towards a diverse audience due to the vast heterogeneity in the Indian population.

On the whole, about 66 per cent of the DD viewers felt that if they subscribed to CATV it would change their life style, while 31.3 per cent of them said that it would not change their life style. About 2.7 per cent of the DD viewers said that they had not given a thought to such an idea.

Table–6.12
Distribution of DD Viewers According to Whether Subscription to CATV would Change their Life Style in the Three Localities

	Locality				
Response	*I*	*II*	*III*	*Total*	*%*
CATV would change life style	40	23	36	99	66
CATV would not change life style	7	26	14	47	31.3
Haven't thought about it	3	1	-	4	2.7
Total	50	50	50	150	100

Further, 80 per cent of the DD viewers in Locality I; 46 per cent in Locality II and 72 per cent in Locality III felt that subscription to CATV would change their life style while 14 per cent in Locality I, 52 per cent in Locality II and 28 per cent in Locality III felt otherwise.

The results indicate that a majority of the DD viewers felt that subscription to CATV would change their life style. Further, majority of the DD viewers in Locality I felt that subscription to CATV would change their life style. Also, majority of the DD viewers in Locality II felt that there would be no change in their life style by subscribing to CATV, as compared to other localities. We had seen in Chapter 3 that majority of the DD viewers of Locality II had earlier been viewers of Cable TV. Therefore, the study suggests that respondents who had earlier been subscribers to CATV felt that their life styles would not change if they subscribed to CATV, but their childrens' studies would definitely be affected.

Data also indicates that among the DD viewers about 31.3 per cent said that subscription to CATV would affect the family interaction patterns as well as interaction with their children while 20 per cent said that social participation at the informal level including family interaction patterns and interaction patterns with children would be affected. Further, 5.3 per cent felt that subscription to CATV would affect social participation at the informal level while only 0.7 per cent felt that it would affect social participation at the formal level. About 8.7 per cent said it would affect interaction with their children only, while 34 per cent either said that it would not affect their social participation at all or they had not given a thought to it.

In Locality I, 40 per cent of the respondent who felt that subscription to CATV will affect them, said that it would affect the family interaction patterns, while 16 per cent said that it would affect interaction with their children only. About 24 per cent said that it would affect social participation both at the informal level as well as family interaction patterns.

In Locality II, 14 per cent said that it would affect social participation at the informal level while 22 per cent said that it would affect family interation patterns. Only 6 per cent said that it

Table-6.13
Distribution of DD Viewers According to the Type of Effect of TV on Social Participation in the Three Localities

Social Participation Level	*Locality* I	II	III	*Total*	%
Formal	-	1	-	1	0.7
Informal	-	7	1	8	5.3
Interaction with children only	8	1	4	13	8.7
Family interaction	20	11	16	47	31.3
Informal and family interaction	12	3	15	30	20.0
No effect/thought	10	27	14	51	34.0
Total	50	50	50	150	100

would affect social participation at the informal level as well as family interaction patterns.

In Locality III, 32 per cent said that it would affect family interaction patterns while 30 per cent said it would affect social participation at the informal level as well as family interaction patterns. Further, 8 per cent indicated that it would affect their interaction with their children only.

It is significant to note that less than half of our respondents i.e., 31.3 per cent felt that if they subscribed to CATV, their family interaction patterns would be affected. In all the three localities the same trend was observed. It was inferred in Chapter 4, that Cable TV had exercised its impact on family interaction patterns. It may be suggested that Cable TV did not have a uniform effect on all the dimensions of social participation. As discussed in Chapter 5 that while Satellite TV exercised no effect on formal participation, it had definitely influenced informal participation among the respondents of Localities I and II. The informal participation of the respondents of Locality III were characterized by strong neighbourhood relations and it was observed that Cable TV had restricted neighbourhood relations especially in Locality III.

Therefore, two segments – *(i)* family interaction patterns and *(ii)* neighbourhood relations were found to be greatly affected by Satellite TV. Data in Table 6.13 also indicates that DD viewers felt that family interaction patterns would be affected with subscription to CATV. These findings substantiate the earlier findings of Chapter 4 and Chapter 5.

Data indicates that 37.3 per cent of the DD viewers said that they were comfortable while watching TV with their family members while 62.7 per cent of the DD viewers said that they were uncomfortable while watching TV with their family members.

Further, 56 per cent of the DD viewers in Locality I; 30 per cent in Locality II and 26 per cent in Locality III said that they were comfortable while watching TV with their family members while 44 per cent in Locality I; 70 per cent in Locality II and 74 per cent in Locality III were uncomfortable while watching TV with their family members.

It was inferred that on the whole a majority of the DD viewers felt uncomfortable while watching TV with family members while locality-wise, majority of the respondents in Locality III were uncomfortable while watching TV with the family members. More respondents in Locality I said that they were comfortable while watching TV with family members as compared to respondents in other localities.

The responsents who said that they were comfortable watching DD programmes with their families remarked that there was nothing obscene on DD as compared to CATV. One respondent said, "DD

Table–6.14
Distribution of DD Viewers According to Whether they Felt Comfortable Watching TV Programmes with their Family in the Three Localities

	Locality				
Response	*I*	*II*	*III*	*Total*	*%*
Feel Comfortable	28	15	13	56	37.3
Feel Uncomfortable	22	35	37	94	62.7
Total	50	50	50	150	100

is clean." Another pointed out, "Nothing is objectionable on DD." Another said, "There is nothing obscene on DD."

Some others said that the Indian society is modern enough not to mind a little of vulgarity and obscenity projected on DD. One respondent from Locality III said, "One should not mind vulgarity and obscenity as it is a part of real life."

A few respondents said that they regulated and restricted the watching of TV by their children so they felt quite comfortable while watching DD. Some parents said that their children did not usually sit with them to watch TV.

One parent remarked, "There is no question of feeling uncomfortable, because children should better get aware of the realities of life from television and not from other sources."

Among those who said that they were uncomfortable watching DD programmes with their families opined that obscenity, vulgarity and love scenes embarassed them and they felt disturbed when their children watched those programmes in their company. There were different reactions of the respondents when they were watching obscene or vulgar scenes based on either songs or films. Some said that when the love scenes appeared, they began to think what would be going on in their children's mind which was quite perturbing. Others said that they tried to divert the attention of their children by speaking loudly, while some others added that they switched off the TV set. In some other families, the children left the TV room and reappeared after the love scenes disappeared. One parent said, "I feel like breaking the TV set when my children watch vulgar, obscene or love scenes."

Data indicates that 68.7 per cent of the CATV viewers felt that their life style would be different if they did not have cable connections while 30.7 per cent of the CATV viewers felt otherwise. Only 0.6 per cent of the CATV viewers said that they did not know if their life style would be different with non-subscription to CATV.

About 96 per cent of CATV viewers in Locality I, 40 per cent in Locality II and 70 per cent in Locality III felt that their life style would have been different had they not subscribed to cable connections. Also, 4 per cent of the CATV viewers in Locality I, 60 per cent in Locality II and 28 per cent in Locality III felt otherwise.

Table–6.15
Distribution of CATV Viewers According to Whether they Felt that Their Life Style would be Different if they did not Subscribe to CATV in the Three Localities

	Locality				
Response	*I*	*II*	*III*	*Total*	*%*
Yes	48	20	35	103	68.7
No	2	30	14	46	30.7
Do not know	–	–	1	1	0.6
Total	50	50	50	150	100

It was inferred that majority of the CATV viewers felt that their life style would be different if they had not taken cable connections. Also, majority of the CATV viewers in Locality I felt that their life style would have been different had they not had cable connections whereas majority of the CATV viewers in Locality II felt that if they did not have cable connections, there would not be any change in their life style.

The respondents who said that their life style would be different without CATV pointed out that there would be more conversations at home especially between the spouses and between parents and children. Most respondents felt that without Cable TV, there would be greater intimacy between spouses and parent-children, which was diminishing day-by-day.

One respondent said, "We would be more intimate and there would be unity in the family." "Family ties have weakened now, he further added. Some parents said that atleast their children would study and listen to their advice.

On the other hand, some others felt that if CATV had not come into their homes, there would be more social activity both indoors and outdoors. A few said that without CATV, they would be absolutely and extremely bored and there would be no entertainment at the home front. One respondent added, "CATV is the best way to pass time and the least expensive entertainment."

A few respondents said that without CATV their life would be different on tremendous dimensions. They would have been less aware, less modern, less advanced and less informed with less exposure had they not subscribed to CATV. One respondent said, "CATV is a boon, without it life would have been miserable."

It was observed throughout that Cable TV had certainly been restricting the physical as well as social interaction among family members, substantiating our findings in Chapter 5. On the one hand, respondents felt that the diminishing levels of intimacy between family members would drastically improve with the withdrawal of Satellite TV from their homes. Majority of the respondents felt that social activity as well as interpersonal and intra-familial ties would improve in the absence of CATV. On the other hand, some respondents felt that CATV had become indispensable and their level of awareness would eventually decline without Cable TV. It was a boon for some while it was an evil for some others. The study suggested that Satellite TV had been perceived both as a positive as well as negative factor by the respondents.

The study revealed that on the whole, 56.7 per cent of the CATV viewers were uncomfortable and 43.3 per cent were comfortable while watching Hindi channels with their family members. In Locality I, 40 per cent; in Locality II, 24 per cent and in Locality III, 26 per cent were comfortable while watching Hindi channels with while their family members. Further, in Locality I, 20 per cent; in Locality II, 76 per cent and in Locality III, 34 per cent were uncomfortable while watching Hindi channels with their family members.

Table-6.16
Distribution of CATV Viewers According to Whether they Felt Comfortable While Watching Hindi Channels with their Family Members in the Three Localities

Locality Response	*Locality I*	*Locality II*	*Locality III*	*Total*	*%*
Feel comfortable	40	12	13	65	43.3
Feel uncomfortable	10	38	37	85	56.7
Total	50	50	50	150	100

The respondents who said that they felt comfortable while watching Hindi channels pointed out that there was not much obscenity and vulgarity on Hindi channels. One respondents said, "We have now got used to the obscenity and vulgarity of the Hindi channels." A few respondents said that there was nothing objectionable on Hindi channels and the their families had an open attitude. One respondent said, "There is a gradual change in the attitudes and the open acceptance of sex is a reality and we are moving into this phase now."

It is important to note here that a majority of the respondents who said they felt comfortable watching television with their families, were from Locality I, where there were multiple TV sets in the house. We have already seen in earlier discussion that different family units, i.e., parents, children, sometimes individuals, were watching TV separately. Hence, there was hardly any need to feel uncomfortable. Some respondents said that they generally selected specific programmes for family viewing, especially for their children.

Among those respondents who said that they were uncomfortable while watching Hindi channels said that the songs of Hindi films were embarrassing as they were filled with vulgar movements. "Intimate scenes are not part of our culture and these should be banned from our media", commented one respondent. Some respondents said that the age differences in family caused embarrassing and uncomfortable moments at home while viewing TV. Some said that advertisements on sanitary napkins and family planning control methods caused extensive embarrassment.

Some respondents said that either they or their children left the TV room on some pretext or the other when vulgar or obscene scenes appeared on TV. Some parents changed the channel with the remote control device and switched back to the same channel after the objectionable scenes were over. Some others switched off the TV set. It was quite astonishing to know that one parent (from Locality II) would ask his children to shut off their eyes and then again tell them to open their eyes when the intimate scenes disappeared from the screen.

The researcher further questioned the respondents on whether they felt comfortable while watching western channels with their families.

Table-6.17
Distribution of CATV Viewers According to Whether they Felt Comfortable While Watching Western Channels with their Family Members in the Three Localities

Response	*Locality* I	II	III	*Total*	*%*
Feel comfortable	17	1	-	18	12.0
Feel uncomfortable	25	14	4	43	28.7
Don't watch Western channels	8	35	46	89	59.3
Total	50	50	50	150	100

The data showed that on the whole, only 12 per cent of the CATV respondents felt comfortable while watching western channels with their family members while 28.7 per cent felt uncomfortable while watching western channels with their family members. About 59.3 per cent of the CATV viewers revealed that they did not watch western channels.

In Locality I, 34 per cent felt comfortable; 50 per cent felt uncomfortable and 16 per cent did not watch western channels. In Locality II, 2 per cent were comfortable; 28 per cent felt uncomfortable and 70 per cent did not watch western channels. In Locality III, 8 per cent felt uncomfortable and 92 per cent did not watch western channels.

It was inferred that majority of the CATV viewers were uncomfortable while watching western channels with their family members. It was also inferred that majority of the respondents of Locality I were comfortable while watching western channels with their family members. It may again be recalled that there were fewer moments when the whole family sat together to view TV in Locality I. Majority of the respondents of Localities II and III were uncomfortable while watching western channels with their family members.

There were very few families among viewers of CATV, who were comfortable while watching western channels with all members of the family. One respondent said, "Everybody is so advanced and has enough knowledge about everything and therefore there is no reason to feel uncomfortable or embarrassed." Some others said that their families were modern in their outlook and had a healthy atmosphere at home so they were comfortable with all programmes on TV. One respondent remarked, "We are very free with our children and there is no generation gap in our family and neither are we narrow minded." Another respondent said, "Sex and intimacy is not part of western culture alone, it is a reality of life, and so it is a part of our culture." "There is no need for embarrassment," he further added.

Among those who felt uncomfortable while watching western channels with their families said that bed scenes, kissing, vulgarity, obscenity, love scenes and intimate scenes caused extensive embarrassment. One respondent said," There is an over exposure of sex in western channels." Another said, "Sex in privacy is part of Indian culture while sex in open is part of western culture." Some respondents said that they did not mind watching western channels with their spouse, but it was not in good taste to watch it with children.

One respondent said, "We feel embarrassed, upset, and disturbed but we are not in a position to ask our children to get out of the room." Some parents said that they changed the channel immediately when 'such' scenes appeared. It was concluded that on the whole, whether it was the Hindi channels or the western channels of Satellite TV, viewers were uncomfortable due to the extensive stress on sex, vulgarity and obscenity on these channels. The study suggested that Satellite TV channels were not meant for family viewing.

The analysis indicated that on the whole, only 13.3 per cent of the CATV viewers and 2.7 per cent of the DD viewers felt that CATV was doing good to our children as well as youth while about 57.3 per cent of the CATV viewers and 66 per cent of the DD viewers felt CATV was doing bad for the children. Also, 24 per cent of the CATV viewers and 8 per cent of the DD viewers felt that CATV was doing both good as well as bad for the children while 5.4 per cent of the CATV viewers and 23.3 per cent of the DD viewers felt that they were unable to give their views to this question.

Table–6.18
Distribution of CATV Viewers and DD Viewers According to Whether CATV was doing Good/Bad to our Children and Youth in the Three Localities

Response	*Locality* I	II	III	*Total*	*%*
Good	9 (-)	3 (1)	8 (3)	20 (4)	13.3 (2.7)
Bad	21 (38)	33 (33)	32 (28)	86 (99)	57.3 (66.0)
Both good and bad	20 (7)	10 (4)	6 (1)	36 (12)	24.0 (8.0)
No comments	- (5)	4 (12)	4 (18)	8 (35)	5.4 (23.3)
Total	50 (50)	50 (50)	50 (50)	150 (150)	100 (100)

The respondents who felt that CATV was good for children, said that if there is controlled and restricted viewing, CATV can produce excellent youth for the country. They identified that CATV makes them have a broader outlook to life and educate them in all respects. One respondent added," CATV is good because you have to keep pace with the world." Another respondent said, "CATV has come as a blessing to our country. We are getting a broader minded society in the making." Another claimed, "Openness and frankness is increasing in families and between friends."

Most respondents said that CATV gives a good exposure to educative programmes, especially scientific programmes. One respondent said, "If we Indians want to compete in the international world, then we have to keep pace with the western world and this can happen through the easiest medium—CATV."

There was an agreement among most respondents that CATV was creating more awareness among children and thereby more conscious children and youth were being produced. They also remarked that CATV was modernizing their children and increasing the knowledge of the youth.

One respondent added, "CATV is very good, but the Indian thinking is not westernized and the Indian society cannot accept the western culture at this juncture." Another respondent said, "If CATV is watched with discretion it can bring positive changes in the family relationships and improve national character." Some others felt that CATV was good entertainment at home. One respondent said," CATV relaxes all the tensions of an individual." Another respondent said," CATV is good because it confines children to their homes."

Some parents felt that CATV is providing good themes in their programmes and delivering good messages for children and youth. The BBC channel was appreciated by most parents for improving and increasing the knowledge of the youth. One respondent added," CATV is good because it not only improves your general knowledge but it adds to personality development."

A few pointed out that CATV is good recreation for the ladies during times when the husband is away from home. They also claimed that CATV improves life style as one gets aware of a wide range of things. One respondent said, "CATV is leading to globalization. Among those respondents who termed CATV as bad for the children and youth emphasized on various negative aspects of the Satellite channels. These negative aspects were categorised so as to get a clear picture of how the respondents perceived the impact of CATV."

Effect of CATV on Childrens' Studies and Health

The most common complaint from parents was that CATV is a hindrance to the academics and career of children. They pointed out that CATV was a colossal waste of time besides curtailing the outdoor and social activities of children. One parent remarked, "CATV is stopping the physical growth of children." "There is no development of children either physically or mentally," claimed a few others. Besides, this, most parents were concerned about the health and eyesight of their children. "Lack of exercise and outdoor activities have contributed to the deterioration in the health of children", parents added.

Most respondents, especially from Ram Darbar, i.e., Locality III were concerned that they were spending their hard earned money on their childrens' studies but their children did not want to attend school and watched CATV at their friends' homes. Some added, "Children are not willing to go to school regularly and they fail in academics." "Careers are being destroyed," parents added.

Another aspect was that children did not pay any attention to food while eating, nor do they eat on the dining table."

Most parents cribbed, "These days children do not know anything pertaining to their studies but know which song is on the top." One mother said, "There is no serial on ZEE TV which does not have an illegitimate child or in which there is no affair between a girl and boy and extra-marital and pre-marital affairs. So how can be expect our children to learn anything good from CATV?" "CATV has created a hysteria. Children pick up those dance numbers, their life style, speaking style and dress sense and to which limit can be reach in controlling them?" questioned a respondent. "My children are dancing all the time with the VTV channel," disclosed a respondent.

There was a general agreement among some respondents that CATV had no informational and educational value. Children watch films all day long with round-the-clock telecast," said a few others. "The increasing number of channels on CATV are ruining the careers of the children as they have no time for their studies", added a parent.

Effect of CATV on the Youth

Most parents who had teenaged children were paranoid with the effect of CATV. Some said that the future of India is destroyed as CATV is promoting criminal tendencies, violence and rash behaviour of the youth. One parent added, "To finish or kill any country, one has to finish the youth of that country. The youth of our country being misled by western countries and our country is finished." Parents also expressed concern over the values projected on the western channels. They said, "The values projected on western channels are different from the Indian value system and now with CATV we are giving them a choice of choosing certain patterns of life. As the mind is tender and children especially teenagers are immature who get infatuated easily, a wrong path and direction is chosen. This is matter of grave concern. Our children are identifying themselves with the stars on TV."

Most parents felt that the youth had become directionless, they have no aim in life, no interest in building a career for themselves and they were neither interested in studying for their regular exams. One mother said, "My son is only squandering money. All that they do is to impress girls. They remove silencers from their motor bikes and horn when girls pass by. We parents are sandwiched like *Kal Aj aur Kal*. "This is the prime effect of CATV," she added.

Another respondent said, "We parents have to search the rooms of our children and take out nude photographs and pictures of girls. We burn them and this has become intolerable now." Another respondent said that their children especially boys are using a lot of perfumes, put their collars up and try to impress girls. "They are desperate to have pre-marital affairs," claimed another respondent. "They leave their homes to attend college but not even 50 per cent of the lectures are attended", added another respondent.

Parents expressed that the brain and mind of the youth are getting polluted. They also remarked that the youth are getting addicted to drugs and cigarettes. One respondent said, "CATV is an addiction. Children cannot resist watching these censored films and they tend to develop rash and violent behaviour. Films like *Insaaf Ka Tarazoo* are not meant for family viewing." "There are aggressions in the temperament of the youth due to CATV and we are producing unpatriotic youth", added another parent.

Vulgarity and Obscenity

One of most disturbing elements seemed to be vulgarity and obscenity projected on CATV. Most respondents were vehemently against the depiction of sex, nudity, lip kissing, love scenes and bed scenes. The respondents felt that western programmes are not meant for family viewing and that their children are getting exposed to wrong things at an early age. This in turn was corrupting the tender minds of young children. One respondent said, "Sex, intimacy and lip kissing will come on the roads and India will become America in a few years from now."

Respondents ridiculed the VTV channel saying that it had sexual tendencies. Others claimed that vulgarity and obscenity are not in tune with the Indian culture. One respondent said, "Vulgarity and obscenity are not meant for Indians as the Indian mentality is full of hypocrisy." Some parents complained that the new generation is exposed to the wrong things at a young age via CATV. One parent remarked, "There is no curtain now between a brother and sister as well as a mother and son. There is open sex on CATV programmes."

As children seemed to be the most effected segment by obscenity and vulgarity on CATV, the respondents were extremely worried about the negative impact of the media. A lady of the household who was also a nursery school teacher related an incident where children of a nursery class of the opposite sex indulged into lip kissing. "This is the effect of CATV", she said. One respondent said, "*Kaliyug* has finally come. Dresses of our Indian heroines are atrocious and the angles from which they display their body are vulgar.". They labelled the CATV for having blue film tendency. The present generation is being explosed to vulgarity and free sex which is having an adverse effect according to a number of respondents. A parent remarked, "If we do not have a CATV connection, people mock at us. It has become a status symbol. We have to accept obscenity and vulgarity."

Effect of the Western Culture Projected on CATV on the Children and Youth

The impact of the western culture was observed on various dimensions. The misbehaviour of children, the increasing generation gap between parents and children, pre-marital relations were some of the reasons for worry by parents.

Parents agreed that their children were rude, disobedient and showed disrespect to elders. Children had become bold and questioned the parents for every little advice given to them. Parents also complained that children wanted more freedom to go to discotheques, join a late night party at their friends' homes which perturbed them. "Indians cannot accept westernization and therefore they should keep CATV away", said a respondent.

Parents also pointed out that children threaten their parents that they would run away from their homes and in some cases they had done it. They also added that children were losing morality, having pre-marital relations and indulging in sexual activities. The awareness of sex through CATV was a grave cause for concern by parents. They said that the over exposure of sexual relations on CATV programmes was leading children to practise them in reality. In a few other cases, parents especially from Localities II and III said that the advertisements on sanitary napkins and family control methods caused much embarrassment as their children asked too many odd questions. One respondent said, "Parents do not have time for children and children don't have time for parents. It's a changing world." "CATV is an evil", he added. CATV is leading to defiance and disobedience to parents. "Girls of our country being affected the most in our country."

Suggestions

Most parents suggested that some restrictions should be imposed on the CATV programmes. Some were of the opinion that CATV should be banned. One parent added, "CATV should be rescheduled to suit children and it should be family oriented and educative."

Some agreed that CATV telecast hours should be limited while some others wanted the VTV should be banned. Some preferred that only restricted transmission be allowed censoring nude scenes. Other respondents recommended that adult films should be avoided while a few suggested that parents should regulate the viewing of their children. Emphasis on educative programmes was suggested by some parents. One respondent said, "Rental charges of CATV should be reduced." A respondent of Locality II said, "We do not have enough food to eat but be have to subscribe to CATV to make our children happy." "CATV is an addiction", claimed most respondents.

It was inferred that majority of the respondents felt that TV had negative aspects as well as positive aspects. The dimensions of negative as well as positive aspects have already been discussed in detail. Among those who said that TV was good, stressed that the educative and scientific programmes had high informational value. On the other hand, the negative effects pointed towards on over dose of sex, vulgarity and obscenity on western channels. However, the study suggested that the impact of the western media on children was a matter of concern among majority of the respondents. Satellite TV was criticised extensively for vulgarity, obscenity, nudity, intimate love scenes, lip kissing, open sex as well as bed scenes. Another important aspect was the studies of children as majority of the respondents felt that the careers of their children were being destroyed. On the other hand, Satellite TV was favoured by some respondents for an increase in the level of awareness, knowledge, exposure to educative and scientific programmes, a cheap means of round-the-clock entertainment at home etc.

However, some of the major inferences drawn in this chapter are:

1. Inspite of parental-mediation in the TV viewing patterns of children, there was a deterioration in the academic performance of children. Viewers of Satellite TV observed that extra-curricular activities were restricted while dress sense, life styles, taste of music, creative power etc., of children were influenced by the western media. Respondents wanted to decrease the viewing duration of their children and the study revealed that regulation of TV was hardly in the control of parents.
2. The viewers of Doordarshan felt that subscription to Satellite TV would affect family interaction patterns—as also suggested in Chapter 4. Satellite TV had weakened inter-familial and intra-familial relationships as well as affected their childrens' studies, for majority of the respondents.
3. Doordarshan viewers on the one hand, pointed out that the programmes on DD were 'clean' while on the other, too many advertisements, advertisements on sanitary napkins and family control methods were not appreciated.
4. Satellite TV was criticised as well as appreciated by majority of the viewers. The study suggested that Satellite TV had both positive as well as negative points. While Cable TV was criticised for the impact of western culture and value system it was appreciated for its educative and informative content.
5. Another inference drawn was that respondents were uncomfortable while watching the western channels with family members especially with children. The study revealed that western channels were not meant for family viewing. Programmes/serials of Satellite TV were ridiculed by viewers as they catered to the urban upper strata of society. These serials depicted pre-marital and extra-marital affairs

as well as projection of sex in a vulgar and obscene manner. The western life style, value system and music were matter of grave concern for parents. Specifically, parents were concerned about the impact of Satellite TV on the studies of children, the increasing misbehaviour, disrespect and rude behaviour of children, and the over exposure of sex on the western channels. However, Satellite TV was indispensable and it had become a member of the family.

7
Inferences and Conclusions

The impact of television has been one of the most frequently debated social issues in India especially after the advent of Satellite TV. No major research has been carried out in the recent years in the country especially on the effects of Satellite TV on social participation. The present study is an endeavour to illustrate the impact of Satellite television on various dimensions of social participation. Initially, this study was designed to undertake a comparative study of Cable TV viewers and non-viewers. The assumption was that TV viewing pre-supposes a certain level of physical immobility of the viewers as they would spend most of their time watching TV programmes. This tendency is expected to curtail social participation of the viewers in a significant manner. Viewers would consequently restrict their outdoor activities, interaction with relatives, friends and neighbours as well as interaction within the family, as they are glued to their TV sets. Further, the round-the-clock entertainment through Satellite TV is expected to isolate individuals from the outside world as well as from their own families. Instead of performing a 'socializing' function, it isolates viewers both physically and socially. The present study is an effort to test this hypothesis. Due to paucity of studies on these issues, the study intended to compare the patterns of social participation among subscribers of Cable TV and others who do not have it. But, during the pilot study it was found that it was not possible to identify any 'non-viewers' since TV had become an essential part of almost every household. Therefore, a comparative study was designed between Cable viewers on the one hand, and the Doordarshan viewers on the other. Such a comparison was justified because at the time the study was conducted, i.e. 1994,

Doordarshan had only two channels (DDI and DDII) with limited hours of telecast in each of the sessions – morning, afternoon and evening. On the other hand, the Satellite TV was offering round-the-clock entertainment programmes. Another important factor in addition to the difference in quantity was the qualitative difference in the content between the two kinds of viewership, especially with a greater content of western culture on Satellite TV. The programmes, themes and life styles projected on western channels were catering to the urban upper strata of society while the Doordarshan programmes were insipid and lack lustre in 'quality' (Sinha, 1996). Hence, in the backdrop of such a situation, it was meaningful to study the impact of Satellite TV on patterns of social participation among viewers.

Previous studies have indicated that patterns of social participation are not uniform among urban-dwellers. The heterogeneity within city-dwellers and the internal variations in terms of age, sex, socio-economic status etc. are important variables to be considered in such a study. For this, three different socio-economic groups i.e. upper, middle and low socio-economic groups, were identified to see the variations in the patterns of social participation among the city-dwellers. Whether the patterns of social participation are uniform among the three different socio-economic groups and whether Cable TV exercises a uniform effect on the patterns of social participation i.e., formal and informal participation within and across families in the three different socio-economic groups, were the issues under focus in this study.

Specifically, the study probed into the demographic profile, the selection of TV programmes, social participation at the formal and informal levels as well as the family interaction patterns and the impact of the western media on children.

The universe of the study comprised of the residents of Chandigarh in three different socio-economic groups. As the housing pattern of Chandigarh is structured on the basis of socio-economic status, three sectors i.e., Sector 9, Sector 22 and Ram Darbar were initally selected. But, during the pilot study it was noticed that there was no Cable operator in Sector 9 and the residents of this sector had either subscribed to Cable TV from the neighbouring sectors or had installed their own dish antennaes. Due to heavy installation charges, most residents were without cable connections. Hence, the researcher also included the two kanal and/or bigger houses of Sector 8 and Sector 18 where there were cable operators. Therefore, the universe for this study comprised of population residing in 2 kanal and/or bigger houses of Sector 8, Sector 9 and Sector 18, which is respresentative of the upper socio-economic group and Sector 22 and Industrial Area B i.e., Ram Darbar which are representative of the middle and low socio-economic groups respectively. These households were stratified on the basis of CATV viewers and DD viewers according to information obtained from cable operators as well as the identification of households with privately owned dish antennaes. The three localities, i.e., high middle and low have been designated in the present study as Localities I, II and III respectively.

In the final stage, 100 households from each of these three socio-economic groups were selected according to the method of systematic random sampling with an equal proportion of CATV viewers and DD viewers. Our sample therefore comprised of 300 households in all. An interview schedule was used to elicit information from the heads of households.

The following hypotheses were drawn for the study:

1. Formal participation has a positive association with income, education and occupation.
2. Viewing Cable TV (with longer duration and variety of channels) would reduce intra-family communication.
3. Viewing Cable TV (within a household) would have the most profound effect on children reflected through both academic and non-academic dimensions.
4. The various socio-economic groups would differ profoundly in terms of the perceived effects of Cable TV on social participation.

In view of the major objectives and the above assumptions, the study attempted to describe the heterogeneity within and between the three neighbourhoods as well as the Cable TV viewers and DD viewers. The demographic profile relating to age, socio-economic status, religion, caste, type of ownership of house, place of origin of respondents revealed that there were considerable variations within the three socio-economic groups as well as between Cable TV viewers and DD viewers. Specifically, the study revealed that majority of the respondents belonged to the three middle–aged categories i.e., 30 years to 59 years – majority of these belonged to the 40-49 years age group category. The mean age in Locality I was the highest while it was the lowest in Locality III. Also, the mean age of the CATV viewers was less than DD viewers in all the three localities. It was inferred that Cable TV viewers were younger than the DD viewers. Further, the study indicated that the respondents of Locality III were younger in age as compared to respondents of the other two localities. Majority of the respondents had a family income of Rs. 5001-10000. The mean income of the respondents in Locality I was highest while it was the lowest in Locality III, which confirmed the selection of the three localities as high, middle and low in terms of economic criterion. The mean income of Cable TV viewers and DD viewers was the same in Locality I while the mean income among the Cable TV viewers was higher than the DD viewers in Localities II and III. This signified that income was not a criterion for subscription to Cable TV among the respondents of Locality I.

The educational qualifications of the respondents further revealed that majority were graduates. It was also observed that while majority of the respondents in Localities I and II were graduates, the respondents of Locality III had their education qualification below matric level. There were no considerable differences in educational qualifications between the Cable TV viewers and DD viewers in all the three localities. The study also suggested that majority of the respondents belonged to the occupational prestige category II (for details of occupational prestige, see Appendix B). It was further indicated by the study that respondents in Locality I belonged to occupations with a higher occupational prestige than the respondents of Localities II and III. The occupational prestige was the lowest among respondents of Locality III. The study also showed that on the one hand none of the respondents in Locality I had lower levels of occupational prestige while on the other hand, there were no respondents in Locality III who had a high levels of occupational prestige. This indicates that the three localities not only differed distinctively in terms of occupational status but there is an association between occupational structures and economic status of respondents. The data also indicated that majority of both the CATV viewers and the DD viewers belonged to occupational prestige Category II. The study revealed that the CATV viewers had a higher occupational status than the

DD viewers indicating a positive association between viewership and occupational status.

The analysis further indicated that three variables, income, education and occupational status were associated with each other among both CATV viewers and DD viewers. The study then, examined the variations in the socio-economic status between respondents on patterns of social participation. But before that the study sought a glimpse on other characteristics like religion, caste, type of ownership of house, place of origin and duration of stay of respondents in Chandigarh.

It was revealed that in all three localities majority of the respondents were Hindus. Further, on the whole there were more CATV viewers than DD viewers among the Hindus while among the Sikhs the reverse was true. The data also indicated that most of the CATV viewers were Hindus. Also, majority of the respondents belonged to the upper castes. However, in Locality III, majority of the respondents belonged to the low caste category (for details of caste categories refer to p. 50). There were a greater proportion of CATV viewers than the DD viewers in the upper caste category in Localities I and II. Further, a similar trend was observed in the low caste category among respondents of Locality III. The study suggested that the upper and middle income groups were dominated by respondents belonging to upper castes while the low income group respondents belonged to the low castes.

Regarding the type of ownership of house, it was important to note the differences in three localities although the sample size was selected on the basis of socio-economic status. The study showed that in all the three localities majority of the respondents owned houses in which they resided. Further, on the whole, the owners of houses were cable subscribers while in Locality III there were more DD viewers who owned houses. The data further revealed that most of the residents of Chandigarh had migrated from Punjab and majority of them had been residing in the city for more than 11 years but less than 20 years. The means duration of stay (in years) in Chandigarh of respondents in Locality II was the highest while it was the lowest in Locality III indicating that the residents of Locality II were staying in Chandigarh for a longer period than the other two localities. It was further indicated that CATV viewers in Localities I and II were staying for a longer duration in Chandigarh than the DD viewers but the reverse was true in Locality III.

The data revealed some major differences in the demographic profile between the CATV viewers and DD viewers as well as in between the three localities. It was concluded that there were some consistent variations between the three neighbourhoods in terms of their income, education and occupational attributes. It was then pertinent to see how these variations in the demographic profile would reflect on the patterns of viewership of TV which was discussed in Chapter 3.

In view of one of the major objectives, i.e., to analyse the association of duration of viewing TV and selectivity of programmes with the socio-economic status, some dimensions and physical factors of the family environment were examined. Further, as the study focusses on the impact of Cable television on social interaction, the number of TV sets as well as space available in a household were crucial factors. This is so because while the possession of a single television set may bring the members together physically, more than one television set on the other hand may increase physical space between them. Similarly, families with more space and greater economic resources may own more than one TV set which may isolate family members both physically as well as socially. The study pointed out that on the whole majority of the respondents owned one television set. In Locality I, more than one-third of the respondents owned two or more TV sets while in Locality II, one-fifth of the respondents owned two or more TV sets. Only one respondent from Locality III owned two TV sets while the rest owned one TV set. Furthermore, Cable TV viewers owned more than one TV set as compared to DD viewers indicating a positive association between viewership and the number of TV sets. Also, an association between the economic status and the number of TV sets with viewership on the one hand and with the space available in a household on the other, was established from the study. (We had seen earlier that respondents of Locality I resided in 2 kanal or bigger houses). The results substantiate the findings of Barrios (1988) that greater the economic resources and space available in a household, the greater the number of TV sets owned by a family.

Further, having inferred that income did not have an association with the subscription of Cable TV among respondents of Locality I, the study probed into the extraneous factors which obstructed respondents from viewership of Satellite TV. One of the main reasons listed out by the DD viewers was their children's studies. The study revealed that respondents of Locality II were most concerned regarding their children's studies as well as expressed grave concern on the obscenity, nudity and vulgarity exhibited on Satellite channels. Also, out of a total of 150 respondents who had not subscribed to Cable TV nearly one-fourth of these DD viewers had earlier remained subscribers of CATV. The withdrawal of subscription to CATV was concentrated mainly in Locality II, wherein nearly half of the respondents of this locality were earlier viewers of CATV. The study also revealed that majority of the DD viewers did not want to subscribe to Cable TV even at a later stage. This indicated that reasons other than their children's studies kept them away from being viewers of Satellite Channels. The reasons according to them was an overdose of obscenity, sexuality and vulgarity depicted on the western channels.

The introduction of television initally made everyone believe that the 'novelty' hypothesis would wear off with the passage of time. But, in most households, TV viewing has become an addiction and the consumption of TV has been steadily rising over the years with an increase in the number of channels as well as round-the-clock transmission on Satellite channels. Further, as viewers tend to exaggerate viewing times (especially when measured in hours) the present study measured the duration of viewing TV according to the number of sessions—i.e., morning, afternoon, evening and late night, the television set was switched on, during one-day. The analysis showed that more than one-third of the respondents watched TV for atleast three or more sessions in a day. It was also inferred that respondents of Locality III consumed more hours of TV than the respondents of the other two localities. These findings substantiate earlier findings by Colomina (1968) and Greenberg and Dominick (1969) that low economic status audience consume more hours of television. Further, as these respondents owned one television set, the family members were bound to watch it together substantiating the view held by Colomina (1968) that the lower socio-economic status audience watch more TV content with their children.

It was also observed that the respondents of Locality II consumed TV content for a lesser duration of time as compared to the other two localities. The study suggested that the upper and low socio-economic groups were heavy consumers of TV content. This indicated that the respondents in these two localities are glued to their TV sets resulting in physical immobility leading to a loss of social activity both with the outside world as well as within the family. These issues were discussed later in Chapter 4.

However, it was interesting to note that as duration of TV viewing increased, there was proportionate increase of Cable viewers. On the whole, majority of the Cable viewers watched TV for a longer duration as compared to DD viewers. It was also observed that Cable TV viewers of Locality III consumed more hours of TV as compared to the other localities. A uniform positive association between duration of viewing and Satellite TV was suggested by the study. Thus, the hypothesis that an increase in the number of channels as well as the availability of round-the-clock transmission leads to an increase in TV consumption has been accepted by the study. These findings indicates that viewers are bound to curtail their physical and social activities within as well as across families. There aspects were richly illustrated in the subsequent chapters.

Further, the analysis also indicated that the duration of viewing TV among the Cable TV viewers was associated with income, education and occupation. The study also showed that CATV viewers with low economic status consumed more hours of TV on the one hand, while on the other, CATV viewers with high economic status watched TV for a lesser duration of time. An inverse association between income and viewership was suggested by the study. Also, income was found to have no association with the duration of viewing TV among the DD viewers while education and occupation were significantly associated with the duration of viewing TV among both the CATV viewers and DD viewers. Subsequently, how the variations in the duration of viewing TV affect the family environment were examined in Chapter 4. But before that, the selectivity of programmes by the respondents were studied to see how the variations in the preferences for specific programmes among family members would affect family life.

Research in communication studies have indicated that the role of primary groups and references groups along with other variables such as education, occupation, gender, age etc., may be significant in inducing variations among the audiences. Preferences for specific programmes may differ according to the socio-economic status, age-groups etc. which contribute heavily in the different patterns of viewership among the recipients of media.

The analysis indicated that the ZEE TV channel which had an overdose of entertainment programmes was the most popular among Satellite TV viewers while DD I channel had popularity among the DD viewers. The results also showed that the variables such as income, education and occupation were associated with the selection of channels among Cable TV viewers while there was no association of these variables in the case of DD viewers. This was because the viewers of Satellite TV had a wide choice of channels to choose from while the Doordarshan viewers were restricted in their choice with the availability of only two channels.

The study further indicated that entertainment based programmes were the most popular among the audience in all the three localities. (This category excluded Hindi film based programmes). Also, the western programmes were popular among the respondents of only Locality I while the Hindi film based programmes were popular mostly among the respondents of Locality III. Further, informative and sports programmes had popularity with some respondents of Localities I and III. It was inferred that in Localities I and II, the respondents were spread over in their choice of programme categories while the respondents of Locality III were stereotyped in their choice of programmes.

Also, the DD viewers preferred informative programmes while western programmes were preferred to a large extent by CATV viewers of Locality I only. This is attributed to the fact that CATV viewers have a wider choice in selection of programmes with the availability of variety of channels. These variations indicate that preference for specific programmes differed according to the socio-economic status as well as the role of primary groups and reference groups which influence viewers for preference of specific programmes. The study also indicates that as the quality of programmes on Doordarshan and Satellite TV differed to a large extent, viewers naturally differed in their selection of programmes. The programmes on Satellite TV are designed for the urban children, urban teenagers, urban youth, urban women and urban adults while the programmes on Doordarshan are oriented towards information, education and also towards development. Further, the two kinds of viewership differed in the quantity as well as the quality of programmes with a greater emphasis of western culture and life style on Satellite TV channels. Hence, CATV viewers and DD viewers differed in taste for programmes. In other words, the study revealed that different people select particular types of media content which is heavily influenced by the socio-economic and demographic characteristics. This theoretical perspective has been accepted by the present study as respondents of the three localities as well as the CATV viewers and DD viewers differed in the selection of programmes. This perspective was further substantiated with the study indicating an association of income, education and duration of viewing TV with the selection of programmes among CATV viewers. Further, income, education and occupation were significantly associated with selection of programmes among DD viewers but not associated with the selection of channels. Also, education and occupation had an association with the duration of viewing TV, among DD viewers. It was also observed that the duration of viewing TV and choice of programmes were significantly associated with each other in the case of both CATV viewers and DD viewers. As the three localities differed in their selection of channels it was pertinent to see in what other ways TV affects family life with different patterns of selection of channels/programmes among family members. Further, how the duration of viewing TV curtails social participation within the family was the focus of Chapter 4.

The relationship between television viewing and family interaction patterns has been a subject of research since the advent of TV. Whether television facilitates closer relationships within families or weakens bonds has been frequently debated. Some communication experts have held the view that television brings in physical proximity and facilitates communication while on the other hand, scholars observed that as a result of physical immobility, there is a reduction in interaction both within and across families. Further, there is an overall decline in the expenditure of leisure time from 'out of home' to 'in home' activities. Television is a primary leisure activity for people indicating that physical and social isolation are bound to occur which leads to a process of 'individuation'.

The study revealed that majority of the respondents both among CATV viewers and DD viewers enjoyed leisure activities which pertained to their ownself, suggesting an isolation among members of the family. It was also observed that more members of the family in Locality III had leisure activities which related to one's ownself as compared to the other localities. Respondents opined that as there was a boom in electronic gadgets, the prime leisure activities of children were 'individualistic' in nature. They also remarked that social activity was curtailed which resulted in a decrease in communication within and across families as viewers interact more and more with the media.

The study suggested an association between Satellite TV and the process of individuation. Further, the study indicated that Satellite TV is a catalytic agent in enhancing isolation within and across families. The perspective which states that TV reduces communication within families has been substantiated while the perspective which states that TV facilitates communication has been rejected by the study. The study stands to further substantiate this perspective with the following inferences.

Further, although our traditional curlture is known for its hospitality, there has been decline in such a hospitality, as more than half the respondents expressed irritation on the arrival of guests while watching an interesting programme. The arrival of guests was not a pleasurable experience for many respondents. The study indicated a significant decline in interpersonal relationships across families. The analysis depicted an inverse relationship between TV viewing and hospitality. The increasing number of channels on Satellite TV resulted in a reduction in intra-familial communication. Also, a number of respondents especially in the upper and middle income groups revealed that it they visited somebody during prime hours of TV, they felt unattended. Instead of getting a welcome, they had to face embarrassment since they disturbed the hosts who were more interested in TV programmes. The respondents revealed that for the fear of being forced guests they avoided visiting people at their homes during prime hours of TV. It was observed that as the TV viewing duration increased consequent to the increase in the number of channels there was a decrease in inter-family communication. The increase in the duration of viewing TV led to a further decrease in physical mobility resulting in a decline in inter-familial relationships.

The study also suggested that on the one hand, TV increased physcial closeness and proximity (especially among the Cable TV viewers of Locality III), while on the other hand TV weakened ties among family members. Further, it was indicated that TV promoted passivity among family members. The time spent interacting with family members was considerably reduced especially among the Cable viewers. Majority of the Cable TV viewers of Localities I and III were of the opinion that TV had contributed to reducing interaction between family members. The study inferred an inverse association between the interaction time of family members and Satellite TV. Hence, the study suggests that TV is a catalytic agent in weakening bonds within and across families. Family members also disclosed that they did not want any interupptions while watching interesting programmes on TV. They also avoided important household issues for discussion as well as outings in favour of watching TV. It was also revealed that children avoided social interaction within as well as across families.

It was also indicated that children exercised maximum control over the TV set in all three localities. Also, the study suggested a positive association between conflicts and the number of TV sets on the one hand and with the number of channels on the other. The frequency of quarrels were maximum between children themselves. It was also indicated that Satellite TV had contributed to disharmony in the husband-wife as well as parent-child relationships. Physical isolation was increasing in families with the increasing rise in the number of channels and the number of TV sets in a household. It can be concluded that the present study substantiates the perspective that TV curtails intra-family communication suggesting a decline in informal social participation within the families.

Results further revealed that many respondents rescheduled their daily activities to watch TV programmes. Respondents did not eat on the dining table while some managed to shift the TV set from the drawing room or lobby into dining rooms and bedrooms. It was also noticed that the Cable TV viewers especially those of Locality III had rescheduled their daily routines. The lady of the household tried to complete her domestic work and cooking while children did their homework early or while watching TV. The study inferred that TV had rescheduled daily routines substantiating the finding of Luthra and Mahajan (1993).

Despite the agreement on the dangers of TV viewing more than 95 per cent of the respondents did not want to change their TV viewing duration substantiating the view held by Leitcher and her associates (1985). It was concluded from Chapter 4 that inter-familial and intra-familial ties had weakened as a result of TV viewing. Further, children emerged as the most prominent segment in the family who avoided household issues, outings, showed disrespect to elders, and ignored guests, due to TV viewing.

The data in the preceeding chapters reflected an impact of TV – whether DD or Cable on the social life within the families. It was evident from the analysis that Cable TV, by restricting the physical mobility of its viewers, would reduce the social participation of people across the families too. In other words, being glued to TV sets during most of the day, inter-familial ties with neighbours, relatives, friends etc. would normally decline. Chapter 5 undertakes an appraisal of this hypothesis. The question posed in this chapter was – Does TV viewing (especially the Cable) in any way affect patterns of social participation among city dwellers? The emphasis on this chapter was upon patterns of social participation across families as the impact of TV on intra-familial interaction was examined. Specifically, in Chapter 5, the nature and degree of formal and informal social participation as well as the impact of TV on these dimensions were studied.

The results showed that formal participation was positively associated with income, education and occupational status as majority of the members of formal organisations belonged to Locality I, substantiating studies by Chandra (1977), Pasricha (1988), Gill (1991) and Gill and Dhawan (1992). It was also observed that memberships in majority of the families were held by the male head of the household. Further, respondents sought membership in entertainment based organisations for dining/playing cards and tambola as well as sports and games. The nature of formal social participation was that majority of the respondents were consumers of services only. Also, the level of participation of the respondents was at the city level and majority of these memberships were held for 5-10 years.

The degree of formal participation was frequent – almost daily among majority of the members. Television did not exercise any affect on formal participation on both dimensions—degree and nature as the type of participation is voluntarily chosen by an individual as well as it is a paid form of social participation. That TV viewing has not affected formal participation in a big way is understandable because members indulge into such a participation by choice. They join formal organisations for achieving some very tangible and concrete ends—ranging from entertainment, physical fitness, to professional development. In the competitiveness world of today, these requirements constitute a top most agenda for an urbanite—especially in an upper income group. It is for this reason that TV or no TV, members of formal organisations maintain regular participation at the formal level. These inferences have been drawn on the basis of our findings in the study.

The informal participation of the respondents of Localities I and II were at the medium level on both dimensions—degree as well as nature (in terms of intimacy of ties). The respondents of Locality III had very strong neighbourhood ties, the study suggested. The quantitative analysis revealed that the degree of informal participation was not associated with the duration of viewing TV both among CATV viewers and DD viewers in the upper and middle income localities. Also, there was no consistent association between income, education and occupation with the degree of informal participation both among CATV viewers and DD viewers. Further, the low levels of degree and nature of informal participation were characteristics of urban dwellers in Localities I and II according to the quantitative analysis. However, the qualitative analysis revealed that majority of the respondents felt that TV had restricted neighbourhood relations. Also, nearly half the respondents did not want to miss TV programmes for the sake of visiting relatives, friends and neighbours in favour of watching TV programmes.

The analysis in Chapter 5 revealed that different trends followed out of quantitative and qualitative investigation of the data. While responses analysed through the use of the index indicated that informal participation had little relationship with TV viewing, indirect questioning of respondents elicited altogether different trends. These responses clearly indicated that television had certainly curtailed their outdoor activities especially in relation to their visits to relatives, neighbours and friends. But the fact remains that this had happened more among the younger generation.

Further, Satellite TV had definitely restricted neighbourhood relations in all the three income groups. It was also inferred that informal participation was affected by Satellite TV in the sense that respondents avoided social visits across families during prime hours of TV. The study suggested that Satellite TV did not exercise a uniform effect on both dimensions of social participation—formal and informal. While formal participation remained unaffected by TV, informal participation across families had been definitely affected by Satellite TV.

Hence, it may be inferred that as the researcher examined the impact of Satellite TV from a macro-level of social participation to micro-level, investigations indicated that Satellite TV had exercised maximum impact on the most crucial unit of the family i.e., children. Therefore, Chapter 6 was designed to study how television affected children, with western media creeping into Indian homes.

Parental mediation in controlling TV viewing among children has been one of the major concerns all over the world. Inspite of this, our study revealed that 95 per cent of the respondents wanted to continue their TV viewing duration. Therefore, the role of parents in this context needs to be examined.

The study indicated that more than half the respondents among both CATV viewers and DD viewers claimed that they regulated TV for their children. There was no significant difference between the CATV viewers and DD viewers in three localities among those who regulated TV for their children. The responses were found to be inconsistent as we had inferred earlier that children had exercised maximum control over the TV sets. Further, inspite of such an observation, more than half the respondents indicated that there was a deterioration in the academic performance of children. Also, the deterioration in the academic performance of the children was more among Cable viewers as compared to DD viewers.

It was also observed that there were more respondents among the regulators of TV who reported a deterioration in the academic performance of children. The study showed that as the responses were inconsistent regarding regulation of TV, deterioration in academic performance was indicated by respondents. This meant that TV was hardly in the control of parents. The study substantiates the findings of Greenberg, Ku and Li (1992) that children are less willing to follow parental rules or obey them. Consequently parents have less control over their children, the study suggested.

The study further revealed that majority of the Cable viewers indicated that TV had an effect on extra-curricular activities, dress sense, life style, taste of music and creativity of children. Respondents complained that their children were swayed away by the western life styles and value system, forgetting their traditional culture. Further, parents wanted that their children should reduce their TV viewing duration but were unable to assert their authority over their children. Parents also indicated that a negative impact of Satellite TV was exerted on the relationship between their children and their friends. Further, parents identified deteriorating standards of the parent-child relationship indicationg disobedience, disrespect, back answering, rude and rash behaviour of their children towards them. The study also indicated that among some respondents, television had contributed in widening the generation gap between parents and children while majority held the view that generation gap was a universal phenomenon.

Majority of the DD viewers were of the view that if they subscribed to CATV, there would be a changer in the life style as well as family interaction patterns. Further, nearly two-thirds of the DD viewers and majority of the Cable TV viewers felt uncomfortable while watching TV programmes with their families. Respondents pointed out obscenity, vulgarity , love scenes and bed scenes which embarrassed them while watching TV with their family members. Although western channels were appreciated by a few respondents for their presentation, photography and information, respondents criticised STAR TV and VTV channels for excessive love scenes, lip kissing and nudity on these channels. Viewers expressed that nudity projected on western channels was not in good taste with the western value system creeping into Indian homes.

Further, majority of the Satellite TV viewers believed that their life styles would be different had they not subscribed to CATV. They also asserted that there would be more intra-family interaction and respect in the husband-wife and parent-child relationships which was diminishing day-by-day.

On the one hand, respondents indicated that CATV was a boon while on the other hand they termed it as an evil. Respondents agreed that if controlled and restricted viewing is practised, then Satellite TV can produce excellent results, creating awareness among children and youth. If watched with discretion, Satellite TV can bring positive changes in the familial relationships, opined respondents. The negative aspects respondents emphasized upon were the academics of children, promotion of criminal, rash and violent tendencies, projection of western culture and values and obscenity, nudity and vulgarity on Satellite channels.

Further, the most disturbing elements identified by respondents was sexuality projected on Satellite channels. Respondents were vehemently against the depiction of scenes with sexual tendencies which were openly viewed in families. Some respondents suggested restrictions while some others proposed a ban on Cable television. Thus, the hypothesis that TV would affect children the most, especially on academic and non-academic dimensions has been substantiated by the study.

Therefore, it is concluded that TV exercised a strong impact on informal social participation within and across families while it did not exercise any effect on formal social participation. Further, it is inferred that most of the viewers perceived Satellite TV as an evil as it destroyed not only the careers of children but the rich traditional Indian culture and value system.

Despite all these tendencies, it remains a fact that those involved in commercialization of Satellite television have been tremendously successful. They have, despite all the problems, been able to induce Cable TV as an unavoidable necessity not only for the children, but for the parents as well. With the growing choice out of a variety of channels and increasing competition among private channels, the viewer is getting more and more enslaved by its glamour.

The present study highlights the need to study the impact of intervening variables on social participation—both within and across families, rather than looking for a unidimensional relationship between urban residence and nature of social participation. While folk-urban continuum perspective remains an important tool to understand changing societies under the impact of urbanisation, the present study underlined the inability of the continuum perspective in acknowledging the role of intervening factors. Findings in our study thus provide a useful insight into the role played by Cable television in transforming the patterns of social participation in an urban setting.

The study partially substantiates the social categories perspective, in that the impact of Satellite TV on social participation is mediated through the social categories. At the same time, however, in certain other dimensions, Satellite TV has been found to exercise a more or less uniform impact irrespective of social class or status for e.g. its impact on children. Hence, the relationship between TV and social participation cannot be understood with the help of any single perspective. Due to the tremendous complexities involved in the phenomena, impact of Satellite TV on social participation—within and outside family, cannot be explained by a single perspective. On the contrary, our findings caution us against formulating any sweeping generalization in this regard.

Theoretical Relevance of the Study

The theoretical contribution of the study lies in its ability to fill in the gaps in existing literature regarding the impact of television at varying levels—micro and macro, formal and informal, intra-familial and inter-familial spheres. Rather than homogenizing the social units which receive the impact, the study is able to specify as to how TV viewing exercises an impact on the urban dwellers through varying socio-economic status. Further, the analysis makes it explicit that TV has affected us most in our informal groupings in that our participation within the family as well as in the neighbourhood has considerably declined due to it. Going further, the study not only reveals the substantial impact exercised by TV within our homes, affecting almost every unit within the family, it also shows how it happens. The role played by the number of TV sets for instance, duration of viewing and viewing patterns in transforming relations between spouses, siblings and between them, is broughout clearly by our findings. Participation in formal organisations on the other hand, which basically tends to be goal-oriented, hardly gets affected by TV viewing because of the professional or other specific goals incurred through such a participation.

The present study therefore helps in laying bare some of the mechanisms through which Satellite TV has been working as an intervening variable in the process of urbanization, in that it leads to specific changes under some given conditions. It prevents us from visualizing any one to one relationship between urban residence on the one hand, and a particular kind of social participation on the other.

To conclude Satellite TV not only makes a differential impact upon different categories of urban dwellers, it also impacts various forms of social participation very differently. Also, the Satellite TV is playing a significant role in transforming the relationships within the family, by hitting directly at parental authority and changing altogether the orientation of children towards social participation. The theoretical relevance of the present study hence lies in going beyond the relationship between Cable television and social participation. It provides insights into the specific conditions under which Cable TV may or may not produce a given impact within the members of a family, as also outside families. The major hypothesis that due to the physical binding of the viewer by Cable TV for long hours, results into a decline in social participation, mainly the informal, has been born out by our findings.

Richness of a research study also lies in its ability to raise some new issues, which may be taken up for future research. This study highlights the need to conduct further analyses as to why Cable TV, which takes a large chunk of a viewer's time, has been invading his participation only at informal level and why it has little effect on formal participation. Whether, this is true only of urban dwellers or it applies to rural dwellers too, is yet to be investigated. These are some of the questions which are posed by the study, to be taken up subsequently.

Appendix–A

INTERVIEW SCHEDULE

1. Demographic Profile

1. Name of the respondent
2. Sex
3. Age
4. Sector
5. Size of the house
6. Type of house

   (i) Own, *(ii)* Rented, and *(iii)* Govt.
7. Religion
8. Caste
9. Place of origin
10. Duration of stay in Chandigarh (in years)___________.
11. Family income per month Rs. ____________________.
12. Are you owner of:

No. of TV sets	1	2	3	4
Dish Antenna		Yes/No		
Cable TV		Yes/No		

13. Are you a viewer of
    (i) Cable TV only
    (ii) Doordarshan only
    (iii) Both Cable TV and DD
    (iv) Neither of the two.

14. If not, why have you not subscribed to CATV?
    (i) Economic reasons
    (ii) Waste of time
    (iii) Nuisance
    (iv) Children's studies
    (v) Any other.

15. Were you earlier a viewer of CATV? Yes/No.

16. If, Yes, why have you withdrawn subscription?

17. Do you still desire to subscribe to it? Yes/No.

18. Do you think ultimately you will have to install it?
    If, Yes, why?
    If, No, why?

19. What are your leisure activities?
    (a) Adults
    (b) Children
    1. Physical activities
    2. Creativity
    3. TV viewing
    4. Reading
    5. Any other.

20. Do you think the leisure activities of your childhood were different from those of your children/children in general? Yes/No. Explain how?

2. Viewership Patterns Among Members of the Household

							Selection		*Duration*
Relation with Respondent	*Sex*	*Age*	*Edn.*	*Income*	*Occupation*	*Working Hrs.*	*Which Channels are Normally Watched in Your House?*	*Which Programmes are Nomrally Watched in Your House?*	*Duration of Viewing TV*
1.							1.	1.	Morning
2.							2.	2.	Afternoon
3.							3.	3	. Night
4.							4.	4.	Whole Day
5.							5.	5.	Till What
6.							6.	6.	time at
7.							7.	7.	night?
8.							8.	8.	
9.							9.	9.	
10.							10.	10.	

3. Formal Participation

Who is Member	*Name of the Organisation*	*Year of Joining*	**Category*	***Area of Operation*	*Only Consumers of Services*	*Contribute Money Only.*	*Contribute Money & Participate Actively*	*Office Holding*	*Time Spent in a Month*	*What is the Type of Activity*
1.										
2.										
3.										
4.										
5.										

***Categories**
1. Religious
2. Political
3. Entertainment
4. Sports
5. Welfare Services
6. Recreational
7. Any other

****Area of Operation**
1. Neighbourhood Only
2. City wide
3. National level
4. International level

3.1 Is any one in your family member of a Sport club, entertainment club, religious organisation or any other formal groups? Yes/No.

3.2 If, Yes, who?

3.3 Do you aspire to be a member of any group? Yes/No.
If, Yes, why?
If, Yes, why?

3.4 Has CATV/DD in any way affected your participation in these organisations? Yes/No.

3.5 If, Yes,
1. You spend lesser time in these organisations
2. You spend more time in these organisations
3. You have withdrawn membership from any of these organisations.
4. Any other

3.6 If, No, why?

4. Informal Participation

4.1 How many relatives other than immediate family members do you have in Chandigarh?
(i) Many *(ii)* Some *(iii)* Very few *(iv)* None

4.2 How often a month do you see them?
(i) Often (once a week),
(ii) Sometimes (once in a fortnight)
(iii) Rarely (once a month or more)
(iv) Never.

4.3 What is the nature of contact?
(i) Casual meeting
(ii) Outings, movies and picnics
(iii) Intimate visiting.

4.4 Has CATV/DD in any way affected your contacts with relatives? Yes/No.

4.5 If, Yes,
1. You have reduced the number of visits to your relatives

2. You have increased the number of visits to your relatives
3. No change
4. Any other

4.6 If, No, why?

4.7 Do you think with CATV/DD you are hardly left with much time for your kinsmen? Yes/No.

4.8 How many friends (but not neighbours) do you have in CHD?
(i) Many *(ii)* Some *(iii)* Very few *(iv)* None

4.9 How often do you see your friends in a month?
(i) Often *(ii)* Sometimes *(iii)* Rarely *(iv)* Never

4.10 What is the nature of contact with your friends?
1. Casual visiting only.
2. Outings, movies and picnics
3. Intimate visiting.

4.11 Has CATV/DD in any way affected your contacts with friends? Yes/No.

4.12 If, Yes,
1. You have reduced the number of visits to your friends
2. You have increased the number of visits to your friends
3. No change
4. Any other

4.13 If, No, why?

4.14 Do you think that with CATV/DD you are hardly left with much time for your friends? Yes/No.

5. Neighbourhood Relations

5.1 For how long have you been staying in this locality? (in years)

5.2 How often do you visit or talk with your neighbours?
(i) Often *(ii)* Sometimes *(iii)* Rarely *(iv)* Never

5.3 How many neighbours are you intimate with?
(i) Many *(ii)* Some *(iii)* Very few *(iv)* None

5.4 Do you and your neighbours take care of each others children, women and old when one is sick or busy?
(i) Often *(ii)* Sometimes *(iii)* Rarely *(iv)* Never

5.5 Do you participate in social group clubs like coffee club, bridge club, tambola or any similar gathering in your locality?
(i) Regularly *(ii)* Sometimes *(iii)* Rarely *(iv)* Never

5.6 Don't you think people are glued to TV sets in the evenings—thus restricting the traditional neighbourhood relations?
(i) Not at all *(ii)* To some extent *(iii)* Definitely yes.

5.7 Has CATV/DD in any way affected your neighbourhood relations? Yes/No.

5.8 If, Yes, in which way?

5.9 If, No, why?

5.10 Do you think that with CATV/DD you are hardly left with much time for your neighbours? Yes/No.

5.11 Are there any specific TV programmes which any one in your family would never like to miss for sake of visiting your relatives, friends and/or neighbours?
(i) Often *(ii)* Sometimes *(iii)* Rarely *(iv)* Never

5.12 Who?

5.13 Do you/your spouse/children feel irritated when guests arrive while watching an interesting programme on TV? Yes/No. If, Yes, specify.

5.14 Do you/your spouse/children avoid visiting people at the prime hours of TV? Yes/No.

6. Interaction Patterns within the Family

6.1 Do you think you would spend more time interacting with your family members if you did not have CATV/DD? Yes/No.

6.2 Do you think TV makes all your family mebers to sit together? Yes/No.

6.3 How?

6.4 Do you think TV has taken the family members away from each other? Yes/No.

6.5 How?

6.6 Who controls the TV set while watching CATV/DD?

6.7 Do you have quarrels over selection of channels?

(i) Often *(ii)* Sometimes *(iii)* Rerely *(iv)* Never

6.8 Has the divergence in selection of channels/programmes affected your relationship with your spouse/children? Yes/No. If Yes, how?

6.9 If someone talks during an interesting programme, what is the reaction of others?

(i) Shut him/her up *(ii)* Indifferent *(iii)* Any other (specify)

6.10 Does your spouse/children switch on the TV set as soon as he/she/they arrive from office/school/college? Yes/No.

6.11 If, Yes, what is your reaction?

6.12 Does your spouse/children avoid any important household issue for discussion for the sake of watching CATV/DD? Yes/No.

6.13 If, Yes, what is your reaction?

6.14 Does your spouse/children avoid outings for the sake of watching CATV/ DD? Yes/No.

6.15 If, Yes, what is your reaction?

6.16 Has CATV/DD

1. Facilitated discussion as a subject of interaction between married couples/parent-children.
2. Reduced conversation between marrried couples/parent-children.
3. Any other.

6.17 Has CATV/DD affected your family interaction pattern in general? Yes/No.

6.18 If, Yes, in which way?

6.19 Have you/your spouse/children rescheduled daily chores for watching CATV/DD programmes?
If, You, specify. Yes/No.

6.20 Would you like to
1. increase viewing hrs—why?
2. decrease viewing hrs—why?
3. continue the same—why?

7. Reactions of Respondents Towards CATV—Impact on Children

7.1 Do you regulate TV viewing pattern of your children? Yes/No.

7.2 If, Yes,
1. Do you switch on the TV set at a particular time?
2. Do you switch over to the channel they prefer?
3. Do you allow them to watch the programme for a fixed period of time?
4. Any other.

7.3 Has CATV/DD affected the academic performance of your children?
1. There is deterioration in his/her academic performance
2. His/her academic performance has improved
3. No change
4. Uncertain
5. Any other

7.4 Has CATV/DD affected you childrens' :
1. Extra-curricular activities
2. Dress sense
3. Life style
4. Music
5. Creativity
6. Any other

7.5 If, Yes, how?

7.6 Would you like your children to change the TV viewing duration?
Yes/No. If Yes, how?
(i) Increase *(ii)* Reduce *(iii)* Continue the same *(iv)* Abstain from viewing totally.

7.7 Do you think CATV/DD has affected your childrens' relationship with their friends? Yes/No.

7.8 If, Yes, how?

7.9 Do you feel that your childrens' behaviour towards you is in any way different from that of your behaviour towards your parents? Yes/No.

7.10 If, Yes, how?

7.11 Do you feel there is a generation gap between you and your children? Yes/No.

7.12 Do you attribute this to CATV/DD? Yes/No.
(Viewers of CATV to proceed to Q.No. IX)

8. For DD Viewers Only

8.1 Do you think subscription to CATV would have changed your life style? Yes/No.

8.2 If, Yes, it would affect your
1. social participation at the formal level
2. social participation at the informal level
3. family interaction patterns
4. interaction with your children.

8.3 Do you feel comfortable watching DD with your family? Yes/No.

8.4 Give reasons.

8.5 What do you like most about DD?

8.6 What do you dislike most about DD?

8.7 Do you think CATV is doing good/bad to our children/

youth? Give reasons.

8.8 Any additional information you would like to add?

9. For CATV Viewers Only

9.1 Had you not had cable connection do you think you life style would have been different? Yes/No.

9.2 If, Yes, in which way?

9.3 What do you like most in western channels?

9.4 What do you dislike most in western channels?

9.5 What do you like most in Hindi channels?

9.6 What do you dislike most in Hindi channels?

9.7 Do you feel comfortable while watching western channels with your family? Yes/No.

9.8 Why?

9.9 Do you feel comfortable while watching Hindi channels with your family? Yes/No.

9.10 Why?

9.11 Do you think CATV is doing good/bad to our children/ youth? Give reason.

9.12 Any additional information you would like to add?

Appendix–B

The arbitary method of classifying occupations into prestige grades has been commonly used in studies on urban communities in India. The main drawback of these methods is that they are not scientifically satisfactory. In the absence of any scientific method of classification, the method used by Victor S.D.'Souza has been used in the present study.

Therefore, in the present study the occupations of respondents were classified into seven prestige categories derived from the study of Victor S.D' Souza.[1]

PRESTIGE CLASSIFICATION OF OCCUPATIONS

Prestige Category I

Doctor
Engineer
Architect
Judge
Magistrate
Managing Director
Defence Officer
Scientist

Prestige Category II

Chartered Accountant
Government Official
Lawyer
Journalist
Professor
Factory Manager
Artist
Editor
Owner of Large Shopping Establishment

Prestige Category III

Contractor
School Teacher

1. D' Souza Victor S. 1968. *Social Structure of a Planned City* Chandigarh, New Delhi. Orient Longman Limited.

Owner of Provision Store
Sales Representative
Insurance Agent
Inspector (Income Tax and Sales Tax)
Military Jawan
Station Master

Prestige Category IV

Office Clerk
Book Seller
Chemist
Electrician (Mechanic)
Photographer
Typist
Railway Guard
Police Constable
Broker
Cashier
Commission Agent
Foreman
Receptionist
Stenographer
Telephone Operator
Surveyor

Prestige Category V

Bus Driver
Carpenter
Mason
Taxi Driver
Black and Coppersmith
Bus Conductor
Chauffeur
Dyer and Cloth Painter
Embroidery Worker
Engine Driver
Engraver
Tailor
Plumber
Metal Worker
Machine Operator
Motor Mechanic
Sweet Meat Maker

Prestige Category VI

Agricultural Labourer
Basket Maker
Bicycle Repairer
Book Binder
Broom Maker
Darner
Domestic Servant
Gardener
Milkman
Peon
Street Hawker
Vegetable Vendor
Watchman
Weaver
Woodcutter

Prestige Category VII

Baker
Baber
Butcher
Coolie
Fisherman
Rickshaw Puller

Show Maker	Shoe Shiner
Washerman	Whitewasher

The occupations of the sample population are classified into seven prestige categories by comparing them with the occupations in the specially graded list of Victor S.D'Souza.

Bibliography

Allan, G. 1985. *Family Life: Domestic Roles and Social Organisation.* Oxford : Basil Blackwell.

Anderson, Nels 1960. "Urbanism and Urbanisation", *American Journal of Sociology,* Vol. LXV, July.

Ang, Ien 1991. *Desperately Seeking the Audience.* London: Routledge.

Atkin, C.K., Murray, J.P. and Nayman, O.B. 1972. "The Surgeon General's Research Programmes of Empirical Findings", *Journal of Broadcasting,* 16, Winter.

Barrios, Leoncio 1988. "Television, Telenovelas, and Family Life in Venezuela", Lull, James (ed.), *World Families Watch Television.* New Delhi: Sage Publications.

Bechtel, Robert B., Achelpohl, Clark and Akers, Roger 1972. "Correlates Between Observed Behaviour and Questionnaire Responses on Television Viewing", Rubinstein, G.A., Comstock, G. and Murray J.P. (eds.), *Television and Social Behaviour,* Vol. 4, Washington D.C : US Government Printing Office.

Becker, Lee 1979. "Measurement of Gratifications", *Communication Research,* Vol. 6, No. 1, pp. 54-73.

Berger, Arthur Asa 1990. "Texts in Contexts". Analysing Media and Popular Culture from a Cross Cultural Perspective," Korzenny, Filipe and Tommey, Stella Ting (eds.), *Mass Media Effects Across Cultures.* International and Intercultural Communication Annual, Vol. XVI: Sage Publications.

Blumler, Jay 1979. "The Role of Theory in Uses and Gratifications Studies," *Communication Research,* Vol. 6, No. 1, pp. 9-36.

Blumler, J. G. and Katz, E. 1974. *The Uses of Mass Communication: Current Perspectives on Gratifications Research.* Beverly Hills, California: Sage Publications.

Bower, Robert T. 1973. *Television and the Public.* New York: Holt, Rinehart and Winston.

Brodie, G.H. and Stoneman, Z. 1983. "The Influence of TV Viewing on Family: A Contextual Framework," *Sociological Abstract.* Vol. 32, No. 1, April 1984.

Bryce, J. 1981. "The Family and Television: An Ethnographic Approach", *Unpublished Doctoral Dissertation.* Columbia University, New York.

Bryce, J. and Leichter, H. 1983. "The Family and Television: Forms of Mediation", *Journal of Family Issues,* Vol. 4, 309-328.

Buley, Jerry 1977." Two-way Cable Television: Some Potential Effects in the Urban Environment", Arnold, W.E. and Buley, J.L. (ed.), *Urban Communication: Survival in the City.* Winthrop Publishers, pp. 127-136.

Cantor, M.G. and Cantor, J.M. 1986. "American Television in the International Market Place", *Communication Research.* Vol. 13, No. 2, April.

Caplow, T., Bahr, H.M., Chadwick, B.A., Hill, R. and Williamson, M.H. 1982. *Middletown Families: Fifty Years of Change and Continuity.* Minneapolis : University of Minnesota Press.

Chafee, S.H., McLeod J. and Atkin, C.K. 1971. "Parental Influences on Adolscent Media Use", *American Behavioral Scientist.* 14, 323-340.

Chandra, Subhash 1977. *Social Participation in Urban Neighbourhood.* New Delhi: National Publishing House.

Chowla, N.L. 1968. "Disturbing Trends in Child TV Viewing", *Times of India,* September 18, p. 8.

Colomina, M. 1986. *El Huesped Alienante,* Maracaibo: Ediciones Universidad de Zulia.

Condry, J. 1989. *The Psychology of Television,* Hillsdale, N J: Lawrence Erlbaum.

Comstock, George 1980. *Television in America.* Beverly Hills, London: Sage Publications.

D' Souza, Victor S. 1968. *Social Structure of a Planned City – Chandigarh.* New Delhi: Orient Longman Limited.

De Fleur, M. 1970. *Theories of Mass Communication.* New York: David McKay.

Dorr, Aimee 1986. *Television and Children: A Special Medium for a Special Audience,* Beverly Hills : Sage Publications.

Dua, Vinod 1992. "A Case for Cable", *Seminar,* Vol. 390. February, pp. 33-35.

Durkheim, Emile 1933. *On Division of Labour in Society,* New York: Macmillan.

Dyal, R. 1992. "Public Response to Cable TV", *Mainstream.* Vol. XXX, No. 2, March, pp. 29-30.

Epestein, S. T. 1962. *Economic Development and Social Change in South India.* Manchester: Monchester University Press.

Feng, J. 1976. *The Effects of Television on Childrens' Behaviour,* Taipee, Taiwan: Wenchin.

Gans, Herbert J. 1968. "Urbanism and Sub-Urbanism as Ways of Life: A Re-evaluation of Definitions in Urbanism", Fava, S.P. (ed.), *Urbanism in World Perspective.* New York: Thomas Y. Crowell Co.

Gill, Rajesh 1991. *Social Change in Urban Periphery.* New Delhi: Allied Pubishers.

Gill, Rajesh and Dhawan, Renuka 1992. "Traditional and Non-Traditional Basis of Social Organisation in an Urban Setting", *Social Action.* Vol. 42, No. 1, January-March, pp. 51-62.

Glass, Ruth 1964. *Urban-Rural Differences in Southern Asia: Some Aspects and Methods of Analysis.* Delhi, UNESCO Research Centre on Social and Economic Development in Southern Asia.

Goode, William J. 1963. *World Revolution and Family Patterns.* New York: Free Press of Glencoe.

Goodman, I.F. 1983. "Television's Role in Family Interaction", *Journal of Family Issues,* Vol. 4, pp 405-25.

Greenberg, B.S. and Dominick, J.R. 1969. "Race and Social Class Differences in Teenagers' Use of Television", *Journal of Broadcasting;* Vol. 13, pp. 1331-34.

Greenberg, Bradley S., Ku, Linlin and Li, Hairong 1992. "Parental Mediation of Childrens' Mass Media Behaviours in China, Japan, Korea, Taiwan and the United States", Korezenny, Felipe and Toomey, Stella Ting (eds.), *Mass Media Across Cultures.* International and Intercultural Communication, Annual, Vol. XVI: Sage Publications.

Gross, L.S. and Walsh, R.P. 1976. "Factors Affecting Parental Control Over Childrens' Television Viewing: A Pilot Study", *Journal of Broadcasting,* Vol. 24, 411-19.

Gupta, G.R. 1976. *Family and Social Change in Modern India,* Bombay: Vikas.

Han, R.H. 1986. "A Comparative Study of Television Watching Behaviour Between Rural and Urban School Children", *Unpublished Masters' Thesis,* Kangwon University: Wonju.

Hatt, Paul K. and Reiss, Albert J. 1951. *Cities and Society: The Revised Reader in Urban Sociology.* Glencoe, Illinois: Free Press.

Himmelweit, H., Oppenheim, A. and Vince, P. 1958. *Television and the Child,* London: Oxford University Press.

Himmelwiet, H. and Swift, B. 1976. "Continuities and Discontinuities in Media Usage and Taste: A Longitudinal Study", *Journal of Social Issues.* 32(4), 133-156.

Hoffman, M.S. and Saltzstein, H.D. 1967. "Parental Discipline and the Child's Moral Development", *Journal of Personality and Social Psychology,* 11(2), 228-239.

Hoselitz, B.F. 1960. *Sociological Aspects of Economic Growth.* Illinois: Free Press.

Howe, Michael J.A. 1977. *Television and Children.* London: New University Education.

Johnson, N. 1967. *How to Talk Back to Your Television Set,* Boston: Little Brown and Co.

Kapadia, K.M. 1956. "Rural Family Patterns", *Sociological Bulletin,* Vol. V, No. 2.

Katz, Elihu 1979. "The Uses of Becker, Blumler and Swanson", *Communication Research.* Vol. 6, No. 1, Pittsburg Press, pp. 74-83.

Katz, Elihu and Lazarsfeld, Paul 1955. *Personal Influence.* Glencoe: Free Press.

Kolenda, P.M. 1967. "Regional Differences in Indian Family Structure", Crane, R.I. (ed.), *Regions and Regionalism in South-Asian Studies: An Exploratory Study.* Duke University, Programme in Comparative Study in Southern Asia, Symposium Papers.

Kunhikrishan, K. 1990. *The Hindu,* Hyderabad Edition, October 7.

Kurain, George 1976. "The Indian Family in Transition: Some Regional Variations", Gupta, G.R. (ed.), *Family and Social Change in Modern India,* New Delhi: Vikas Publishers.

Lambert, R.D. 1962. "The Impact of Urban Society Upon Village Life",

Turner, Roy (ed.), *India's Urban Future*. Bombay: Oxford University Press.

Lauer, Robert H. 1992. *Perspectives on Social Change,* Allyn and Bacon.

Lazarsfeld, Paul F. 1949. "Current Trends in Social Psychology", *Communication Research.* Vol. 2, No. 1, Pittsburg Press, pp. 233-248.

Lee, C.C. 1980. *Media Imperialism Reconsidered: The Homogenising of Television Culture,* Beverly Hills: Sage Publications.

Leichter, H., Ahmed, D., Barrios, L., Bryce, J., Larsen, E. and Moe, L. 1985. "Family Contexts of Television", *Educational Communication and Technology Journal,* 33, 26-41.

Lerner, Daniel 1958. *The Passing of Traditional Society: Modernizing the Middle East.* Glencoe, Illinois: Free Press.

Lewis, Oscar 1965. "Further Observations on the Folk-Urban Continuum and Urbanisation with Special Reference to Mexico City," Hauser, Philip M. and Schnore, Leo F. (eds.), *The Study of Urbanisation.* New York: John Wiley and Sons, INC.

Lull, James 1990. *Inside Family Viewing Ethnographic Research On Television's Audiences.* London: Routledge.

—1988. *World Families Watch Television.* Beverly Hills: Sage Publications.

—1980. "Family Communication Patterns and Social Uses of Television", *Communication Research,* Vol. 7, No. 3, July.

—1980. "The Social Uses of Television", *Human Communication Research,* Vol. 6, pp. 197-209.

Luthra, Nirupama and Mahajan, Amarjit 1993. *Family and Television: A Sociological Study.* New Delhi: Gyan Publishing House.

Lyle, J. and Hoffman, H.R. 1972. "Childrens' Use of Television and Other Media", Rubinstein, E.A., Comstock, G.A. and Murray, J.P. (eds.), *Television and Social Behaviour,* Vol. IV, pp. 129-256, Washington, D.C : Government Printing Office.

Maine, Henry. 1961. *Ancient Law.* London, J. Murray.

Mander, Jerry 1978. *Four Arguments for the Elimination of Television,* New York: Quill.

Massing, H.H. 1986. Decoding Dallas, *Society,* November-December.

McLeod, J.M., Atkin, C.K. and Chafee, S.H. 1972. "Adolescent and Self-support Measures from Maryland and Wisconsin Samples",

Comstock, G.A. (ed.), *Television and Social Behaviour.* Vol III, pp 173-238, Washington D.C. Government Printing Office.

McLeod, J.M., Fitzpatrick, M.A., Glynn, C.J., and Fallis, S.F. 1982. "Television and Social Relations: Family Influences and Consequences for Interpersonal Behaviour" in *National Institute of Mental Health, Television and Behaviour: Ten Years of Scientific Progress and Implications for the Eighties.* (DHHS Publication ADM 82-1196), pp. 272-286, Washington D.C : Government Printing Office.

Medrich, E.A. 1979. "Constant Television: A Background to Daily Life", *Journal of Communication.* Vol. 29, pp. 171-76.

Messaris, P. 1983. "Family Conversations About Television", *Journal of Family Issues,* Vol. 4, pp. 293-309.

Millikan, Max F. 1961. "The Most Fundamental Technological Change", Johnson L.B. (ed.), *Communication and Change in Developing Countries.* Honolulu: East-West Centre Press.

Mitsuya, K. 1988. "What is Television for Elementary School Students?", *NHK Monthly Report on Broadcast Research,* pp. 26-45.

Mohr, P.J. 1979. "Parental Influence of Children's Viewing of Evening Television Programmes," *Journal of Broadcasting.* 23(2), 213-228.

Moody, Kate 1980. *Growing Up on Television – The TV Effect.* New York: Times Book Co., INC.

Morley, David 1988. "Domestic Relations: The Framework of Family Viewing in Great Britain", Lull, James (ed.), *World Families Watch Television,* New Delhi: Sage Publications. Beverly Hills.

Narayanan, Andal 1987. *Impact of Television on Viewers: A Case Study of Bombay TV Viewers.* Bombay: Somaiya Publications.

Noelle-Neumann, E. 1981. "Mass Media and Social Change in Developing Societies", Katz, E. and Szecsko, T. (eds.), *Mass Media and Social Change,* London: Sage Publications.

Ogburn, F. William 1938. "Social Change with Respect to Culture and Original Nature", Lauer, R.H. (ed.), *Perspectives on Social Change,* Allyn and Bacon.

Olsen, Marvin E. 1968. *The Process of Social Organisation.* Holt, Rinehart and Winston Publications.

Pascricha, Seema 1988. "Formal and Informal Participation Among City Dwellers: A Study in Chandigarh", *Upublished Master's Thesis.* Department of Sociology, Panjab University, Chandigarh.

Patri, Vasantha R. 1992. *The Hindustan Times*, New Delhi Edition, August 25.

Rao, M.S.A. 1970. *Urbanisation and Social Change: A Study of a Rural Community on a Metropolitan Fringe*, New Delhi: Orient Longman Ltd.

Redfield, Robert 1947, "The Folk Society", *The American Journal of Sociology*, Vol. 52, January.

Research Group on Adoloscence and Television 1984. *High School Students and Television China News Year Book*, pp. 296-300.

Riley, John W. and Riley, White M. 1959. "Mass Communication and the Social System", Merton R.K. *et. al* (eds.), *Sociology Today*. New York: Basic Book.

Robinson, J.P. 1981. "Television and Leisure Time: A New Scenario, *Journal of Communication*, 3(1), 120-130.

—1972. "TV's Impact on Everyday Life", Rubinstein, E.A. et. al (eds.), *Television and Social Behaviour*, Washington D.C : US Government Printing Press.

—1969. "Television on Leisure Time, Yesterday, Today and (Maybe) Tomorrow, *Public Opinion Quaterly*, 32, pp. 21-22.

Rogge, Jan-Uwe 1989. "The Media in Everyday Family Life", Seiter, E., Borchers, H., Kreutzner, Cr. and Worth, E.M. (eds.), *Remote Control TV, Audiences and Cultural Power*. London: Routledge.

Sammuelsson, Kurt 1961. *Religion and Economic Action: A Critique of Max Weber*. Trans, Geoffery E. French, New York: Haper and Row Publishers.

Schiller, H. 1976. *Communication and Cultural Dominations*. White Plains, New York: International Arts and Science.

Schramm, Wilbur 1967. "Communication and Change in the Developing Countries", Johnson, L.B. (ed.), *Communication and Change in the Developing Countries*, Honolulu: East-West Centre Press.

Schramm, W., Lyle, J. and Parker, E. 1961. *Television in the Lives of Our Children*. Stanford, CA: Stanford University Press.

Schramm, Wilbur and Ruggles, Lee W. 1967. "How Mass Media Systems Grow", Johnson, L.B. (ed.), *Communication and Change in the Developing Countries*. Honolulu: East-West Centre Press.

Sharma, K.N. 1975. *Institutions Networks and Social Change*, Simla: Indian Institute of Advanced Study.

Sharma, Roop 1992. *The Hindustan Times*, New Delhi Edition, August 25.

Sheehan, P.W. 1983. "Age Trends and the Correlates of Children's Television Viewing", *Australian Journal of Psychology*, 35(3), 417-431.

Singer, J. and Singer, D. 1977. "Television: A Member of the Family", *National Elementary Principal*, 56, March, pp. 50-53.

Sinha, Arbind 1996. "Development Dilemmas for Indian Television," French, David and Richards, Michael (eds.), *Contemperory Television Eastern Perspectives*, New Delhi: Sage Publications.

Sjoberg, Gideon 1951. "Pre-Industrial City", Hatt, K. Paul and Reiss, J. Albert (eds.), *Cities and Society*, Glencoe, Illinois: Free Press.

Srivastava, U.K. 1986. "National Cost of Television in India in 2000 A.D.: Socio-economic and Political Implication and Issues", *Paper Presented at the XV General Assembly of the International Association for Mass Communication Research*, New Delhi, August.

Steiner, Garry A. 1963. *The People Look at Television*. New York: Alfred A. Knoff.

Swanson, David 1979. "Political Communication Research and the Uses and Gratifications Model: A Critique", *Communication Research*, Vol. 6, No. 1, pp. 37-53.

Szalai, Alexander 1972. *Daily Activities of Urban and Sub-Urban Populations in Twelve Countries*, The Hague: Mouton.

—1972. *The Use Of Time*. The Hague: Mounton and Co.

Tonnies, Ferdinand 1940. *Gemeinschaft and Gessellschaft*. New York: American Book Co.

The Tribune. Chandigarh Edition, December 21, 1992.

Thomas, Sari 1990. As Quoted in Mohammadi, Downing J., Ali Mohammadi and Annabelle Sreberny, *Questioning the Media*, Thousand Oaks: Sage Publications.

Unnikrishnan, Namita and Bajpai, Shailaja 1996. *The Impact of Television Advertising of Children*, New Delhi: Sage Publications.

Veblen, Thorstein 1904. "The Theory of Business Enterprise", Lauer, Robert H. (ed.), *Perspectives on Social Change*. Allyn and Bacon.

Weber, Max 1958. *The Protestant Ethic and Spirit of Capitalism*. Trans. Jalcott Parsons, New York: Charles Scribner's Sons.

Webster, J. 1986. "Audience Behaviour in the New Environment", *Journal of Communication*, Vol. 36, 77-91.

Williams, F., Phillips, A.F. and Lum P. 1985. "Gratifications Associated with New Communication Technologies" in Rosengren, K.E., Wenner L.A. and Palmgreen, P. (eds.), *Media Gratifications Research*, Beverly Hills, CA: Sage Publications.

Williams, T.H., and Handford, A.G. 1986. "Television and Other Leisure Activities", Williams ,T.H. (ed.), *The Impact of Television: A Natural Experiment in Three Communities*, pp. 143-213, Orlando, FL: Academic Press, INC.

Winick, Mariann Pezella and Charles, Winick 1979. *The Television Experience – What Children.* See. Thousand Oaks : Sage Publications Ltd.

Wirth, Louis 1938. "Urbanism As a Way of Life", *American Journal of Sociology*, Vol. 44.

Wu , J.S. 1985. "Viewing of Childrens' Shows on Television by Elementary School Students," *Journal of Teachers College of Taiwan*, 1(8), 289-338.

Yadava, J.S. and Reddi, U.V. 1988. "In the Midst of Diversity: Television in Urban Indian Homes", Lull, James (ed.), *World Families Watch Television*, New Delhi: Sage Publications.

Yorburg, B. 1983. *Families and Societies: Survival Or Extinction?* New York: Columbia University Press.

Index